The Economics of
American Universities

SUNY Series
FRONTIERS IN EDUCATION
Philip G. Altbach, Editor

The Frontiers in Education Series draws upon a range of disciplines and approaches in the analysis of contemporary educational issues and concerns. Books in the series help to reinterpret established fields of scholarship in education by encouraging the latest synthesis and research. A special focus highlights educational policy issues from a multidisciplinary perspective. The series is published in cooperation with the Graduate School of Education, State University of New York at Buffalo.

The
ECONOMICS of
AMERICAN
UNIVERSITIES

Management, Operations,
and Fiscal Environment

Stephen A. Hoenack
and Eileen L. Collins

STATE UNIVERSITY OF NEW YORK PRESS

Published by
State University of New York Press, Albany

For information, address State University of New York
Press, State University Plaza, Albany, NY 12246

Library of Congress Cataloging-in Publication Data

The economics of American universities : management, operations, and
    fiscal environment / Stephen A. Hoenack and Eileen L. Collins,
    editors.
        p. cm. — (SUNY series, frontiers in education)
    Includes bibliographies and index.
    ISBN 0-7914-0028-X. — ISBN 0-7914-0029-8 (pbk.)
    1. Education, Higher—Economic aspects—United States—Congresses.
2. Universities and colleges—United States—Administration—
Congresses. 3. Universities and colleges—United States—Finance—
Congresses. I. Hoenack, Stephen A., 1941-   . II. Collins,
Eileen L. III. Series.
LC67.62.E26 1990
378.73—dc19   88-39385

10 9 8 7 6 5 4 3 2 1

Contents

Introduction

STEPHEN A. HOENACK

Universities are central to the achievement of many individuals' highest personal aspirations as well to the accomplishment of important policy goals. As a group, universities provide access to most professional and managerial labor markets and play a crucial role in developing the scientific knowledge underlying technological advancement in an increasingly internationally competitive economy. They are where society stores and advances knowledge in the humanities and social sciences. Most of these institutions have emerged from their enormous growth and transition since the Second World War as vital and reasonably fiscally sound organizations, even after recent years of leveling or declining enrollments and funding.

It is probably incorrect and perhaps alarmist to state, as many have, that American universities face a crisis, whether fiscal or academic. Yet there are problems concerning these organizations that deserve serious, if dispassionate, attention. Perhaps the most important of these is universities' heavy dependence on public funding, a condition that applies to private as well as public institutions due to the receipt by private universities of federal research and student aid expenditures. This dependence inevitably makes university funding subject to political influences. The direct competition with other public goals and the effects of politicians' short-term responsiveness to interest-group pressures makes universities' income uncertain; yet at the same time they face large fixed costs in serving some of society's most enduring purposes.

There are legitimate concerns about the substantive contributions that universities make. These organizations are expensive, difficult to understand well enough to evaluate, and, like many service entities, subject to low productivity growth. They can appear to be elitist while having the potential to contribute significantly to social mobility. When these institutions receive increased instructional or research funding, it is sometimes hard to tell whether the result is what the funders want or what the institution wants. For example: How much does instructional

1

funding from state governments elicit research as well as instructional outcomes? What are the teaching and basic research outcomes of federal funding for research? And to what extent does student financial aid alter socioeconomic access to higher education? The economist places these questions under a broad heading labeled "Supply behavior of higher education institutions."

The explosive growth of universities' roles during the fifties and early sixties was followed by an interest in improving their management. The Department of Defense had been experimenting with Program Planning and Budgeting Systems (PPBS), and the idea of employing information systems that could improve the management and accountability of universities briefly became popular. Considerable effort went into attempts to design uniform methods of measuring costs in these institutions, and the federally funded National Center for Higher Education Management Systems additionally devoted efforts to measuring outcomes and assigning costs to them. Not much came of this work for a combination of two reasons: 1) resistance (and lack of incentives) to change, and 2) the absence of a conceptual framework about educational production processes and about supply behavior within universities and in service organizations generally. Without the understanding imparted by such a framework, there was little logical basis for supporting the proposed new information systems in the face of self-serving criticisms of them.

The early attempts to improve decisionmaking in higher education were made without sufficient knowledge. It is possible that implementing these systems could create perverse incentives and thereby worsen decisionmaking. For example, it was widely feared that pressure on institutions to lower their measured costs could result in reductions in quality rather than the intended increases in efficiency. In a similar manner, the recent attempts of federal officials to control higher education institutions through "jawboning" will surely be fruitless or even harmful without incentives based on a reasonably sophisticated analysis of behavior within universities.

Universities are complex organizations and the first steps in improving their responsiveness to society's demands for their services should be close study of their production processes, their incentives and governance structures, their costs and supply behavior, and their student attendance demands and funding environments. Over the last twenty years, a handful of economists, many of whom were involved in the early PPBS experiments, have been working on these questions. The papers in this volume summarize much of this work and interpret from an economic perspective related research in other disciplines. These papers were originally commissioned by the National Science Foundation (NSF) for two seminars in the summer of 1986, which were organized by Eileen L. Collins of the NSF.

A key concept in the microeconomic analysis of any organization is the production function. There are alternative ways of employing scarce inputs such as the time of teachers and the uses of space to produce outputs such as learning outcomes. A production function for any set of outputs produced together is information about possible ways of employing inputs to produce the outputs. Efficient production involves the utilization of inputs from the set of production possibilities represented by the applicable production function in such a way as to maximize the value of outputs achieved. Perhaps more interesting, long-term growth in productivity requires expanding knowledge about production possibilities, i.e. new production functions.

An organization's underlying production functions can say a great deal about it. In particular regard to universities, when production possibilities are well known only to the employees directly engaged in productive activities, it would be very costly for others to become sufficiently informed to place useful controls on their activities. The resulting discretion held by employees will be increased when important outputs and the most productive inputs are intangible. The fewer the incentives for employees to experiment with production possibilities, the lower the productivity growth. When the same input applications (e.g., time spent working with graduate students) produce multiple outputs (e.g., learning and research outcomes), they will tend to be produced together.

In spite of the complexity and obscurity of university production functions, there has been a significant amount of interest among researchers in describing them and even attempting to measure them. In this volume, David S. P. Hopkin's paper, "The Higher Education Production Function: Theoretical Foundations and Empirical Findings," describes and evaluates this research and concludes that "less ambitious and more discrete" efforts have a better chance of being informative for policy purposes than attempts to characterize entire production functions. For example, he proposes studies of "the cost-effectiveness of alternative technologies for instruction" and of alternative methods of organizing research teams.

Research is a crucial and little-understood product of universities. Specific issues in the production of research are analyzed in Frederick E. Balderston's paper "Organization, Funding, Incentives, and Initiatives for University Research: A University Management Perspective." Balderston goes well beyond the usual assertion that research and instruction are produced jointly and explores alternative means of organizing applied and basic research activities, including those with an interdisciplinary focus. This paper also analyzes university incentives vis-à-vis research, and relates them to the possibility of using different methods of organizing research.

Because the production functions for university outputs impart discretion to faculty, the nature and quantity of the institution's instructional and research outcomes reflect the choices of these people, as well as those made by administrators and others outside the university. The choices made by academic personnel are not unconstrained, however. Any organization must be responsive to the demands facing it. Universities are usually concerned with the demands of students and those of outside funding organizations. Public universities are normally even more concerned with the demands of their legislatures. Faculty decisions are nonetheless often most immediately constrained by internal university governance structures. These structures encourage individual faculty to pursue stated or implied goals that are determined within the institution. For example, faculty salaries and unit budgets may be based in significant part on research productivity even in institutions whose external funding is largely determined by their enrollments.

The importance of goals determined within an organization is a function of the degree of discretion its personnel have to pursue them. Academic personnel often have considerable discretion to pursue their goals. Two important questions are: 1) What are these goals? and 2) How do they compare with those of the constituencies of higher education? The paper "Participant Goals, Institutional Goals, and University Resource Allocation Decisions" by Howard P. Tuckman and Cyril Chang addresses these questions. The authors summarize and interpret the extensive literature on the subject and also interpret how the goals of individuals are reflected in the demand and supply relationships that help determine university organization and resource choices. The authors conclude that institutional goals can be usefully formulated, but that the role of these goals in resource allocation depends on the nature of the budget process.

In turn, goals are reflected in choices. Estelle James' paper, "Decision Processes and Priorities in Higher Education," focuses on the ways decisions are made in higher education. The author pays special attention to those decisions in which faculty are given discretion over an institution's research and instructional outcomes. A number of models of university decisionmaking have been based on the assumption that it is possible to formulate specific institutional objective functions which then can be maximized within known limits. In other models, university decisionmaking is analyzed as being more decentralized with varying degrees of underlying political behavior. James interprets both literatures and discusses proposals made by several authors for improving decisionmaking within universities.

University decision processes and the costs of information about their activities underlie these institutions' supply behavior. This behavior determines the amounts that external constituents must pay for the instructional and research outcomes they desire, i.e., the costs of these outcomes faced by the institution's clientele. These costs constitute the university's income, part of which is allocated to functions (such as internally funded basic research activities) that reflect faculty discretion rather than the demands of clients. In "Higher Education Cost Functions," Paul Brinkman summarizes the extensive literature on these costs, including his own research on economies of scale in higher education. Brinkman presents many conclusions on how the instructional costs faced by students and external funders vary with the size and characteristics of institutions. These results will be valuable to higher education planners and administrators. My own paper, "An Economist's Perspective on Costs within Higher Education Institutions," explores how two concepts from economics affect cost analysis in higher education. These are: 1) opportunity costs, and 2) the idea that university costs paid by their constituencies include the resources absorbed by faculty members' discretionary activities. Literature on higher education costs is interpreted with these concepts.

From an economic point of view, the most important aspect of the environment facing higher education institutions is the demands of their constituencies. Demand reflects willingness to pay for services rendered, not necessarily the total value to society of these services. There are two reasons for a possible divergence between demand and social value. First, aspects of higher education such as spillovers of teaching onto research, which in turn affect technology in the economy, can provide benefits which would be impossible or prohibitively costly to measure well enough to assess user charges for them. The second reason is that the willingness to pay for higher education is below what it otherwise would be because increments of an individual's earnings cannot serve as readily marketable collateral for student loans.

Because the willingness to pay for higher education can be observed, it is possible to use available data on enrollments, tuition, and other variables to make inferences about the demand functions facing universities. Based on the recent extension of economic theory of investment behavior into choices involving human capital, economists have specified variables in equations representing the demand behavior of students. William E. Becker's paper, "The Demand for Higher Education," provides the most comprehensive and analytical survey available of the extensive literature on the topic. His paper separately considers models based on grouped data (e.g., enrollment ratios) and data representing individual choices, and Becker makes a distinction between studies that make inferences about demand functions facing individual institutions, and those inferring more aggregative relationships which concern themselves with demands facing categories of institutions (e.g., public universities). Professor Becker also explores the implications of existing research on student demand for financial aid policies.

The combined demand-and-supply forces facing higher education as a whole determine: 1) the flows of resources to this sector of the economy; 2) the adaptations of higher education institutions to these flows; and 3) the success of universities in increasing services in response to new demands. There has been much discussion about the possibility of 'fiscal distress' in higher education, an ill-defined concept that is intended to reflect institutional difficulties in adapting to changes in external funding. Joseph Froomkin's paper, "The Impact of Changing Levels of Financial Resources on the Structure of Colleges and Universities," provides an overview of trends in income and expenses for American colleges and universities over the last twenty years. Froomkin thoughtfully interprets these data to infer how higher education as a whole adapted to shifts in funding. He concludes that all institutions had difficulty balancing their budgets during the early 1980's, and that: "During this period of penury, budgets were balanced mostly at the expense of faculty compensation. Other functions of the university, such as construction, renovation of facilities and maintenance also suffered. Most institutions managed to protect their instructional programs and, as far as we could determine, shifted resources from declining programs to new, emerging fields, mostly in science."

All in all, Froomkin suggests that higher education as a whole has emerged in reasonably good condition from a period of unanticipated revenue shortfalls and cost increases. He clearly points out, however, that some institutions have had greater difficulties than others. Paul Brinkman's paper, "College and University Adjustments to a Changing Financial Environment," focuses on the diversity of institutions in terms of both their own funding situations and their capabilities to make adjustments. He documents the variation in fiscal changes facing universities, analyzes the different economic and social forces underlying these financial impacts, and describes the types of institutional responses—also within a conceptual framework. For example, he presents data classifying proportions of institutions having varying positive and negative percentage changes in revenues, discusses impacts of governmental policies on funding, and explores the diversity of institutions' capabilities to use tuition increases as a means of overcoming shortfalls of revenues from other sources. Brinkman's paper concludes with a separate analysis of the specific impacts of institutions' fiscal situations on their science and engineering programs.

The papers in this volume do not cover all of the available economic research on universities and they raise a few new research questions. In addition, economics has not yet proven its value as a research tool for making inferences about a number of important, policy-relevant topics in higher education.

One major area of research not covered here is the estimation by many economists of rates of return to education at this level, and comparisons of these rates with those at other educational levels. Recent surveys of research on this topic include Bowen (1977) and Leslie and Brinkman (1988). A particularly relevant example of this research remains Solmon's (1975) study of the impacts of institutional quality on students' subsequent earnings. Most of the research on returns to higher education deals with the earnings gains captured by students, not their nonmonetary gains or the possible external gains (or losses) to others that result from the behaviors of students for which they are not compensated (or taxed.) There may also be direct external gains or costs from the educational process, but, despite assertions that they exist (usually as benefits), there is little convincing evidence about them. The available evidence on external returns is also surveyed in Bowen (1977) and Leslie and Brinkman (1988). Much of the work on returns to higher education is subject to "selectivity bias." This phenomenon occurs when those going to college would, if they did not attend, still earn more or create more external benefits than those not going to college.

Most economic research on the demand for higher education relates to the demands of students as can be noted from William Becker's survey. There has been much less research on the important demands of governments at all levels for higher education. Some examples of research in this area include: Clotfelter (1976), Grubb (1988), and Hoenack and Pierro (1990). Another underresearched topic is the willingness of donors to provide funds to universities in response to their instructional and research outcomes.

There has been a significant amount of economic research on universities and higher education issues in other countries, including the many institutions throughout the Third World. References on this topic include Psacharopoulos and Woodhall (1985), Psacharopoulos (1980), and Coombs (1985). Much of this research provides a useful comparative perspective. For example, in other countries, research activities are often more separated from instructional functions than they are in the United States.

Another important topic on the economics of higher education is the financial aid system: how it works and what are its effects. There has been a considerable amount of interest in this topic in recent years on the part of such well-known economists in the field as W. Lee Hansen and Michael S. McPherson, whose work is not in this volume. Recent research on financial aid is described in a special issue of *Economics of Education Review* (1988) and Leslie and Brinkman (1988). The studies in the present volume suggest several directions for future research. These include advancements in our understanding of institutional supply behavior, specific studies on methods of organizing instructional, research, and nonacademic support activities within universities, and improved modeling of demand-and-supply behavior.

There are some other areas not dealt with in this volume where economics has the potential to make a useful contribution. One such research frontier is learning behavior. This topic has too long been left to psychologists and noneconomist educational researchers in spite of some pioneering efforts by economists (McKenzie and Staaf, 1974). Economics has a contribution to make in this important area because of its focus on incentives and policy-controllable inputs. Another core area largely overlooked by economists is the organization of teaching and the development of curriculum. It is widely believed that these crucial functions of universities should be left entirely to the instructor's discretion. It is easy to see why such discretion exists (the nature of production functions and costs of information in higher education), but there is a lack of theoretical or empirical justification for such a practice. Indeed, the absence of productivity growth in higher education, as in many other service industries, and the relatively limited use of economically available technological improvements adaptable to education lead one to suspect that this practice should be modified. It may be, for example, that some of the concepts of what is referred to as mastery learning or outcome-based instruction (Jones and Spady, 1985, Rubin and Spady, 1984, and Spady, 1982) can be applied to improve learning in higher education as well as at earlier levels and perhaps also as a means of introducing effective teaching incentives (Hoenack, 1988) in higher education.

Little is known also about the means by which higher education contributes to economic development and to regional success in attracting business investments. There have been many flawed empirical attempts to investigate this topic. All of these attempts point to the need for an improved conceptual framework for analyzing the causal relationships between the activities of higher education institutions and events in the economies that surround them.

It is hoped that the papers in this volume will encourage researchers to investigate these and other topics. Such work has the potential to improve further our understanding of the behavioral relationships within universities that reflect their responses to public policies.

CHAPTER 1

The Higher Education Production Function: Theoretical Foundations and Empirical Findings

DAVID S. P. HOPKINS

This paper reviews the literature of educational economics for evidence concerning the higher education production function. The results from a large number of sources are synthesized and presented in a systematic way so as to reveal what is known and what is not known about the character and form of the production function. From this synthesis, we derive a set of important unanswered questions and suggestions for future research.

The Production Function in General Form

The production function is intended to represent the process by means of which an institution—here, a college or university—transforms inputs (typically labor and capital) into outputs. In order to specify the function at all precisely, we must be able to: a) identify and quantify all relevant inputs and outputs, and b) describe the relationship between inputs and outputs in mathematical terms.

The general mathematical formulation is given in Hopkins and Massy (1981). Let

$$\underline{Y} = (Y_1, Y_2, \ldots, Y_m) \text{ be a vector of outputs, and}$$

$$\underline{X} = (X_1, X_2, \ldots, X_n) \text{ be a vector of inputs.}$$

The production process is described by one or more functions of the type

$$(1) \qquad\qquad F^k\,(\underline{Y},\underline{X}) = 0.$$

To be a true production function, F^k (. , $\underline{X}$) should represent the *maximum* output $\underline{Y}$ obtainable from the inputs $\underline{X}$. The output measures must relate to the three primary missions of the higher education institution, namely, the transmission of knowledge (instruction), the creation of new knowledge (research), and so-called public service. One aspect of the diversity of the higher education industry in the U.S. is that different institutions place differing degrees of emphasis on these three missions; yet the research mission is clearly not limited to the major research university just as the public service mission is not limited to the publicly funded institution. Thus, most institutions have more than one major mission and, hence, a plurality of important outputs.

As Hopkins and Massy have pointed out (1981), the intangible features of both the inputs and outputs of the higher education production process are every bit as important as (many would say much more important than) the more tangible, easily quantifiable ones. These authors go on to identify a set of inputs and outputs similar to those shown in Table 1. They do not, however, carry the analysis any further in terms of specifying the exact functional form in (1) that relates these specific inputs to these specific outputs.

At this point, it would be well to observe that no researcher to date has successfully characterized the production function in terms as precise as the set of input and output variables listed in Table 1, and it is doubtful whether anyone ever will. The reasons for this are many, but they all boil down to the fact that the technologies of instruction, research, and public service are poorly understood, and the tools for estimating the requisite functional forms and coefficients are woefully inadequate to the task. To be more specific, not only are we lacking appropriate measures of quality, but the very nature of the interactions between, for example, teaching and research is difficult to express in mathematical terms. Definition of these intangibles can at least be approached by capturing these more subjective variables in a utility function that is optimized, as proposed by Hopkins and Massy (1981) and Garvin (1980), but that still does not solve the problem arising from the joint production of teaching and research. Another related problem for the economist is that, in the absence of any uniform, exogenously provided set of prices for the inputs and outputs of higher education, there is simply no way to escape the multidimensional character of the production function and all of the specification and estimation problems that it entails. Finally, we note that the concept of a true production function is based on an optimal technology, one that achieves maximum levels of output for a given set of inputs. Yet, as Levin (1976),

TABLE 1

Identification of Inputs and Outputs of Higher Education

	Tangible	*Intangible*
Inputs	New students matriculating	Quality and diversity of matriculating students
	Faculty time and effort	Quality of effort put forth by faculty
	Student time and effort	Quality of effort put forth by students
	Staff time and effort	Quality of effort put forth by staff
	Buildings & equipment	Quality, age, and style of buildings; age and quality of equipment
	Library holdings and acquisitions	Quality of library holdings and acquisitions
	Endowment assets	
Outputs	Student enrollment in courses	Quality of education obtained
	Degrees awarded	Quality of education obtained
	Research awards, articles, and citations	Quality of research performed (also quantity)
	Services rendered to the general public	Quality of services rendered
		Goodwill
		Reputation

*Adapted from Table 3.1 in David J.P. Hopkins and William F. Massy *Planning Models for Colleges and Universities*, Standard University Press. Copyright 1981.

among others, has pointed out, there is no reason to believe that the educational enterprise has been operating on the efficient frontier of production possibilities; and there are many reasons to believe that it has not. This means that, even if we were able to specify the true and complete functional form, we would still be unable to estimate the true coefficients of the model from any existing set of data.

It is apparent, therefore, that all efforts to date directed at specifying and estimating the higher education production function have provided only partial results. For example, quality measures have often been omitted, and most empirical studies have focused on the instructional production function alone without regard to the research objective, either on its own or in interaction with the instructional objective. Yet there are a great many such efforts reflected in the literature, and we shall summarize the important results below. First, however, it is useful to describe research concerning the nature and measurement of inputs and outputs.

Identification and Measurement of Inputs and Outputs

For purposes of estimating the production function for instruction, it is imperative to separate *student* input characteristics (e.g., numbers of students, aptitudes, family backgrounds, etc.) from *institutional* characteristics, such as faculty size and quality. Solmon (1973) has proposed specific measures of quality that can be used to characterize both student and institutional inputs. On the output side, nearly all researchers take some form of standardized test scores as a proxy for the amount of knowledge gained by students through the process of instruction. Astin (1973) has argued that attempts to develop a single overall measure of educational output are unrealistic; what is needed instead is a battery of measures that are sufficiently broad to capture the major outcomes of the educational process. He states, for example, that it is probably not sufficient to measure just the change in *mean* test scores resulting from students' college experience, since other features of the distribution of test scores, such as the variance or spread, may be just as important.

Perhaps the most ambitious effort to date to catalog the myriad outputs of higher education is represented by Western Interstate Commission for Higher Education (WICHE) (1970). The complete list of proposed output measures is shown in Table 2. Unfortunately, by concentrating solely on quantifiable measures, these authors have practically neglected the all-important quality dimension in their proposed output variables for research and public service. As Attiyeh has pointed out, "The number of pages of published research reports or the number of patents applied for or any other simple measure does not tell anything about the quality of research done in a university" (Lumsden, 1974, p. 6).

A somewhat more complete set of output measures for graduate education and research may be found in the National Research Council's (NRC) 1982 *Assessment of Research-Doctorate Programs in the United States.* This document gauges doctoral programs at American universities according to eighteen separate variables which are arrayed along the following six dimensions: program size, characteristics of program graduates, reputational survey results, university library size, research support, and publication records. Several direct measures of quality are included, especially in the reputational survey results. It is significant, however, that the NRC made no attempt to combine these variables into a single, composite indicator of university output.

TABLE 2
An Accounting Structure for the Outputs of Higher Education:
One Proposal

Instructional Outputs

Variables	*Source of Measures*
Cognitive Attributes of Students:	
Level of General Knowledge	Test Scores
Level of Knowledge in Chosen Field	Test Scores
Basic Language Arts Skills	Test Scores
Critical Thinking and Reasoning	Test Scores
General Intelligence	Test Scores
Affective Attributes of Students:	
Self-concept	Questionnaire Responses
Satisfaction with Educational Experience	Questionnaire Responses
Citizenship	Questionnaire Responses
Values	Questionnaire Responses
Achievement Motivation	Questionnaire Responses
Tangible Attributes of Students:	
Earning Power	Placement and Employment Data
Awards	Number and Stature of Awards
Affiliations	Number and Kind of Affiliations
Avocations	Number and Kind of Hobbies
G.P.A.	Academic Record Data
Level of Educational Attainment	Academic Record Data
Flexibility of Employment	Placement and Employment Data
Areas of Career Interest	Questionnaire Responses

Institutional Environment Outputs

Variables	*Source of Measures*
Academic Environment Attributes:	
Rate of Student Success	Dropout Data
Mean Time to Reach Degree	Student Record Data
Faculty Turnover	Faculty Record Data
Faculty Availability to Students	Student Questionnaire
Academic Resources Available	Library Data
Quality of Instruction	Faculty & Student Questionnaire
Academic Aptitude Mix	Entering Student SAT Scores
Student Stress	Student Questionnaire
Faculty Stress	Faculty Questionnaire

TABLE 2 *(continued)*

Institutional Environment Outputs (continued)

Variables	*Source of Measures*
Social Environment Attributes:	
Degree of Social Activity on Campus	Activity Records and Questionnaire
Racial Mix	Student & Faculty Records
Socio-Economic Mix	Student Records
Family Attitude Characteristics	Questionnaire
Social Involvement of Student Body	Questionnaire
Per cent Resident (on campus) Students	Housing and Student Records
Rate of Marriage Among Students	Student Records
Physical Environment	Physical Plant Data and Questionnaire

Research Outputs

Variables	*Source of Measures*
Reorganization of Knowledge	Number of new books, textbooks, etc.
New Inventions and Developments (Applied Research Products)	Number of patents, adopted procedures, etc.
New Ideas and Concepts (Pure Research Outputs)	Number of articles, papers, awards, citations, etc.
Personal Involvement of Students and Others (instructional spinoff)	Number of hours involvement on projects by students, industry, personnel, etc.

Public Service Outputs

Variables	*Source of Measures*
Student Involvement in Community	Hours of time, type of project, questionnaire
Faculty Involvement in Community	Hours of time, type of project, questionnaire
Cultural Activities Available	Number, type, duration, attendance, participation

TABLE 2 *(continued)*

Public Service Outputs (continued)

Variables	Source of Measures
Recreation Activities Available	Number, type, duration, attendance, participation
Continuing Education Activities	Number, type, duration, enrollment, quality, and satisfaction, questionnaire
Social Criticism	Amount, frequency, intensity, effects of confrontation —Students and Community —Faculty and Community
Personal Services	Number of health care patients, counseling patients, psychological testing, legal advice requests, etc. (dollar value of such services)
Indirect Community Benefits	Students available as employees, drawing power of the community as a place of residence for professional and skilled persons
Community Psychic Income	Public pride, awareness that expertise is available if needed
Product Testing	Number and types of products and materials tested for government and industry

Source: WICHE (1970).

The Relationship Between Inputs and Outputs

Production Functions for Instruction

We begin this summary of the empirical findings concerning the production function of higher education by limiting ourselves to the instructional objective alone, unrelated to any other objectives, since most of the empirical work to date has been carried out in this domain. These studies may further be categorized according to the predominant level of analysis, that is, whether the model is intended to represent the production process of an entire institution or of a single academic department, or the learning process of an individual student. Of course, the models and results in this section are directly applicable to those institu-

TABLE 3
Measures Compiled on Individual Research-Doctorate Programs
in the Social and Behavioral Sciences

Program Size[1]
01   Reported number of faculty members in the program, December 1980.
02   Reported number of program graduates in last five years (July 1975 through June 1980).
03   Reported total number of full-time and part-time graduate students enrolled in the program who intend to earn doctorates, December 1980.

Characteristics of Graduates[2]
04   Fraction of FY1975-79 program graduates who had received some national fellowship of training grant support during their graduate education.
05   Median number of years from first enrollment in graduate school to receipt of the doctorate—FY1975-79 program graduates.[3]
06   Fraction of FY1975-79 program graduates who at the time they completed requirements for the doctorate reported that they had made definite commitments for postgraduation employment.
07   Fraction of FY1975-79 program graduates who at the time they completed requirements for the doctorate reported that they had made definite commitments for postgraduation employment in Ph.D.-granting universities.

Reputational Survey Results[4]
08   Mean rating of the scholarly quality of program faculty.
09   Mean rating of the effectiveness of the program in educating research scholars/scientists.
10   Mean rating of the improvement in program quality in the last five years.
11   Mean rating of the evaluators' familiarity with the work of the program's faculty.

University Library Size[5]
12   Composite index describing the library size in the university in which the program is located, 1979-80.

Research Support
13   Fraction of program faculty members holding research grants from the Alcohol, Drug Abuse, and Mental Health Administration, the National Institutes of Health, or the National Science Foundation at any time during the FY1978-80 period.[6]
14   Total expenditures (in thousands of dollars) reported by the university for research and development activities in a specified field, FY1979.[7]

Publication Records[8]
17   Number of published articles attributed to the program faculty members, 1978-80.
18   Fraction of program faculty members with one or more published articles, 1978-80.

[1]Based on information provided to the committee by the participating universities.
[2]Based on data compiled in the NRC's Survey of Earned Doctorates.
[3]In reporting standardized scores and correlations with other variables, a shorter time-to-Ph.D. is assigned a higher score.
[4]Based on responses to the committee's survey conducted in April 1981.
[5]Based on data compiled by the Association of Research Libraries.
[6]Based on matching faculty names provided by institutional coordinators with the names of research grant awardees from the three federal agencies.
[7]Based on data provided to the National Science Foundation by universities.
[8]Based on data compiled by the Institute for Scientific Information.

Source: *An Assessment of Research-Doctorate Programs in the United States: Social and Behavioral Sciences,* © Copyright 1982, by the National Academy of Sciences.

tions classified as "predominantly teaching institutions," whereas the interactions of instruction with research must be considered in the case of more research-oriented universities.

At the *institutional* level, the grossest form of production function can be represented by unit-cost ratios, such as dollar expenditures for instruction per student credit hour. Such ratios are often used as crude productivity indices (Wallhaus, 1975). In these instances, the sole measure of input is cost and the sole measure of output is credit hours. The implicit production function assumes a single-efficient-point technology with constant returns to scale; that is, it is of the form

$$(2) \qquad\qquad y = ax,$$

where x = total expenditures on instruction and y = number of student credit hours produced.

A somewhat more sophisticated form of the instructional production function is expressed in Gulko and Hussein (1971). There, output is measured in terms of student enrollments, inputs are faculty and staff full-time equivalents and other university resources, and the level of aggregation is a cluster of academic departments representing a "discipline." The model takes the simple linear form:

$$(3) \qquad\qquad \underline{x} = A \cdot \underline{y},$$

where, now, $\underline{x} = (x_1, x_2, \ldots, x_n)$ is a vector of resource requirements, $\underline{y} = (y_1, y_2, \ldots, y_m)$ is a vector of student enrollments by level and major discipline, and $\underline{A} = [a_{ij}]$ is a matrix of input-output coefficients, such as the ratio of full professors in economics to upper-division undergraduate history majors. It is implicit in (3) that for any given set of outputs, there is a unique set of inputs, although the reverse is not true.

As I have pointed out in my article "On the Use of Large-Scale Simulation Models for University Planning" (Hopkins, 1971), this formulation of the university production function is simply not credible. Not only does it fail to take account of the university's research objective, but the implicit assumption of a single-efficient-point technology with constant returns to scale is patently unrealistic at this level of disaggregation. Hence, the aptness of such a model in describing the higher education production function is limited to institutions in which faculty are paid only to teach quite rigidly prescribed classes and students are severely restricted in their choices of which classes to take.

A somewhat different approach to representing the instructional production function for a university is given by Oliver and Hopkins (1976).

By introducing a time dimension, these authors portray the production process as a network of cohort flows in which students enter the system at various levels (freshman, undergraduate transfer, graduate student, etc.), remain for a certain period of time (cumulatively, that is—attendance is not assumed to occur in consecutive time periods) and then either graduate or drop out. A simplified representation of the network is shown in Figure 1. Outputs are represented in terms of degree-earners and dropouts, not just student-years of enrollment at the institution, while inputs are new matriculants in various degree programs plus the resources (faculty, staff, facilities, etc.) provided by the university. One particularly interesting feature of the model is that it explicitly accounts for the feedback effect whereby undergraduate enrollments create demand for graduate research assistants which, in turn, leads to requirements for new graduate admissions. Once again, the technology of

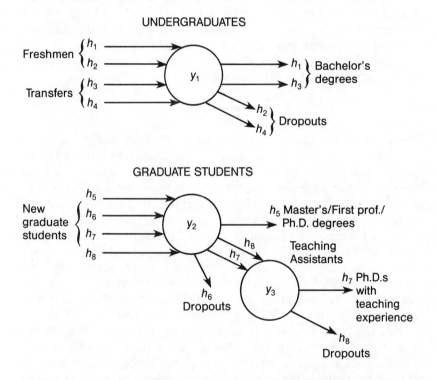

FIGURE 1. Network representation of the eight-cohort model. Reprinted from Figure 5.3 in David S.P. Hopkins and William F. Massy, *Planning Models for Colleges and Universities*, Stanford University Press. Copyright 1981.

instruction is represented by a matrix of faculty-student ratios, but in this case, the small dimensionality of the matrix (3 x 4) makes it feasible to vary its coefficients so that, in this sense, the model is neither linear nor does it assume a single efficient point.

One limitation of this model is that the flow network is assumed to be in equilibrium. That is, the flow rates of student cohorts, along with all behavioral and technological constraints, are fixed from one year to another. A time-varying version is given by Radner and Miller (1975, Chapter 10). While their model was formulated to represent the production function of the entire system of higher education, in which teachers are produced in one time period to instruct students in another, it is applicable to a single institution if one allows for an inflow of teachers from outside that particular institution.

An interesting application of production theory at the individual departmental level is given by Breneman (1976). His work is aimed at explaining the Ph.D. degree-granting behavior of academic departments in a prestigious university. A simple input-output structure of the following type is used to describe the Ph.D. production process (which we assume to be in equilibrium):

let

x = number of new matriculants per time period (input)
y_1 = number of successful degree-earners per time period (output)
y_2 = number of degree program dropouts per time period (output)
s = number of students enrolled in the degree program
f = success rate of matriculants (ratio of degree earners to new matriculants)
l_1 = average length of time to the degree
l_2 = average length of time to dropout.

From these definitions, we can write:

$$(4) \qquad\qquad y_1 = f \cdot x$$

and

$$(5) \qquad\qquad s = l_1 y_1 + l_2 y_2.$$

Breneman studies variations in the parameters f and l, which he assumed to be easily manipulated by the faculty, to differences in departmental prestige, demand for the Ph.D. output, and the amount of resources provided to the department. His chief hypothesis was that a faculty's concern over the prestige of their department would limit the production of Ph.D.'s in situations of limited demand for the product, regardless of the enrollment level, since prestige is directly related to the placement of graduates in other top schools. Although Breneman cites a variety of evidence in support of his theory, the evidence is certainly not conclusive.

Next, we turn to a brief review of production models which use the individual student as the unit of analysis. In all such models, educational output is measured in terms of level of student achievement in one or more categories or, better, in terms of the *change* in level of student achievement that results from the schooling process. Here, *student achievement* is typically measured in terms of standardized test scores. Within this category of models, we must distinguish between those that relate student achievement to a variety of school-related and non-school-related inputs, and those relating student achievement to investment to the student's time. Models of the former variety are represented generically by the following set of simultaneous equations:

$$(6) \qquad\qquad A^k_{it} = f(\underline{b}^t_i, \underline{e}^t_i, \underline{s}^t_i),$$

where

A^t_{it} = is the achievement level (or change in achievement level) in area k of student i at time t,

$\underline{b}^t_i$ = $(b^t_{i1}, b^t_{i2}, \ldots, b^t_{il})$ is a vector of background characteristics for the ith student at time t (ideally containing some measure of innate ability),

$\underline{e}^t_i$ = $(e^t_{i1}, e^t_{i2}, \ldots, e^t_{im})$ is a vector of environmental influences affecting the ith student at time $\underline{t}$ and

$\underline{s}^t_i$ = $(s^t_{i1}, s^t_{i2}, \ldots, s^t_{in})$ is a vector of school-related variables for student i at time t.

Obviously, the production function described in (6) can only be derived empirically if the functional form can be specified and its coefficients estimated from available data. Generally, the function is assumed to be linear (or log-linear) in all the independent variables, and the coefficients are estimated from large data bases using (simultaneous) least-squares regression.

A great deal of work was carried out during the 1960s and 1970s using the model formulation and estimation methodology described above for the purpose of estimating the 'school effect' on achievement in the primary and secondary schools. (One of the first such efforts led to the widely referenced and highly controversial Coleman Report, 1966.) This work has been well summarized and subjected to extensive critique by Cohn (1979), Hanushek (1979), Heim and Perl (1974), Lau (1979), and Levin (1976), among others. In spite of numerous attempts that were made over a period of some twenty years to relate various achievement measures to various characteristics of the student, his or her environment, and the schools, the results are often contradictory and largely inconclusive. It is not difficult to imagine the reasons for this, as the methodology can do nothing to reject, or even to indicate, the misspecification of variables and functional relationships. Yet our understanding of the true learning process is extremely limited and, hence, does not lead us to a unique specification of the appropriate production function.

The above model and approach have been applied directly to higher education in at least two instances. The often-referenced work by Astin (1968) attempted to relate social backgrounds and ability levels of college students and several measures of the quality of the college which they attended to their achievement scores on the Graduate Record Examination. The results were somewhat disturbing in that, once student ability and background had been taken into account, no differential effect from attending a highly selective (and presumably expensive) institution could be discovered. Manahan (1983) performed a similar analysis on a much more microscopic level. Using data obtained from a class in economics taught at Illinois State University in the fall of 1978, he found some positive association of change in standardized test scores with "quality of instruction," as measured by attendance and class participation. These studies are obviously subject to the same form of criticism as those performed using data from the primary and secondary schools. Suffice it to say that no reliable estimates of the true production function for individual student learning have been derived to date.

A different tack is taken in Becker (1983) and in Polachek, *et al.* (1978). These authors postulate a relationship between a gain in knowledge or achievement (the output variable) and the amount of time that a student invests in the learning process. Becker's production function is of the Cobb-Douglas variety and uses a measure of precourse aptitude along with time allocated to the course as inputs. Polachek, *et al.*, use a more general constant partial elasticity of substitution form with three input variables (single measure of precourse aptitude plus separate measures of time allocated to classroom instruction and studying out-side of class). The latter authors were able to fit their model to data obtained from a special survey of students enrolled in a first-year eco-nomics course at the University of North Carolina at Chapel Hill. The results yielded some interesting figures on the marginal product of one hour's worth of class attendance versus the marginal product of the same amount of time spent studying. These figures are probably not general-izable to other situations, however, nor does the model account for any differences in output that relate to institution-specific variables such as method of instruction, quality of teacher, etc.

Some more recent studies analyze the substitution possibilities of new technologies in the individual instruction process. For example, Lewis, *et al.* (1985) report some evidence on the substitutability of computer-assisted instruction (CAI) for independent study time in terms of a student's gaining mastery of a fixed set of course material. These authors go on to report, however, that practically no current data exist on the cost-effectiveness of this instructional method compared with that of any others.

The Joint Production Function for Instruction and Research

In our rather extensive review of the literature, we were unable to locate any evidence (either theoretical or empirically based) concerning the production function for university research alone. We did, however, find several works dealing with the *joint* production of instruction and re-search. Models that incorporate the major interactions between instruc-tional and research activities of faculty and students obviously are nec-essary if we are accurately to describe the production function of the research university. Yet the current state of understanding of these interactions—at least in any quantitative sense—is quite rudimentary.

A simple theoretical framework is provided by Nerlove (1972). This author examines the joint production of undergraduate education and graduate education coupled with research. He postulates that the pro-duction possibility curve must be the shape displayed in Figure 2. This curve shows a region close to each axis, in which the two outputs are postulated to be complementary to one another (more output of both is feasible under a fixed resource constraint), and a wider region in the middle in which the two function as substitutes. It is important to note that the outputs depicted along the axes of Figure 2 are intended to be measured in "quality-adjusted" units so that increases in output occur whenever quantity *or* quality is increased.

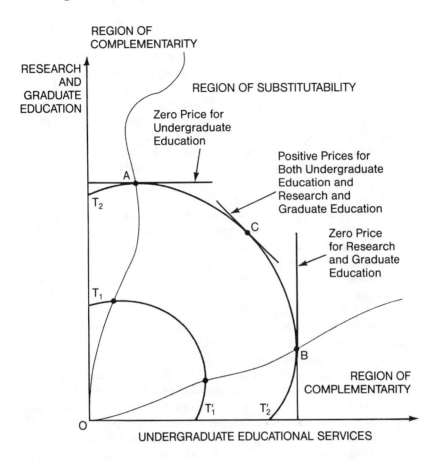

FIGURE 2. Combinations of undergraduate education and of research and graduate education showing the regions of complementarity and the region of substitutability

Source: Reprinted from Figure 1 in Nerlove (1972). ©1972 by The University of Chicago.

One inference drawn by Nerlove from his model is that it is more efficient to produce learning and new knowledge in the same institution than in entirely separate ones. This conclusion follows from the complementary supposedly exhibited between teaching and research when either activity is largely subordinate to the other one. Presumably, this concept of complementarity lies at the very heart of the existence of the research university.

Empirical models of the joint production function are extremely rare in the literature. Two particular attempts at direct estimation are reported by Southwick (1969) and Sengupta (1975). These two authors tried to fit numerous models to a statistical data base covering a variety of input and output measures for sixty-eight land grant colleges and universities over a six-year time period. Unfortunately, no model that was specified would fit the data with any reasonable degree of statistical significance, and so one must conclude that the variance in output measures (student enrollments and research expenditures) was largely explained by factors other than the input variables that were included in these various models.

Of course, even if we were successful in fitting such a model to real data, there would be no guarantee that the result would represent the efficient frontier of production possibilities. In fact, following the reasoning advanced by Cootner (1974) and the evidence presented in Carlson (1975), we expect that it would not, in which case we would only have succeeded in modeling the inefficiencies of the current educational system. This observation, coupled with the usual problem of specification errors has probably kept most researchers away from attempting to estimate the university's production function by any such direct means.

Another approach to modeling the joint production process is given in Chapter 5 of Hopkins and Massy (1981). Built upon the earlier work of Oliver and Hopkins, this effort was largely undertaken for the purpose of developing a framework for computing the full costs (direct and indirect) of instructional outputs. The model recognizes five general classes of faculty activity (classroom teaching and preparation, teaching outside the classroom, joint teaching and research, pure research, and administration) and develops a weighting scheme for apportioning total faculty effort among the five categories. Implicit in the weighting scheme are the trade-offs among teaching effort, research effort, and joint teaching/research effort. Yet, since these tradeoffs are all expressed in terms of faculty *input* variables, they do not tell us anything about the real tradeoffs of interest, namely those between teaching and research *outputs* for fixed faculty inputs.

Another means of examining the tradeoffs implicit in the university production function is through the formulation of economic models of individual faculty behavior. One such model is described in Becker (1975). In this paper, it is assumed that a professor chooses an allocation of his or her time among teaching (T_1), research (T_2), and leisure activities (T_3) to maximize a utility function $U(.\ ,\ .\ ,\ .)$ defined in terms of teaching output (Q_1), research output (Q_2), and leisure-time consumption (Q_3). The output variables are further assumed to be linear functions of the time allocations and, in the case of leisure time only, of income (Y):

(7)
$$Q_1 = a_{11}T_1 + a_{12}T_2$$

(8)
$$Q_2 = a_{21}T_1 + a_{22}T_2$$

(9)
$$Q_3 = bY + a_{33}T_3$$

(Note that the "technology" coefficients, a_{ij}, do incorporate the 'jointness' between complementary teaching and research activities.) Finally, income itself is expressed as a function of the individual's output levels of teaching and research:

(10)
$$Y = w_1Q_1 + w_2Q_2$$

This system of equations is easily manipulated to yield an expression for the professor's production possibilities for a fixed amount of total time (T) in the form:

(11)
$$T = h_1Q_1 + h_2Q_2 + h_3Q_3$$

where the h are themselves explicit functions of the coefficients a_{ij}, b and w_i. From this expression we can see that the terms of trade among Q_1, $(Q_1$, and Q_3 are fixed (e.g., $dQ_2/dQ_1 = -H_1/h_2$) and the respective signs of the coefficients h_1 and h_2 indicate whether teaching and research are economic complements or substitutes. No data are reported by Becker, however, that would enable us to determine the nature or magnitude of these trade-offs in output space.

Directly related to Becker's work are several published reports that evaluate the relationship between research productivity and teaching effectiveness at various specific institutions (see, for example, Bresler, 1968, Hayes, 1971, and Voecks, 1962). The specified intent of these articles was to determine whether performance in research is positively or negatively correlated with teaching effectiveness in the university setting. Unfortunately, the results are quite mixed, with some schools exhibiting a positive correlation, others a negative one, and still others none that is measurable. Once again, the difficulties inherent in defining and measuring such concepts as 'teaching effectiveness' and 'research performance' in stark statistical terms have hindered us from compiling the evidence that we seek.

In summary, it is widely believed that teaching and research are at least partially complementary activities in the university setting. Several different attempts have been made to model the exact nature of the interaction between the two, yet none has succeeded in quantifying this joint production relationship in a way that would permit one to draw hard inferences based on real data about the economic 'terms of trade.' Thus, the empirical evidence we seek concerning the exact nature of the joint production process for instruction and research is still missing.

Economies of Scale in Higher Education

We turn finally to a review of the evidence concerning economies of scale in the production function of higher education. It is necessary to state at the outset that no evidence about economies of scale in university research could be found in any of the literature reviewed for this paper. Several efforts have been made, however, to determine whether economies of scale exist in the overall instruction process.

The Carnegie Commission on Higher Education (1971) explored the relationship between costs per student and institutional size using a national data base of colleges and universities. The data revealed a generally declining trend in unit costs with increasing size; this trend was especially pronounced for institutions with enrollment of under one thousand. These results suggest that there are increasing returns to scale for dollar expenditures as a function of enrollment over quite a broad range of institutional sizes.

This work was extended by Radner and Miller (1975) who performed a number of cross-sectional and longitudinal studies of faculty-student ratios as a function of institutional size. Here, again, student enrollment was used for the scale variable, while inputs were faculty rather than expenditures (although one would expect these two input variables to be highly correlated). Results were obtained from a national data set, stratified by type of institution, and showed for undergraduate-only institutions definite increasing returns to scale up to an enrollment level of between three and four thousand students. These increasing returns to scale were more pronounced for the private schools in the group than for the public ones. On the other hand, despite the authors' heroic efforts to examine the relationship of faculty inputs to size and several other variables at the public and private Ph.D.-granting institutions in their sample, they could discern no significant economies or diseconomies of scale for such institutions with respect to either undergraduate or graduate enrollment levels.

In addition to the studies already cited which draw evidence concerning economies of scale from a data set consisting of a wide number and variety of institutions, there is one published study that focuses on the same issue at a single institution. Dunworth and Bottomley (1974) formulated a cost model in terms of enrollments for the University of Bradford in the United Kingdom. Total costs per student were broken down into teaching costs, administration, student services, library costs, and capital and maintenance costs. The authors then studied potential economies that might arise from such strategies as increasing enrollments in specific disciplines with slack teaching capacity, increasing the utilization of expensive facilities (e.g., laboratories) through enrollment increases, and introducing alternative teaching structures (such as reduced number of contact hours per student, fewer courses offered, etc.). The analysis assumed that the proportions of time given to research and public service activities by the faculty were to remain constant at their then-current levels. Using real data from their university campus, the authors found a considerable potential for economies of scale that could be realized through better utilization of facilities and course offerings. These results should serve as yet another reminder of the hazards of using actual data on faculty-student or cost-student ratios as measures of efficient technological production possibilities in higher education!

In summary, there is considerable evidence for the existence of economies of scale for instruction in institutions of higher education. This evidence is found both in studies of aggregate 'productivity ratio' statistics across a large number of institutions, and of single institutional data on utilization of facilities and courses of instruction. The evidence is stronger in the case of institutions devoted primarily to teaching than it is for universities having a major research objective as well. Although intuitively one knows that economies of scale probably exist in research as well, no quantitative studies of the nature and extent of such economies were found in the higher education literature.

Suggestions for Further Research

Clearly, additional research is needed before we can specify the production function for higher education, or at least characterize the important trade-offs among inputs and outputs in anything other than purely qualitative terms. The following suggestions are made in recognition of the extreme complexity of the task, including the immeasurability of the many of the critical factors that enter into or result from this particular production process.

First, it does not appear particularly fruitful to examine any further the direct relationship between instructional output, as measured by student test scores, and variables representing attributes of the student and the institution. Such efforts have failed in the past due to inaccurate or incomplete specification of the 'learning model,' and any empirical basis for correct specification is still missing. Unless and until educational psychologists can reduce the learning process to quantitative terms with a high degree of accuracy, efforts by economists in this area will remain largely empty exercises in statistical manipulation.

We do not mean to suggest, however, that institutions should refrain from studying the impact of variables within their control upon the results of educational and research activities. Indeed, one area in which further research is badly needed is in the cost-effectiveness of alternative technologies for instruction. For example, in spite of the fact that many labor-saving devices have been recently invented in the form of computer-assisted learning devices and educational programming on television (including videotaped lectures given by the foremost authorities in many fields), the technology of instruction at most colleges and universities has scarcely been affected. The predominant mode of instruction remains face-to-face interaction between an instructor (often a highly paid member of the senior faculty) and a group of students in the classroom setting. Given the recent innovations referred to above, it would seem important to study alternative configurations of the instructional process in order to determine whether economies can be achieved through some substitution of capital for faculty labor without reducing educational effectiveness. Of course, one must be careful in conducting such studies to evaluate the quality of instruction along with its more measurable attributes.

Second, it is apparent that our ability to identify and measure the outputs of research is even more limited than in the area of instruction. Undoubtedly, this will remain an elusive problem, especially where the results of basic, as opposed to applied, research are concerned. We simply lack the means to define a 'quantum' of knowledge produced which could serve as a common unit of measurement across all disciplines or even across research teams operating in the same discipline. Neither can we anticipate future payoffs from basic research.

Here, again, we would propose less ambitious and more discrete efforts to study the production function for research in higher education. For example, we should be able to collect data on specific research teams in different disciplines within the same university. These teams are typically comprised of one or more faculty senior investigators, professional research associates, postdoctoral fellows, technicians, and students. What role is played by these actors individually and collectively and how do they contribute to the overall result? What would it mean to

TABLE 4
Summary Table of References on the
Higher Education Production Function

	Instruction Only	*Instruction and Research*
Outputs		Wiche [1970]
Production Functions:		
A. Institution Level	Gulko & Hussein [1971] Hopkins [1971] Oliver & Hopkins [1976] Radner & Miller [1975]	Carlson [1975] Cootner [1974] Nerlove [1972] Sengupta [1975] Southwick [1969]
B. Department Level	Breneman [1976]	
C. Individual Faculty		Becker [1975] Bresler [1968] Hayes [1971] Voecks [1962]
D. Individual Student	Astin [1973] Astin [1968] Becker [1983] Coleman [1966] Hanushek [1979] Heim & Perl [1974] Lau [1979] Levin [1976] Lewis, *et al.* [1985] Manahan [1983] Polachek, *et al.* [1978] Solmon [1973]	
Economies of Scale		Dunworth & Bottomley [1974]
General		Cohn [1979] Garvin [1980] Hopkins and Massy [1981] Lumsden [1974] Wallhaus [1975]

substitute more or less of one kind of labor input for another? How does the quantity and quality of capital inputs (facilities and equipment) affect the result? These are obviously terribly important questions in the present era of tightly constrained resources, and yet little is known about the major substitution effects.

Our suggestion is that the most fruitful avenue to explore for this kind of information is at a quite microscopic level within the institution, rather than in terms of global variables representing a conglomeration of disparate research activities across the institution. Alternatively, one might examine alternative approaches to investigating the same research problems across institutions. Data on measurable inputs might be manipulated in an effort to estimate the "efficient frontier," as in Carlson's work on identification of efficient points for instruction (Carlson, 1975). Of course, one would need to make the somewhat rash assumptions that output is constant across the institutions and that at least some of the research programs reflected in the data set are operating at or near the efficient frontier.

Finally, we would suggest that some further efforts to understand the joint production of instruction and research also be directed at the more microscopic level within the institution. Data, both quantitative and qualitative, might be obtained reflecting on the nature of the interactions taking place among faculty, undergraduates, graduate students, and postdoctoral associates within individual academic disciplines. These data could then be related to a set of locally defined outcomes for the purpose of illuminating the contributions made by each participant in the joint educational and research process.

The studies proposed above would be designed to increase our knowledge about the higher education production function, which, one must admit, is rather low at present. It is important that our expectations not exceed our capabilities. It would be a mistake to imagine that any amount of data analysis could lead to the complete specification of the production function and, hence, enable us to examine with any precision trade-offs in input and output space in quantifiable terms. There are simply too many intangibles relating to the abilities of various key actors to contribute to the process of education and research in ways that never will be very well understood. Thus, the most we should hope for is a better *qualitative* understanding of the production process in different kinds of institutions and in different disciplinary areas within those institutions. Whether this information will be sufficient to produce wise decisions about the very important trade-offs being faced by makers of national policy remains to be seen.

Organization, Funding, Incentives, and Initiatives for University Research: A University Management Perspective

FREDERICK E. BALDERSTON

The major universities in the United States are preeminent in graduate education and research in the scholarly disciplines and the professions.* Combining a wide range of academic programs and linking the conduct of large-scale research with graduate education, American universities differ from institutions in Europe and the Soviet Union, where a great deal of research is done in separate institutes and academies while instruction of students is the dominant function of universities. American analysts of higher education regard this multiplicity of functions in the U.S. universities as a strength. However, the research universities of the U.S. compete to some extent with other producers of research. Therefore, universities must demonstrate their effectiveness in the research enterprise if they are to retain their dominant role in basic research.

University Research: Changes in Funding Composition

The aggregate of federal basic research funding has risen, in current dollars, by fifty-eight percent from 1982 to 1987, to a projected total of $8.6 billion in the president's fiscal year 1987 budget.

The increase of total federal research and development funding is even more spectacular, including as it does enormous increases for new weapons systems. It will total more than $44 billion for fiscal year 1987. But, in the category of basic research, the '6.1' item of the Department of Defense (DOD) budget has grown to approximately $1 billion, and almost half of this is received by universities, not by defense contractors or federal laboratories (American Association for the Advancement of Science [AAAS], 1987).

In 1985, 51.6% of federal agency obligations for basic research went to universities, 25.2% to freestanding federal laboratories, 6.6% to industry, and 16.6% to other performers, including federally financed research and development centers (FFRDCs) operated by universities. The total amount of these federal obligations was $7.787 billion in 1985 (see National Science Board (NSB), 1986a, App. Table 2.15 and App. Table 2.13). Thus, universities received approximately $4 billion in federal obligations for basic research in 1985.

Universities also receive substantial funding from the much larger applied research and development components of federal research and development. In 1984, of $8.3 billion from all funding sources spent on research and development by doctorate-granting institutions, 33.4% was spent on applied research and the rest on basic research. (NSB, 1986a, App. Table 5.19). Universities received a total of $5.5 billion in federal research and development funds in that year; and, as 1984 was not very different from 1985, we can conclude that universities received about $1.5 billion in federal funds for applied research in 1985.

The overall increase in basic research funding is differentially spread across federal agencies. The National Science Foundation (NSF) had a fiscal year 1986 budget of $1.5 billion and a proposed increase of 9.8 percent for fiscal year 1987. The National Institutes of Health (NIH), on the other hand, received a small absolute reduction for fiscal year 1987, and it was anticipated that this would fall heavily on the project funding of faculty principal investigators rather than on the national biomedical institutes. The Department of Transportation (DOT) and the non-weapons portion of the Department of Energy (DOE) received very deep percentage reductions—30 to 40 percent (AAAS, 1987).

These changes in federal-agency funding may profoundly affect university research in particular fields. Portions of the biological sciences that draw heavily from NIH and chemical engineering research related to fossil fuels components of the DOE budget were hit by severe reductions in recent years. Dr. Neil Smelser testified, on behalf of a National Research Council (NRC) committee to a congressional committee, on the extreme volatility of NSF funding for the social and behavioral sciences. In 1985 dollars, funding in this area fell by 24 percent between 1976 and 1985, resulting in the shortening of the average grant interval to 1.2 years for approximately the same number of grants. This area's fraction of the NSF budget also fell, from 7.8 percent to 5.7 percent.

Modes of University Response to Funding Variations

One way to manage effectively in the face of sharp variations in public funding is to assemble the political leverage necessary to reduce the variations. Universities do lobby energetically, but universities, like manatees, swim rather slowly and are gentle beasts. On the whole, they are unlikely to succeed in asserting control over the political environment of federal research funding, although they can and do exert influence when they draw attention to their research contributions (Baker, 1985).

The other approach is to build precautionary buffers, and then act decisively in response to funding variations. Universities rarely have enough working capital to build buffer reserves. Their decentralized budgetary structures, in turn, do not enable them to adjust personnel and programs as quickly as business corporations do. Thus, a university department, or organized research unit (ORU), facing a sharp reduction in agency funding typically faces an emergency, and the sudden shrinkage of staff and budgets produces wasteful dislocations (*New York Times*, 1986).

The Conduct of Academic Research

Fundamental research is by definition a high-risk activity: uncertain in definition of the problem to be investigated; uncertain in duration and cost to achieve results; and uncertain in the implications of the results both for the structure of knowledge in the discipline and for the practical uses to which the new insights may eventually contribute. The great rewards of the contributor to fundamental knowledge are, first, the exhilaration of discovery, second, the approbation of expert colleagues in the discipline who can appreciate what has been discovered, and, third, professional recognition in the form of advancement in rank, salary, facilities, and responsibility.

Business corporations generally prefer to leave the funding and conduct of basic research to universities and concentrate their research and development investments in applied research and the development of products and processes toward commercialization and market success. In some fields, however, the traditional boundaries between the role of the university and the role of the commercial user are changing radically.

The dominant paradigm for the translation of new knowledge into things of value is from basic research to applied research to development to commercial introduction. But in recombinant-DNA research and in semiconductors, for example, this more-or-less leisurely progression has compressed in time and blurred the sequence of development. Newer university-industry relationships are emerging, as will be discussed below.

There is an alternative paradigm for the development of new knowledge. This is exemplified by the pattern that developed in agricultural research, beginning with the Hatch Act of 1887 and continuing with subsequent state and federal enactments. Because agriculture was highly dispersed and largely conducted in small-scale enterprises, government came to provide the applied research and problem-solving that no single farmer could afford. With this support, American agriculture became extraordinarily strong and scientifically progressive.

The agricultural experiment station at each land-grant university includes cooperative extension services for a continuous link between basic science and day-to-day farm operations. Some funds are devoted to basic scientific research, especially in the life sciences, even though applied research and field assistance are the mission-oriented parts of the research system (University of California, 1980).

In this alternative research paradigm, a new problem or an unmet need on the farm or in the marketplace comes to the attention of the agricultural extension specialist, a problem-solver in the field, who reports the problem back to the experiment station scientists. They assign the problem to a team of applied-research scientists. This team has access to basic researchers who do long-term research in plant genetics, entomology, or other disciplines. Their work is also sometimes enlivened by the unresolved field problems with which they are confronted for advice and help. When a promising solution to the problem has been developed in the laboratory, it is field tested and then disseminated to any who are interested in using it.

In varying forms, the problem-first paradigm prevails in many mission-oriented research organizations. Research at many frontiers between science and technology may well follow this paradigm. University researchers normally concentrate, however, upon the applied science problems that are beyond the immediate horizon of technological possibilities. By avoiding—as industrial firms cannot—preoccupation with the very next generation of a product or service, university researchers strengthen the long-term progress of technology.

The following examples illustrate changes in methods of research and funding that are likely characterizations of future trends in the organization of university research.

Examples of University-Industry Cooperation

The Microelectronics Laboratory of Berkeley, as a case in point, receives part of its funding from NSF and part from the Defense Advanced Research Projects Agency (DARPA). A major component of the lab's support, however, comes from twenty companies, each of which contributes $120,000 per year, and more than one hundred companies whose contributions are in the $10,000 to $50,000 range. The lab also receives matching funds from the State of California which have been specially allocated (U.C., 1982, 1985-86).

The laboratory asks for the involvement of corporate scientists in the periodic definition and formulation of research problems, and there is provision for periods of visitation by these scientists if they can be spared from their company work. The laboratory however, operates as an open facility, on the principle that the stimulus of free circulation of ideas is highly productive, whereas restrictions on the discussion of work in process or the dissemination of research results would be stultifying. The faculty and students of the lab also seek wide contacts with academic scientists across the campus, as the new problems that come on the agenda require fresh insights and leads from basic science.

The Center for Integrated Systems at Stanford University, in a similar pattern, received capital grants of $750,000 each from a number of companies for its laboratory building. This building was designed with the expectation that the infrastructure and equipment requirements for research within it may change rapidly. Large between-floors spaces permit installation of ducts, wiring, and other service systems as the focus of experimental methods changes in the multi-disciplinary teams that are housed there. Sponsoring companies contribute substantial annual support grants for operations, and these funds are joined with federal and university support funds.

A major company sometimes has a cooperative relationship with a research group at an institution. MIT established a long-term research relationship with DuPont. Hoescht AG, the German chemical company, established a laboratory for recombinant DNA research at the Massachusetts General Hospital and pledged $10 million per year for five years to attract an outstanding director and provide facilities.

These relationships with a single sponsor, like the governmental support that a university program may receive from a single-mission agency of the federal government, entail certain risks of intrusion and control. (See Day, 1976, for a study of contrasts between the client-focused ORU and other research organizations.)

The sponsor may demand prepublication clearance of research papers and other reports, or may seek other proprietary advantages from the relationship. In one instance, the industrial sponsor had the right to maintain in residence at the university laboratory two of its own staff scientists.

In principle, the fruits of basic research become public domain, and the researcher has not only the right but the duty to publish and discuss results freely with other scientists. This 'public goods' view of fundamental knowledge differs from the corporate justification of research and development as an investment in new products or processes whose uniqueness is to be protected where possible because that uniqueness imparts increased market value.

In the semiconductor industry and some other industries, patents and copyrights are relatively easily circumvented. The race for competitive advantage is always to the swift, and a bit of lead time with the best new ideas is the main source of competitive strength. The two laboratories at Berkeley and Stanford, each supported by numerous industrial sponsors, may help their respective sponsors to maintain state-of-the-art currency by working on the more basic problems that have to be solved in order to permit the specific development of commercial products some years in the future. The hypothesis underlying the open-lab approach is that the best work can be done only if there is full and free scientific communication—between scientists in the same and different universities, and between the university scientist and the industrial scientist. This conflicts with the instinct for control that lies behind industrial secrecy and the secrecy associated with national security. If universities accept industrial support with restraining conditions on publication and free discussion, they not only create internal philosophical tensions, but they may also prevent their own scientists from making the fullest possible contributions.

Nelson and Winter (1982) find that patent controls and other restraints on the spread and use of knowledge work to increase private economic gain in some industries more than in others.

It appears certain that university-industry relationships will increase in number and size. Some universities have produced guidelines for such cooperative arrangements (see U. C. 1982).

Research Consortia, Institutes, and University-Affiliated, Federally Funded Research Facilities

Facilities and equipment of great size and cost have become necessary in high-energy physics and in astronomy, with other related disciplines also involved. Total federal obligations to support the major university-affiliated FFRDC's amounted to $2.75 billion in 1983 (National Science Board [NSB], 1986a, App. Table 5.24). Of this total, however, a significant portion consisted of classified weapons research and development at Lawrence Livermore Laboratory and at Los Alamos Scientific Laboratory, whose combined budgets totaled a little over $1 billion.

When a very-large-scale facility is created, it requires expert operating management to minimize downtime and to schedule experiments by scientists from a variety of institutions. The funding agencies are quite naturally interested in assuring that there is maximum use of these one-of-a-kind facilities. Budget crunches such as that caused by the March 1986 Gramm-Rudman Act cut impair utilization of these facilities because operating support must be reduced. Of greater long-range concern is delay in funding major improvements to existing facilities, and the deeper question of whether to even attempt funding for the largest of them all, the Superconducting Supercollider (SSC).

Each university's scientists stand in an uneasy relation to these major facilities: knowing that shared use is necessary, yet concerned about whether the funding of such facilities cuts into the normal flow of project grants. The debate over the SSC includes suggestions that the U. S. try to interest European countries in a cooperative, multinational venture to share the enormous ($4 billion or more) cost and not to jeopardize the regular base of basic research funding. (NSB, 1986b).

New regional research institutes such as the Institute of Physics at Santa Barbara and the Mathematical Sciences Research Institute (MSRI) at Berkeley are NSF—financed consortia. These bring together senior experts and junior researchers around one or more themes of frontier-level research each year. Such institutes are clearly an enrichment of research opportunities for the individuals concerned, and MSRI seeks to provide stimulus to institutions in the region by arranging for its fellows to lecture at numerous locations each year. MSRI, in particular, has avoided any accumulation of permanent research staff, and its practice is to appoint fellows on one-year rotations. This approach minimizes any danger that such an institute could go stale or could drift into the European model of the research institute with permanent career staff, separated from the universities.

As the research enterprise becomes more complex, consortia and special institutes will probably grow in number. The universities will have to be alert to the positive effect these can have on faculty research productivity and equally alert to possible diversion of faculty energies or creation of competing research organizations.

Incentive Structures in Universities

Incentives for Graduate Study

Attracting the very ablest young people to graduate preparation for scholarly careers is a traditional concern of the universities. It is also a proper national concern, given the national role of the major universities and the critical need for new talent to ensure the future of basic research and teaching. Talented young Americans veered away from study for the doctorate in the late 1970s as the message about the Ph.D.

glut came through. Government policy changed drastically, with a decline in federally funded fellowship awards in all fields (science and nonscience) from 51,000 in 1968 to 6,000 in 1981 (NAS, 1983a, 1985, 1986).

Doctoral students are important in the internal economy of the research university, however, both as teaching assistants and in the research process. When qualified domestic students were not available, universities reached out to admit a growing proportion of foreign students (Froomkin, 1983). In 1980, foreign students received 46 percent of the doctorates granted in engineering, 27 percent of those in math and computer sciences, and 23 percent of those in the physical sciences. More ominous, "The number of engineering doctorates conferred on foreign students actually declined during the five years ending in 1980. The proportion increased because of a sharp decline in the number of U. S. citizens seeking doctorates in engineering" (NAS, 1983a, p. 82). As of 1983, foreign students represented 42 percent of all full-time graduate enrollments in engineering, 40 percent in mathematics, 38 percent in the computer sciences, and 29 percent in the physical sciences. (NSB, 1986a, p. 101).

Greater participation of female students in doctoral education in science and engineering commenced in the early 1970s. From 1980 to 1983, female enrollment increased by a further 7 percent. (NSB, 1986a, p. 100). A difficult problem remaining is the attraction of greater numbers of talented minority students into graduate education. This is necessary to redress serious underrepresentation of minorities in college and university faculties as well as to provide broader opportunities for these students themselves. Special fellowship programs are assisting in this process of recruitment.

For new doctoral students generally, portable NSF doctoral fellowships remain highly prized, and some other federal funding agencies are providing increased graduate student support (Colvig, 1986). But the problems of financial support during doctoral study remain a worry for talented candidates for science and engineering doctorates, and such support needs to be visibly increased. Beyond this, many recognize the difficulties of the current and recent generations of new Ph.D.s in obtaining attractive academic placement on completion of their degrees.

It appears clear that the 1990s will see a broad increase in the annual number of faculty vacancies as the faculty demographic pattern —currently a nonsymmetric age distribution—shifts to accommodate increased retirement rates (NSF, 1985; Congress, Office of Technology Assessment, 1985). In order to present a valid and convincing picture of career opportunities for future academic scientists and engineering doctorates, it would be a good idea for the NAS and other capable agencies to develop field-by-field and year-by-year projections of the nationwide demand for academic placement of new doctorates. This, together with reasonable assurances concerning future real incomes of academic scientists and other scholars, might help to convince greater numbers of the highly talented to turn toward doctoral study (Balderston and McPherson, 1980).

Incentives for Faculty

A faculty member is appointed and promoted in a research university according to his or her fulfillment of criteria of teaching, research, and public service. The most important of these—for tenure, reputation, and mobility—is, of course, research. Especially in the pretenure stage of career, it behooves the junior faculty member to provide evidence of individual creative achievement. The academic department is both the traditional setting for this work and the agency sponsoring the eventual candidacy for tenure, for this is where the faculty member holds appointment.

The candidate finds that time is short—often, three to six years, depending upon the rules of the university—to prove scholarly achievement and so justify advancement in rank and promotion to tenure. Sympathetic and able mentors in the department can help with the choice of research topics that can yield outstanding results in time for the tenure decision. Such choices are often crucial early career decisions.

Much important work in science and engineering consists of team efforts, led by a senior faculty investigator, bringing together a variety of specialists. (This pattern is less frequent in the social sciences and all but unknown in the humanities.) The young researcher must often be judged according to the quality of results in such collaborations and according to testimony concerning the role that he or she has played. Promotion and tenure-review committees prefer the easier task of evaluating individual publications for which the candidate is solely responsible. But team participation must nonetheless be evaluated fairly and fully if that is the necessary research mode in the field.

Research teams for problem-oriented research are often assembled from several departments, and the members spend protracted periods—up to several years—in a multidisciplinary team that is independent of departmental control. Unless the senior members of the team are on good terms with the junior researcher's academic department, such research participation may be a career risk, no matter how exciting are the topic and the context of research. One method of reducing this risk is for the candidate and the department to agree from the beginning on a procedure for periodic review of progress and for clarifying, to the department, how the candidate's research contributions are to be evaluated. It is also important for those administrators and faculty who are involved in the review and approval of advancement decisions to educate themselves concerning the modes of research that are necessary responses to the new types of challenging research problems.

Broad opportunities for original work in early career are of such importance that a new program of Presidential Young Investigator (PYI) awards has been initiated in the NSF. Because the young investigator might not ordinarily be able to garner adequate funds for research equipment and assistance, the PYI grant provides an unusual opportunity. The base grant is $25,000 per year for the research interval, plus up to $37,500 per year. The latter portion, however, is contingent on the candidate's success in attracting research grants or gifts from industry sources. If everything falls together, though, the young investigator has a research fund of $100,000 per year, which is a substantial boost to potential achievement. In engineering and applied science fields where senior faculty have many industry contacts and, as mentors, can help the PYI recipient to find industry support, this program has apparently succeeded well. Young researchers in some other fields, however, such as psychology or the theoretical sciences, have much more difficulty, both because the senior mentors cannot be so helpful in generating contacts and because it is difficult to evoke positive interest from industry donors in research that is remote from industrial application.

A high-quality academic research unit generally needs a mix of seasoned and energetic senior faculty and the very ablest, most daring young research minds. When the process works as it should, the senior faculty members bear the burdens of administrative leadership and reputational visibility, and the junior faculty members, as they prove themselves, contribute exceptional research findings.

Seed Money, Tide-Over Money, and Money in Unsupported Fields

In all the fields of scholarly work, stretching beyond the hard sciences and engineering through the social sciences, humanities and the old and newer professions, young investigators (and some older ones) need access to institutionally administered seed money. A new research area may need to be cultivated and 'proven up' for some time before it is ready to be described in a formal proposal that will be evaluated by peer review panels. A young investigator may simply not have a research record to demonstrate ability, no matter how attractive the prospectus for the work is. The university should assemble resources to provide such seed money, and it should work out simple procedures for application and for prompt approval decisions (National Commission on Research [NCR], 1980).

The faculty researcher who does normally have grants from outside the university sometimes finds that grant funds do not arrive one after another in the smooth order that is desirable for the conduct of research. The granting agency may suddenly fall into budgetary difficulty, or priorities may shift away from the area of work that has been supported. The university should be prepared to reinforce the institutional loyalties and incentives of the investigator by providing 'tide-over' funds for at least a limited period, so that the investigator can avoid the sudden abandonment of the research effort and the dispersal of the research team.

Finally, as is well known, some scholarly fields receive little or no external support, whether from federal agencies or from private foundations and donors. Yet the scholars in these fields need encouragement, and they need some resources to facilitate their work. Institutionally administered research-grant programs are needed as a response to these needs.

All three types of research support—seed money, tideover money, and money for unsupported fields—need the institutional leadership, and initiative of the university's central administration, for the external sources that may sometimes be available cannot be reached by the faculty researchers. Tapping these sources requires, not the typical project grant proposal, but some form of organized solicitation of alumni or other interested patrons of the institution. In addition, universities may provide some seed money by earmarking part of the indirect cost recovery money for this purpose or by setting up a research fund with the proceeds of patent royalties.

Institutional Incentives and Initiatives

The focus of the nation's basic research and cost of its educational leadership is on the three hundred doctorate-granting universities. The subset 'Research Universities I'—approximately eighty institutions—produces most basic research findings, receives most of the federal funding for basic research, and awards most of the doctorates in all scholarly fields. Of these eighty universities, approximately half are private and half are public (major campuses of some multicampus state university systems count as separate universities).

Doctorate-granting institutions that are not in the category of Research University I are generally striving to get there. And some public universities not now empowered to give the doctorate on an independent basis are seeking that authority (see State of California [SC], 1985-86).

How Many First-Rate Universities Does America Need?

One ceiling on the number of first-rate universities in the United States is provided by the amount of funding available for academic research and development. This grew remarkably (in 1972 dollars), from $1.1 billion in 1961 to $2.6 billion in 1968. It then grew very little for a decade, and thereafter expanded to an estimated $4.1 billion (still in 1972 dollars) in 1985 (NSB, 1986a, App. Table 5.20, p. 279). In current dollars, the 1985 estimate is $9.6 billion. While the federal component is, at $6.1 billion, almost two-thirds of the 1985 total, its growth in percent, has been less than that of support from the other sources: industry, foundations, and institutional funds (which includes state government funds). The doctorate-granting institutions account for 99 percent of the total of academic research and development funding. Further, one hundred of these three hundred universities accounted for 84 percent of the total, a proportion which has remained essentially unchanged over the years" (NSB, 1986a, p. 107.)

Masked beneath these growth figures is the pattern of only partial NIH and NSF support of qualified research investigators, as only about a quarter of approved grants could actually be funded. Nonfederal support cannot be expected to make up the difference (Kaiser, 1985).

There seem to be two possible modes of further development in the absence of a violent deviation from current trends. The first would be for the doctorate-granting institutions to continue competing for all the forms of support in a marketlike fashion. The second would be for these institutions—or at least more of them—to adopt more selective institutional strategies, so as to concentrate their institutional resources and their priorities upon a limited range of programs, and then to build more aggressively toward excellence in research and graduate education in that more limited domain of activity (Balderston, 1985). Given the wide distribution of undergraduate majors over the disciplines, a selective strategy would deny to some faculty groups and departments the opportunity to participate directly in the education of the next generation of advanced academic scholars. This would be a bitter pill—so bitter, in fact, that few university presidents are eager to dispense it.

Multicampus public university systems have the opportunity to sharpen developmental priorities by assigning appropriately specialized missions to their newer and smaller campuses, so that each of these will become strong in selected graduate areas instead of establishing small, low-quality beachheads in every field. The State University of New York does stratify its many campuses so that four of them—Albany, Buffalo, Stony Brook and Binghamton—are designated research university campuses. Some other multicampus systems give very special priority to a particular central or main campus. In some other instances, however, there is no plan for assignment of functions, and the campuses compete as though they were separate institutions. The University of California system does this in the academic disciplines, but there are controls by the Regents of the University and the California Postsecondary Education Commission on the establishment of new professional schools (Balderston, 1974, 1985).

There are serious defects of the first mode of adjustment—generalized competition—because it results in a large commitment of national, state, and private resources to graduate programs that do not meet generally agreed standards of excellence and that, in most cases, have no discernible route to the significant improvement necessary to become excellent.

There is a case for regional economic and social development centering upon strong higher education institutions, although it has been difficult to prove through economic analysis that investment in a strong regional university has been the cause of rapid regional economic advance. Nevertheless, some state governments may be pursuing a sensible developmental policy, as in the efforts over a twenty-five year period by public and private sector leaders in North Carolina to develop the Research Triangle.

Given the slow real growth of federal funding of basic research, however, it will be difficult for any large number of state initiatives to match federal research funding on the large scale that is required for world-class performance. Congress could once again spread out federal research funds through political allocation to the regions of the country. This would displace the current system of allowing the funds to go through peer review project grant channels and through quality-focused panels for the larger, multiuniversity research equipment installations. But regional reallocation of this kind would, unfortunately, weaken the leading universities whose performance is critical to the entire society (U.S. General Accounting Office, 1986).

To encourage more selective focus of academic priorities by each university or university system, one could imagine a special series of federal or foundation-sponsored institutional grants available to public or private universities with the condition that applicants undertake a self-study and assemble five-year or ten-year plans specifying which doctoral programs they would consolidate or abandon in return for strengthened, one-time support of the most promising and critically needed. For example, to facilitate the strategic redirection of American dental schools, the Pew Trust has provided a number of leading schools with two-phased planning grants so that they can redefine their activities for a very different future.

Resources and Flexibility for Institutional Initiatives

Lack of flexibility—and the need for more of it—is a common theme in the numerous commission and committee reports on the problems of the universities (Peterson, 1986). The availability of funding from many sources confers great advantages upon American universities, allowing them largely to direct their own operations and develop their own academic programs. No single funding source, however, is committed to or interested in providing the cushion of funds needed for the adjustment and redistribution of universities' operations and programs. The state governments are hard pressed to provide base budgets at adequate standards; to offer discretionary funds beyond this would run counter to the usual rules of political and bureaucratic control, even if the funds could somehow be found. Private universities are scrambling to maintain their competitive capabilities; funds set aside for discretionary flexibility would be a luxury to most.

Typically, each level of administration, from project to department to college to president's office, seeks to push rigidity to another level while retaining as much flexibility as possible for itself. It is a natural but ultimately self-defeating process.

Private foundations have tended away from higher education, focusing instead on research programs in which their boards become interested or for which they believe there is an especially urgent social priority (Cheit and Lobman, 1979). Private foundations could well consider 'flexibility grants' to universities in whose quality they have confidence. Federal research-funding agencies are now providing some enrichment funds along with their project grants, and this approach could and should be expanded. Given the source in funding for basic research, these moneys could be restricted quite legitimately to seed-money uses, to the purchase of equipment, and to the provision of special support to graduate students and postdoctoral associates. This is what the major universities would undoubtedly do with more money in any case.

Every university would benefit from flexibility money, and the distribution of such funds would surely have high social as well as institutional benefits at the margin. Again, flexibility grants could be tied to a university's self-study and its determination of selective development strategies.

Indirect Cost Recovery

All major universities have disputes with the federal government over the 'overhead rate,' as faculty researchers often (erroneously) call it. Incentive questions arise at several levels in connection with this problem of indirect cost recovery. First, Federal Circular A-21 sets the procedures for the accumulation of cost pools (for example, a pool for the totality of library costs, another for all maintenance and operation of physical plant, etc.) and the extent of research usage of the resources within each pool is then estimated to determine the amount of each type of indirect cost. The accounting and management problems are complicated enough, however, to leave considerable room for argument. The two cognizant federal agencies for determination and oversight of indirect cost recovery are the DOD and the Department of Health and Human Services (DHHS). They apparently differ somewhat in their practices, so that a university assigned to one of these agencies may have a different situation than a university assigned to the other.

In 1983, the NAS Ad Hoc Committee on Government-University Relations gathered expert opinions on the subject. Among the useful suggestions intended to partition this area of detailed and contentious argument by setting some agreed and uniform rate of indirect cost recovery on certain parts of the federal total. For example, it was suggested that program funds exclusively or largely devoted to graduate student training be separately provided for (NAS, 1983a).

The situation is exacerbated at the moment by the intention of the Office of Management and Budget (OMB) to 'find' $100 million by cutting back on indirect cost recovery. Even if the previous efforts to work through cost determination problems were imperfect, it seems peculiarly burdensome, according to David Packard and others, to use this approach for budget-cutting (see Culliton, 1986). Indirect cost recovery rates are said to be much higher for industrial contractors with the federal government than for universities. Once the current budget crunch is behind us, perhaps it will be possible to arrive at some new approaches to this problem.

As it is, public universities face a basically different situation than do the private universities. Private institutions regard indirect cost recovery as a matter of insuring the basic fabric and services of the institution — the library, the accounting system, departmental administration, etc. — and they claim that their base budgets would be disastrously impaired if rates were reduced or capped (Stanford University, 1985; MIT, 1985). Public universities, on the other hand, receive state appropriations for most of the basics. Indirect cost recovery, as viewed by many state authorities, is simply federal reimbursement for the portion of these services that are used in federally-funded research activity. By this reckoning, the state government would be entitled to capture all or nearly all of the moneys paid as indirect cost recovery.

Most states share to some extent with their public universities, so that part of the recovered funds can be retained for university uses. Even so, the public universities, as a group, have negotiated rates that are considerably lower than those of the major private institutions. One analysis showed that, of thirty high-volume (in total research dollars) university campuses, the average indirect cost recovery rate of the private universities was 63.6 percent in 1986, as against an average of 42.8 percent for the public university campuses. If the public universities were allowed to keep more of the funds recovered, or more above some base dollar figure, they would probably work harder to get larger cost recovery.

In both the public and private universities, however, indirect cost recovery is universally unpopular among faculty research investigators. Partly this is due to the practice of some research funding agencies, including NSF, of making total-cost awards, in which overhead costs are subtracted from the amount available for use by the principal investigator. But another reason, much closer to home, is that the faculty investigator usually has the sense that funds the university receives have simply vanished into the administrative maw, with no discernible benefit to the project, the department, or any tangible activity that is of interest to the academic process (*Chemical Engineering News*, 1984).

Some of the ammunition for federal attacks on the universities' practices regarding indirect cost recovery has come from faculty members antagonized by what they feel is unfair allocative treatment. This aspect of the incentive (or disincentive) system is troubling because it makes antagonists out of energetic and devoted leaders in the universities. Perhaps a bit of balm could be applied in the form of an increase of a certain percentage in each university's rate, to be devoted to meeting the funding deficiencies for research equipment. But any scheme of this sort must be deferred until the current budget crunch has passed.

Conclusions and Suggestions

From the above discussion of organizational and funding problems, it can be concluded that universities and their funding sources should be explicit in providing funds and organizational arrangements for greater flexibility, and that universities and their funding sources should see that they provide positive incentives for the good performance of individuals, departments, and research units.

Incentives for the Individual Investigator

First, the individual faculty investigator would often benefit if, instead of annual grants or other grants for a small, stated number of years, federal

granting agencies would agree to finance *a stream of work*, with simplified annual progress reports and a final stage of research indicated by
the fulfillment of that workstream. Some approximation of this exists
now, with the practice by one agency of providing a ten-year grant after
the faculty investigator has proven his or her research productivity in
one or two grants for shorter periods. But the problem, in essence, is
that any arbitrary time period may be incorrect with respect to the
research process itself, even though it may be organizationally and
budgetarily convenient. The prospects for arranging this sort of change
will be poor as long as the funding agencies are under significant budgetary pressure, as they now are.

Second, institutionally controlled research funds under the discretionary direction of skilled senior academic research administrators are
needed so that there can be access to project support that is based on
more flexible, risk-oriented criteria than those normally employed by
peer panels for extramural funding. Some of the multiprogram, federally funded research and development centers can perform this function, providing support for the high-risk idea that would not likely pass
muster in a formal proposal to a peer review panel. There is a shortage
of philosopher kings, however, and not very many universities have
immediate access to an administered research agency with a large
funding base. Nevertheless, a university that wanted to provide a basis
for awarding high-risk research funds could seek a special research
endowment to experiment with the mode of administering the annual
income as grant funds.

Flexibility in Research Organization

Organized research units (ORUs) need to be more easily formed, or, if
licenses to do business are bureaucratically restricted, then ORUs need
to be flexible in adapting to changing research agendas. ORUs need
greater flexibility in arranging the affiliation of appropriate people from
the various disciplines who contribute to the research agenda. Greater
flexibility in allocating facilities and equipment is also very much needed.
Such flexibility of research organization is difficult to achieve and still
more difficult to sustain. Periodic evaluation of the vitality of the ORU
and the significance of its field of focus is one definite aid. A university
often provides a core budget for an ORU—an amount sufficient to keep
an office operation going. The ORU is then expected to serve as domi-
cile for extramural grant funds secured by faculty investigators, and these
funds defray research expenses. University funds may be provided if the
research organization has institutional responsibility for maintaining a

research collection, or, as in the case of state universities, if the state government mandates the provision of research activities in agriculture, industrial relations, or some other area of social importance. But ordinarily, an ORU's loss of impetus is signalled by a persistent decline in extramural grant support, and it is then time for a searching review by the university administration.

In the periodic review of ORUs, two cases need to be distinguished: that in which, as above, such principal investigator brings in his or her own project funding; and that in which there is either state-mandated research funding or an institutional commitment by the university to develop a major research thrust. In the latter case, the ORU stands or falls on the collective performance of the unit, rather than on the performances of independent investigators.

Given that core funding is a valuable asset to those interested in the ORU, however, there is natural resistance to its dispersal and the reallocation of these funds. Thus, active oversight and administrative initiative are required.

The typical practice of universities is to allocate office and laboratory space through administrative negotiation, not to regard space as an economic asset that should be priced and budgeted. An academic department or research organization has little or no incentive to admit excess capacity or to give up space unless forced to do so. Dollar budgets for administrative support, on the other hand, are usually watched carefully and managed in a more thrifty fashion. Putting the allocation of space in a more disciplined, market-like framework would make departments, ORUs and other units behave somewhat more rationally.

Strategic Direction of the University: Selective Priority

A deeper issue is that of institutional leadership in the determination and support of academic and related research priorities. In many respects, the development of a university over time is evolutionary: the result of step-by-step actions to appoint faculty, resolve curricular disputes, respond to proposals for new degree programs, or, occasionally, establish a new school or college. Traditional departmental organization, with the department consisting of colleagues defined as peers within the same discipline, does not lend itself to rapid shifts of direction. In this evolutionary mode, the university expects of its administrative leadership a balanced, reflective, and calm approach to the allocation of available resources and the solution of problems.

There is, however, an increasingly strong case to be made for a more active approach. The more rapid pace of adjustment in labor markets and social developments in the wider society makes it necessary to anticipate a wider amplitude of fluctuation of enrollments in both undergraduate and graduate degree programs in the disciplines. The professional schools face even more rapid adjustment requirements, both to variations of enrollment interest and to the more rapidly changing needs, demands, and perceptions of their client professional markets. (It was only yesterday that *everyone* wanted to go to medical school, and only the day before yesterday that *nobody* wanted to enroll in engineering!)

Building and rebuilding of curricula, faculty, and academic organizations becomes a strategic necessity in such a world of change. For the major university, the research enterprise faces a similar acceleration of changes, partly because shifts in instructional organization are coupled to changes of instructional requirements in graduate education and the professions, and partly because progress within disciplines continually modifies the research agenda itself.

The NAS assessment of quality in graduate education provides a status report as a starting point in the major disciplines and in engineering (NAS, 1983b). But this only points to strength or weakness, and in a rather conventionally defined way. The university's administration and faculty leadership, taking their own more detailed assessments, need to determine whether to allocate heavy efforts to rebuild a weak department or, alternatively, to reduce it or consolidate it with related fields.

Each professional school needs a similar periodic assessment and a determination of its direction of development. A professional school may be guided budgetarily by the 'every-tub-on-its-own-bottom' principle, but it also needs to look far enough ahead to provide leadership and initiative to its professional field.

Research and research organization feed strength (or convey weakness) to the existing disciplines and the professional schools. Thus, if it is determined that a field needs reorganization and strengthening, there should be simultaneous determination of priorities for faculty appointments, research subsidies and facilities, and research directions.

Dynamic Adaptation as Knowledge Expands:
Offsetting Increased Instability

New discoveries eventually result in the reorganization of what needs to be taught and learned. New fields such as biophysics, biostatistics, and psycholinguistics are testimony to this. As time goes on, some of these become formal academic departments, with permanent curricular and faculty responsibilities on their own. But the sheer volume of new discovery and its quickening pace require much more flexibility in the conduct of research than is generally needed or feasible in the organization of academic departments. Ever since it was made famous by Vannevar Bush, we are used to the notion of "the endless frontier" of science. But new discovery is making the stock of knowledge change in dimension as well as amount. New interconnections between fields, of a technique invented in one field for investigation of a problem in another, and new challenges to existing paradigms of explanation: All of these require us to anticipate that research will confront a continually increasing range of important open questions.

There is some upper limit on the sensible size of any one university. Thus, no matter how daring its faculty and how ebullient and entrepreneurial its president, each university will have to reconcile itself to not doing everything. Rather, its fruitful course will be to choose significant areas within its existing capabilities and push those hard toward distinctive contributions.

Proliferation, mutations of fields, and increasing complexity appear certain to characterize the search for knowledge. The areas of science, engineering and social science that depend squarely on computation and online control and interpretation are indicative of this future.

We have seen that it would be desirable for the good functioning of the universities to have greater continuity, stability and flexibility. It is ironic, or perhaps it is only justice or a cosmic joke, that the pace of change induced by expanding knowledge increases instability in the institutions and working lives that create this knowledge.

John von Neumann predicted that, while the onrush of technology would confer great blessings upon mankind, it would also increase the risks of many types of social and political instability. This instability comes not only through the heightening power of military technology, but also through the expansion of capabilities of the numerous new technologies that push us near the confining limits of space on the earth itself (von Neumann, 1955/1986). As we consider how universities contribute to the increasing stock of knowledge—and thus, according to von Neumann's speculation, increase instability—we should assure that the research agenda includes the production of insights that will help us to offset and reduce the hazards that are created by our ingenuity!

Participant Goals, Institutional Goals, and University Resource Allocation Decisions

HOWARD P. TUCKMAN and CYRIL F. CHANG

While many researchers have studied both the ideal and the actual goals of participants in the higher education process, surprisingly little has been written about how these goals affect the resource allocation decisions made by universities.* This chapter makes a first step toward defining the relationship between institutional goals and resource allocation decisions.

A Model of Efficient Resource Allocation

Economic theory provides a rich framework for analyzing economically efficient resource allocation (Ferguson, 1969). The economic model assumes a decisionmaker who pursues a set of goals for his or her own satisfaction subject to one or more constraints (see chapter 4 by Estelle James). The goals are not realized all in one piece, but rather in small increments. Each increment realized results in an increase in the decision-maker's satisfaction (or utility). If, for example, the goal is to educate more students, each additional student added to the university's enrollment increases the satisfaction of the decisionmaker. The same is true if the goal is to improve the quality of the educational offerings of the university. A one-point increase in the entering SAT scores of students is associated with a finite increase in the decisionmaker's satisfaction.

Satisfaction is maximized when the decisionmaker allocates resources to each goal in such a fashion that no other combination of resources gives rise to a higher level of total utility, given the constraints. At this point, equilibrium is reached and resource allocation patterns remain stable unless new goals are introduced, and/or the utility function of the decisionmaker changes (see Kohler, 1986). The economic model has been applied by economists in a wide variety of contexts including law, education, health care, and environmental protection.

53

Application of the economic model to the resource allocation process at universities involves at least four assumptions: 1) A set of goals can be identified which result in increases in the satisfaction of decisionmakers. 2) Where multiple decisionmakers are involved, a means can be found to select from among the myriad of sometimes conflicting goals of participants. 3) Sufficient goal stability exists that the optimal resource allocation is not constantly changing. 4) Increases in the resources devoted to pursuing goals can be related to recognizable outputs. This chapter explores the use of these assumptions beginning with an identification of the interested parties in the resource allocation process and the goals normally attributed to them.

The Goals of the Major Parties

Over the years, a considerable literature has developed on the goals for higher education (see Tuckman and Chang, 1988). Bowen (1980), for example, claims to have found more than fifteen hundred goal statements in historical and contemporary sources. Despite this richness on the subject, the literature lacks a consistent set of definitions of the terms *aim, purpose, mission, goals, objectives,* and *priorities.* To facilitate discussion of the resource allocation issues, we begin our discussion with a short vocabulary. A *purpose* is an object or aim to be reached or accomplished. It represents an organization's reason for existence. A *mission* is a statement of educational philosophy which provides a long-term sense of institutional identity. Missions and purposes serve to guide and assist decisionmakers in the process of goal selection and affect resource allocation only in a very broad sense. For example, at a university with a regional mission, a decisionmaker might deny resources to a program which primarily serves a national clientele. The goals of a university are more likely to have a major effect on resource allocation than its mission or purpose because they are more concrete.

Fenske (1980) defines university goals as statements of purpose that fall between broad statements, such as those found in mission statements, and specific descriptions of university operations. Goals can be framed either for the long or the short term, although the vocabulary in this area is not standardized. For example, Pratt and Reichard (1983) argue that goals provide direction for periods of two or more years while objectives are more specific statements for periods of one year or less. In contrast, Elgart and Schanfield (1984) define mission and objectives as ends to be achieved in the long run and goals as ends to be reached more immediately.

Goals can also be either general or specific. For example, a general university goal is to increase the quality of its educational offerings. A specific goal is to increase the average GMAT score of its graduates by fifty points. (It should be noted that the strategic planning literature often refers to highly specific goals of this type as objectives, in contrast to the authors discussed above.) The more general the goal, the more likely it is to encompass several specific goals. Thus, the goal of improving quality for the university may encompass a set of goals for each curriculum and/or field offering. In this paper, we use the term *generic goal* to refer to a general goal which encompasses a set of specific goals.

A large number of interested parties have an effect on university resource allocation decisions. Each of these parties has a set of generic goals which govern their actions toward universities and which give them satisfaction when the goals are realized. The ten major participant groups are: (1) students, (2) faculty, (3) administrators, (4) trustees and governing boards, (5) professional and accrediting agencies, (6) society at large, (7) federal funding agents, (8) state funding agents, (9) philanthropic institutions, and (10) private industry. The sections that follow identify the major generic goals of each of these groups.

Student Goals

To facilitate cognitive learning:

To acquire from a university verbal and quantitative skills, a base of cultural and factual material, the ability to think logically, intellectual tolerance, esthetic sensibility, creativeness, intellectual integrity, and wisdom.

To promote emotional and moral development:

To search in a conducive university setting for self, psychological well-being, human understanding, valid and internalized values and moral principles, religious interests, and refinement of taste, conduct, and manner.

To achieve practical competence:

To acquire from a university skills to fulfill the need for achievement, future orientation, adaptability, leadership, citizenship, economic productivity, sound family life, consumer efficiency, fruitful leisure, and health.

To attain direct satisfaction and enjoyment:

To have an environment conducive to learning how to gain satisfaction and enjoyment from life both during college years and later.

To avoid negative outcomes:

To have an environment which encourages the learning of how to resolve conflicts in college and later years.

Faculty Goals

To facilitate cognitive learning for self:

To function in an environment which facilitates the continued acquisition of new verbal and quantitative skills, knowledge from existing data bases, creative skills, and wisdom and renewal of skills that have deteriorated or become obsolete.

To increase emotional and moral self-development:

To work in an environment conducive to learning how to adapt to life-cycle changes, to changes in personal circumstance, and to social and economic forces that affect self-concept and psychological well-being.

To contribute to student learning:

To work in a setting which encourages the preparation of written and verbal materials designed to improve or augment student learning, design new courses and improved curricula, disseminate knowledge and wisdom outside the university through articles, public appearances, consulting, etc.; to be encouraged to preserve knowledge for future generations through textbook preparation, creation of archives or museums, etc.

To contribute to the creation of new knowledge:

To work in a university which creates an incentive to restate existing knowledge in ways which provide new insights, criticize existing knowledge in ways which suggest ways to improve upon it, pursue and discover new knowledge through conceptualization, data collection, experimentation, mathematical derivation and/or statistical analysis.

To achieve professional recognition and prestige:

To have an incentive to serve in an officer capacity in honoraries, national academies, or professional societies; to receive citations in national journals or indices, appointments to decisionmaking committees at universities, national, state, local or private organizations, consultantships, editorial positions, and other service or awards that either lead to or recognize the faculty member's achievements.

To achieve economic success:

To be recognized by the university with salary increases, promotions, sabbaticals, and university and/or outside grant-funded support for graduate students, equipment, laboratories, and other related resources.

To realize non-work-related satisfaction and enjoyment:

To be a happy person outside the office.

Administrator Goals

To achieve self-cognitive learning:

To have an institutional incentive to acquire verbal, management, and organization skills, knowledge from relevant data bases, creative skills, and skills for dealing with both people and situations.

To pursue emotional and moral self-development:

To work in an environment conducive to acquiring skills that will help adapt to changes in the organization, in life cycle, in personal circumstance, and to other factors affecting self-concept, human understanding, values and morals, and psychological well-being.

To contribute to student and faculty learning:

To work in an environment which encourages stregthening the curriculum and instruction process through new or improved course offerings, hiring of better faculty, acquisition of better instructional facilities, development of support systems to facilitate learning, and implementation of programs designed to upgrade and motivate faculty.

To insure the perpetuation and growth of the institution:

To receive recognition for enhancing the reputation of the university, building or securing its financial base, improving its competitive position, increasing its chance of survival, and enabling it to occupy new niches in the educational marketplace.

To insure efficient management of the institution:

To improve communications among participants, increase resource accountability, streamline operations, raise productivity, motivate faculty and staff, and otherwise insure efficient operation of the university.

To achieve professional recognition and prestige:

To have an incentive to serve in an officer capacity in professional associations, on boards of directors of businesses, charities, hospitals, or educational committees, accreditation boards; to be appointed to national task forces, to state and local civic organizations, and other related appointments; to receive awards for administrative achievements and other public acknowledgements of professional accomplishment.

To achieve economic success:

To secure salary increases, solicit offers from more desirable institutions, offers of consultantships, and increased job perquisites.

To realize non-work-related satisfaction and enjoyment:

To be a happy person outside the office.

Trustee and Governing Board Goals

To insure survival and growth of the institution:

To enhance the position of the university by overseeing its financial base, fund-raising activities, and to enhance its reputation in the region and the nation.

To insure efficient management of the institution:

To oversee the activities of the president of an institution to achieve sound management and accountability, avoid unnecessary duplication of function (public institutions), and require efficient operation.

To represent alumni or state interests:

To insure that the university's reputation is not allowed to diminish, that alumni concerns are heard and addressed, and that alumni and public needs are met.

To encourage preservation and dissemination of culture.

To encourage discovery and dissemination of new knowledge.

Many trustees and governing boards also share one or more of the societal goals listed below.

Professional and Accrediting Board Goals

To work for the preservation and growth of institutions of higher education.

To encourage preservation and dissemination of our cultural heritage.

To encourage discovery and dissemination of new knowledge.

To improve the quality of higher education offerings.

To realize specific goals of members.

Society Goals

To preserve and disseminate cultural heritage:

To have universities discover, preserve, and make available to the public the many facets of human culture.

To encourage discovery and dissemination of new knowledge:

To have universities create new knowledge and advance philosophical and religious thought, literature, and the fine arts in order to increase our satisfaction and enjoyment from living in a world of advancing knowledge, technology, ideas, and arts.

To encourage discovery, recognition, training, and placement of talent:

To have universities identify bright young minds, teach and assist them to develop, point them toward appropriate fields of study, and to encourage them to assume productive societal roles.

To advance the social welfare:

To have universities adopt programs which increase economic efficiency and growth, enhance national prestige and power, enable progress toward solution of social problems, improve the motives, values and other aspects of the emotional and moral development of individuals, and enable progress in human equality, freedom, justice and related aspects of our social system.

To assist society in achieving positive and avoiding negative outcomes.

Federal Funding Agent Goals

To promote equality of opportunity:

Insure equal access to universities for qualified students of every race, creed and color.

To provide student financial aid to the needy:

Insure that qualified students are able to receive a university education.

To promote and encourage research:

Encourage research that is national in character and that can potentially contribute to the basic knowledge and/or well-being of society.

To finance innovation:

Increase the diversity of research, course offerings, options available to students, faculty, and society.

To assure efficient use of federal funds:

To eliminate wasteful duplication, practices leading to under- or over-utilization of resources, use of funds for improper purposes, and other practices impeding efficient use of federal funds.

State Funding Agent Goals

To protect the rights of citizens in the educational process:

To promote and insure fair treatment, adequate educational standards, and equal and reasonable access to universities for all citizens of the state.

To assure efficient use of state funds:

To eliminate wasteful duplication, practices which lead to underutilization of resources, use of funds for improper purposes, or other practices that hamper efficient use of state funds.

To train citizens to meet state needs:

To educate a large proportion of those in the state eligible for higher education; to educate over a large part of a citizen's lifetime, provide higher levels of training than otherwise attainable in the state, provide expertise to help solve social problems, provide training for state manpower needs.

To coordinate the sources of postsecondary education:

To expand the range of postsecondary choices available to students including nonformal and traditional forms of instruction.

To protect the diversity of university offerings:

To preserve the unique character of different institutions and provide meaningful choices to those planning to attend college.

Goals of Philanthropic Institutions

To upgrade the quality of instruction:

To fund specific programs to improve teaching techniques, provide new forms of instructional material, encourage learning of specific types of knowledge, etc.

To insure equal access to education:

To provide various scholarship and loan programs to insure equal access to qualified minorities.

To direct students and faculty toward fields in short supply:

To provide funds to researchers for better data on occupations in short supply or for training in fields judged critical to the operation of the economy but where shortages of personnel exist.

To direct research toward fields of concern to the social welfare.

To improve the quality of campus facilities:

To fund new buildings, equipment, laboratories and other campus projects that upgrade the quality of the university physical plant.

Private Industry Funders Goals

To upgrade the level of manpower available to industry:

To educate persons able to solve complex problems, familiar with existing knowledge bases, and conversant with changing technologies.

To create and disseminate new knowledge:

To encourage usable basic research, solve problems not dealt with by industry, foster innovation, and create a knowledge base useful in the future.

To provide greater awareness of the economic system:

To fund teaching and research projects designed to acquaint students with the advantages of market-oriented systems.

The Role of Institutional Goals

While the above goals are meaningful and important to the persons and groups that hold them, the question arises as to which goals, if any, will be adopted by the university. No university will adopt all of the above goals both because of their sheer number and because some of the goals are contradictory. A choice must be made as to which of the goals are most important from an institutional perspective, and which best reflect the mission and orientation of the institution.

The problem of how institutional goals can be selected by individuals is addressed by Hoenack and Berg (1980). These authors argue that a group which attempts to define a set of institutional goals cannot derive mutual objectives from individual objectives unless: (1) The objectives of one individual dictate the objectives of the group, (2) a set of objectives is imposed on the group or, (3) individuals are induced to accept a set of objectives (e.g., a party with control over resources induces cooperation through an implied or actual commitment of resources). To these authors, mutual consent is derived by compensating individual members of the group to endorse objectives other than their own.

Institutional goals can be derived in several ways; from the mission statement of the institution, from statements of the president and the leadership, from the institution's planning office, from committees formed for accreditation or strategic planning, and/or from efforts to meet the demands of external funders. It should be clear, however, that the existence of a set of goals does not mean that they are embraced by all of the participants in university activities or that they have any impact on the ongoing operations of the institution.

At present, surprisingly little empirical research provides insights into the way that institutional goals are formulated or the extent to which they are espoused by participants in the higher education process. Instead, a majority of the literature contains three competing strands of thought. The first argues that institutional goals cannot be defined, the second that while such goals can be identified they are not used, and the third that formal goals cannot guide decisionmaking.

An example of the first perspective is Wallin (1983) who argues that universities are "leading actors in search of their parts." In contrast, Gardner (1965) sees institutions shaped by the "unintended consequences of millions of fragmented purposes," and Bowen (1984), a believer in goals for higher education, notes that "academic administration consists not of a long-range planning based on reliable prediction but of adjustments to a continual succession of surprises." An implication of these arguments is that while institutional goals can be identified, they may not be stable or consistent.

A second group of authors argues that institutional goals do not meaningfully affect resource allocation. For example, Rugg, Warren, and Carpenter (1981) argue that the diversity and pluralistic nature of the comprehensive university makes the development of specific institutional goals difficult, if not impossible. Moreover, the absence of consensus among the participants lessens or negates the impact of the goals on decisionmaking. A different line of argument comes from Pratt and Reichard (1983) who maintain that while many institutions develop goals, few assess how well these are achieved. Institutional goals which exist on paper but which are not operational are unlikely to affect resource allocation.

A third approach taken by Conrad (1974) distinguishes between formal goals and operative goals. The latter emerge from the process of daily decisionmaking and give the university "directionality" and "continuity," but these are a by-product of the operation of a university rather than a determinant of the direction it takes. Conrad also argues that the operative goals of an institution cannot be predicted in advance. An implication is that a utility function for the institution arises from the past rather than as a plan for the future. The allocation of resources that emerges in Conrad's world is a viable one but there is no assurance that is optimal.

Summarizing the above, we find that literature offers few insights beyond the conclusion that university goals exist. The issue of how the multiple—and sometimes conflicting—goals of interested parties are melded into a set of institutional goals that can guide resource allocation remains an area for fertile research.

The Stability of Institutional Goals

To exert a long-term influence over resource allocation decisions, institutional goals need to be reasonably stable over time. This section reviews several factors which contribute to goal stability.

Stability of the decision process:

Institutional goals are more likely to be stable if the persons or groups that formulate these goals remain constant through time than if these people change frequently. Stability is also more likely if the weights given to the preferences of participants in the resource allocation process are not subject to frequent modification. Instability is especially likely to occur if the decision rules used to weight the goals of the participants are not well established or if an institution continually redefines its goals and purposes.

Stability of the environment:

Institutional goals are shaped by social, political, economic, intellectual, moral and other environmental conditions. Changes in any of these conditions can affect the goals of the institution. For example, changes in labor markets can cause a university to redefine its goals for individual programs or for research. A university which specializes in engineering may be forced to change its goals when engineering jobs grow scarce. Likewise, a university that wishes to reduce the size of its education school may find it necessary to redefine this goal if a teacher shortage arises. A number of medical schools have closed their dental schools in recent years because of a shortage of high-quality new applicants, and many nursing schools have been forced to shrink because of an absence of candidates.

Changes in political and social conditions also affect both the institutional goals and the weights given to participants in the resource allocation process. For example, several authors note the shift in administrative goal-setting from within the university to external sources (Berdahl

and Gove, 1982; Perkins, 1984). Likewise, the change in student attitudes away from socially oriented pursuits towards business had a substantial impact on the resources directed towards the business school
vis-à-vis the rest of the university. While universities may reach more
slowly than society at large to changing conditions, their goals are not
independent of what is happening around them.

The validity of the goals:

Institutional goals are more likely to be stable if they are widely held by
the participants in the university, if they are perceived as fair, and/or if
they are consistent with the traditions or mores of the institution. They
are less likely to be stable to the extent that they reflect a weakly
supported compromise, are held by a few persons in the university community (particularly if these persons are not directly connected with the
decision process), and/or are imposed by external parties with a short-
term commitment to the university. Goals defined in an autocratic manner may be stable if the autocrat is firmly entrenched and a consistent
party to the resource allocation process.

The generality of the goals:

General goals are more likely to be stable than specific goals for at least
three reasons: (1) It is easier to gain and maintain support for a general
goal statement because the persons who support it are less likely to be
concerned about (or aware of) its effect on their self-interest than if the
statement were specific. (2) General statements are less likely to be
affected by changes in the environment than specific ones and hence
may be more resistant to change. For example, a university which has a
goal of maintaining a quality student body will be less likely to change
that goal than one that promises to recruit three hundred Merit Scholars
or to fund one hundred minority students each year. (3) Because general
goals are less binding on decisionmaking than specific ones, pressures to
modify or eliminate these are less likely than for specific goals

Absence of goal conflict:

Where one participant's goal is achieved at the cost of another's, the
latter may continue to challenge that achievement even long after it is
accepted at the institutional level. Depending on the rules of the game,
goals which conflict may be less stable than nonconflicting ones if the
strength of the opposing parties changes through time. When resources
are scarce, goal conflict is inevitable. The nature of the process for
resolving these conflicts and the stability of the weights given to participant goals affect the stability of institutional goals.

Stability of external funding sources:

Universities attract the attention of external funders for at least five reasons: (1) They are involved in the creation of knowledge and external funders wish to change the direction of (or improve the quality of) universities' inquiry and/or to acquire the specific knowledge they generate. (2) They provide trained labor and external parties want to influence either the quantity, quality, or type of labor universities produce. (3) They are a prime problem-solving source which may provide a solution for the problem of an external funder. (4) They are repositories of knowledge and a funder would like to see certain knowledge disseminated. (5) A funder likes what a university does and wants it to do more.

Except in the case of reason 5, when a university contracts to accept funds provided by an external source, it admits a new participant to its goal-setting team. This member can be a source of instability if it is an inconsistent source of funds and/or if its goals change frequently. For example, the impact of federal funding on both research and graduate studies support has been well documented in the literature. Changes in federal policy have caused instability in the direction of university research, staffing patterns, ability to fund graduate students, and overall institutional support (Fallows, 1983; Freeman, 1971; Zumeta, 1985). The external agent also affects institutional goals through the regulations it imposes. Likewise, public institutions have found themselves heavily impacted by state efforts to impose external goals on them. A substantial literature questions the advisability of allowing external entities to define university goals (e.g., McPherson, 1983; Perkins, 1984).

The literature is strangely silent on whether external funders successfully change the goals of universities and whether they realize their goals by funding universities. A number of studies of individual projects have been undertaken by the funders who paid for them, ranging from job training, to economic development, to postdoctoral programs. Thus far, however, no researcher has rendered a definitive judgement on the overall effect of the external funders on a university.

A Critical Evaluation of the Economic Model

The economic model of resource allocation assumes that a decision-maker takes a bundle of resources available to him or her and allocates it in a way that maximizes his or her satisfaction. An implicit assumption of those who seek to directly apply the economic model to the university setting is that increases in the resources devoted to institutional goals cause increases in output, and these increases in output in turn translate into increases in decisionmaker satisfaction. The difficulties and problems in applying the economic model are addressed below.

Identification of Outputs

Although some researchers employ an educational production function to relate inputs to outputs, the technical and substantive problems implicit in the use of this approach are serious (Becker and Waldman, 1987). The key problems can broken down into three areas: how to measure, what to measure, and how to relate inputs to outputs.

Cohn (1979) writes that "it is much easier to specify the kinds of educational outputs than to define them in precise terms." While a thorough review of the problem of *how to measure* university outputs requires too much space to present here, it is useful to explore a few select issues. First, yardsticks are not available to measure such outputs as moral development, satisfaction or enjoyment with life, education-induced equal opportunity, and good citizenship. In part, this is because most of the outputs of the educational process are intangible and, in part, it is because researchers cannot agree on the appropriate output measures. Second, a need exists to measure some outputs which are invisible to the decisionmaker. A student may know that his education has made him more worldly or self-confident, but how does the decisionmaker quantify these changes? While anecdotal data may be satisfying, they do not lead to the maximization of satisfaction envisioned in the economic model.

Third, certain disagreements must be resolved before measurement of some of the outputs can begin. Is good citizenship achieved if a student stays out of jail, votes, campaigns for a political candidate, or passes an attitude test? Should one measure be used to capture this output or are many required? The answers to these questions are highly subjective and the questions themselves resist scientific investigation. Fourth, the intellectual changes which education produces are particularly difficult to measure when they occur with a lag. A student's intellectual perspective often matures several years after graduation. At that point, it may be hard to measure the influence of a university education. Fifth, it may be too costly to measure all of the outputs of a university even if adequate measures can be found. A problem then arises as to which outputs to measure. Anything less than total measurement will understate the actual outputs of a university yet we lack the data to determine which outputs can safely be ignored.

Finally, learning does not proceed from a zero base but from the level students have reached at the time when their formal instruction begins. Since learning is incremental, and since saturation occurs as student understanding of a skill increases, it is difficult to identify what a university education contributes to learning, particularly if students are at different skill levels. Problems of this type continue to plague researchers despite many attempts to address them in the last few years.

A different set of issues arise in the area of *what to measure*. While attempts to measure learning have received considerable attention, it is not clear that agreement has been reached on the appropriate measures of student performance (Cohn, 1979). A number of basic skills tests claim to measure the same output but the research community is not unanimous as to which is the most accurate. Unfortunately, the choice of measure affects one's conclusions regarding outcome effects. Disagreements over the proper measure escalate when attitude change is involved (Mann and Fusfeld, 1970). In this case, the experts disagree as to the "right" attitudes as well as to how these should be measured. Moreover, because a comprehensive university provides courses covering a large range of attitudes and beliefs, a vast number of questions are required to cover the full range of attitude changes which a university produces.

Disagreements also arise when output measurement is extended to behavioral change. The goal list presented above indicates that some participants have a strong desire to see universities produce specific behavioral changes. It is clear, however, that the changes which the various participants seek sometimes conflict. Should universities encourage students to attend graduate school or to enter the business world, to address social needs or to pursue self-interest, to question or to problem-solve, to invest or to consume? While it is tempting to suggest that a university should measure all its outputs, this is impossible. The sheer number of outputs of a comprehensive university insures that an attempt to measure them all will fail. Issues then arise as to which changes should be measured and to what biases are introduced by ignoring the non-measured alterations in behavior that the university produces.

Difficulties also exist in *relating the inputs of universities to the outputs*. Studies suggest that teacher characteristics and skills have different effects on student learning depending on the home background, personality, abilities, and prior skills of students (Coleman, 1966; Mayeske, 1972). Even if one output level is selected and carefully defined, a given level of university inputs may produce several output levels, depending on the characteristics of the students being educated. Decisionmaker satisfaction is dependent not only on the level of financial resources devoted to an output but also on the characteristics of the persons used to produce that output. The state of our knowledge is not sufficient to enable decisionmakers to identify an optimal student-faculty mix. Yet, the type of mix is a determinant of many of the outputs that universities produce.

Finally, additional problems arise in relating inputs to outputs where the desired output occurs when a threshold is reached. Two problems arise here: how to identify the threshold and what to do about the students who pass it before entering the university. For example, assume that a student either is or is not a good citizen. Some students will be good citizens before they arrive at a university, some will be on the threshold of becoming good citizens, and others will require considerable instruction to cross the threshold. A problem exists in determining which students have crossed the threshold prior to the arrival at the university. If those who were good citizens on entry are not removed before output is measured, the university will be credited with a higher level of output than it deserves. Indeed, by recruiting only these students, a university could appear to produce many good citizens when it is in fact the beneficiary of somebody else's efforts. A second problem relates to the most efficient way to educate good citizens. Presumably, the most efficient approach is to educate students up to the point where they cross the threshold since education beyond this point is wasteful. If the threshold cannot be identified, an optimal resource allocation to citizenship education cannot be found.

Relation of Outputs to Decisionmaker Satisfaction

Suppose that the problems discussed above are resolved, that a given set of outputs $X_1, \ldots, X_n$ is defined, and that a decisionmaker or decision-making group is identified. The problem is then to determine a set of weights, $A_i, \ldots, A_n$ relating the outputs of a university to levels of its decisionmakers' satisfaction. A set of valuation problems arise concerning how to connect diverse and sometimes intangible outputs to decisionmaker satisfaction. The problems are highlighted with an illustration. Assume that a decisionmaker's satisfaction from managing the institution is derived from the production of four outputs. Output 1 is the total number of faculty publications at a university, serving as an indicator of the discovery of new knowledge. The assumption is made that the more a faculty member publishes, the higher the decisionmaker's satisfaction. Equal weight is given to applied and basic research, to short and long articles, to descriptive and theoretical pieces, and to manuscripts in top and in mediocre journals. Output 2, designed to capture the university's contribution to advanced training, is defined as the percentage of students who graduate and continue for an advanced degree. No adjustment is made for the quality of students and all graduate degrees are treated as equally important to the administrator. These are compromises made in recognition of the complexities of a more sophisticated approach.

Output 3 measures the moral development of administrators on a scale of 1 to 100 and is based on questions developed by a group of theologians and philosophers. Implicit in its use is the assumption that a movement from 5 to 6 has the same value as a move from 91 to 92. Output 4, an indicator of the university's success in meeting state needs, is defined as the number of graduating students entering a set of desirable jobs (as defined by a committee convened for this purpose) divided by the number of students that might potentially enter these jobs. Because this measure does not distinguish among jobs, a student entering a social work position has the same value to the decisionmaker as a student taking a job in environmental regulation. An increase in any of the four outputs causes an increase in the decisionmaker's satisfaction.

The economic model presumes that a decisionmaker takes a given bundle of resources and allocates it across the four outputs to maximize his or her satisfaction. It ignores the fact that the decisionmaker must make a subjective estimate as to how well each output measure serves as a proxy for what it represents. If the estimation is incorrect, the allocation is not optimal. Given the intangible nature of the outputs, the chance that the estimation will be wrong is substantial. Second, the decisionmaker is assumed to have a knowledge of how a change in each output impacts his or her satisfaction. Given the nature of the outputs of the university, many of the effects of output changes are subtle, indirect, and subject to change. The more subtle the change, the more resources the decisionmaker must use to determine the impact of a change in that output on his or her satisfaction level. This suggests that outputs with recognizable effects may be favored over those which require time and money to trace.

The diverse set of measurement scales of the four outputs also pose a problem. For example, a decisionmaker may ask what an additional ten thousand dollars of input yields in terms of output. Suppose that the answer is a choice between ten new publications, a two-point increase in moral development, a one-percent increase in student continuing to graduate school, or a 0.8-percent increase in students in desirable jobs. The difficulties in weighting these disparate outputs, particularly when many outputs are involved, make it difficult to arrive at an optimal resource allocation. Somehow the 0.8-percent increase in students in desirable jobs must be weighed against ten new publications. This is asking a great deal of the decisionmaker, particularly when very large numbers of outputs are involved.

The problem is compounded when uncertainty is introduced into the analysis. In the academic world, it is unlikely that a decisionmaker can say with certainty that ten thousand dollars will produce ten new articles or that it will insure that a fixed percentage of students choose a job valued by the state. Instead, the decisionmaker faces a set of probabilities that each uncertain output will be attained. The final resource allocation must take these into account if it is to be optimal. Finally, if some outputs are left out, as is likely to be the case for reasons discussed above, the resulting allocation will not be optimal.

The difficulties involved in measuring, weighting, and relating the alternative outputs to satisfaction are sufficiently serious that the economic model is impractical for application in the near future. This does not mean that the model should be abandoned. Instead, the principles which underlie it should provide the basis for the second-best solutions used to allocate university resources.

Goal-Based Resource Allocation

This section discusses the key elements of goal-based allocation schemes and raises four issues: (1) how the categories used in the process play a role in determining whether institutional goals will be recognized; (2) the role of process in determining who will participate in resource allocation and the weights given to each party's views; (3) the effect of the review process on priorities; and (4) how the nature of institutional goals determines whether they affect resource allocation. The section ends with a brief discussion of a second-best solution which integrates the principles of the economic model into the resource allocation process.

The Alternative Resource Allocation Approaches

The economic model reflects the economist's belief that resources should be directed toward the attainment of ends which increase decisionmaker satisfaction. While the logic behind this argument is compelling, many institutions base their budgeting on noneconomic approaches.

Decades of work have gone into defining and evaluating various budgeting schemes, the most popular of which are organizational or functional. *Organizational approaches* allocate resources on the basis of the management entities which comprise the organization; usually departments, colleges, institutes, personnel, etc. Thus, yearly allocations are made to Psychology, Management, Astronomy, etc. *Functional approaches* allocate funds based on the functions an organization performs. Funds are provided for teaching, recruiting, faculty training, student guidance, etc. These approaches predominate because they are easy to implement, complementary to institutional management goals, and often based on many years of use.

In contrast, *output-based budgeting* enables the decisionmaker to decide among conflicting programs, however subjectively, based on what is believed to be the best mix of programs for a university to perform. In the last few decades, three types of output-based schemes have been introduced; program budgeting, management by objectives, and zero-based budgeting. The program budgeting approach identifies the desirable programs of the university and budgets in a manner which supports these programs. This framework offers the greatest opportunity to link institutional goals to specific program outputs because it requires the institution to think through the programs which are most closely tied to its goals. In addition, by budgeting funds directly to programs which meet university goals, it assigns the job of weighting and valuing these goals to the budget process.

Management by objectives (MBO) involves the formulation of a set of objectives to be funded for accomplishment by the institution. Each year the decisionmaker has the opportunity to determine how well the objectives are carried out. The objectives can be programmatic, in which case they may be based on institutional goals, or they may reflect management or accounting goals. This approach bases resource allocation on purposeful behavior but such behavior need not be programmatic or strategic in nature. MBO provides an opportunity to introduce institutional goals but it does not guarantee that these will be utilized.

Zero-based budgeting (ZBB) addresses institutional goals less directly. Since the objective is to evaluate what is gained or lost if a particular item is removed from the budget base, the budget categories are the key consideration. If the initial unit is programmatic then the gain or loss is to the program; if it is organizational, the gain or loss is to the organizational entity. For example, if loss is defined in terms of number of Merit Scholars, ZBB can be related to program goals; if loss is defined in terms of number of political science courses taught, this approach is less likely to facilitate the introduction of institutional goals into the budget process.

Strategic business unit (SBU). Budgeting by SBU focuses on the products and services that an organization produces. Given the intangible nature of university outputs, these are usually defined in terms of fields, degree levels, and/or types of research and service. This approach also emphasizes the competitive strengths and weaknesses of each SBU. Because the emphasis is on the identification of specific services for specific markets, it ignores many of the intangible goals defined in earlier sections. Outputs such as the moral development of administrators, intellectual development of students, and improvement of citizenship are difficult to integrate into this framework. SBU budgeting is effective in raising organizational consciousness of threats and opportunities in the business environment. It has also made large organizations more aware of the individual services and products they produce. It has not been used widely in higher education because it does not work well where the products are educational services produced in a largely non-competitive setting.

The above discussion underscores the importance of the basic budgeting unit in determining whether institutional goals will guide resource allocation. The more management-oriented the budget, the less likely it is that these goals will impact resource allocation; the more programmatic the basic unit, the more likely it is that the decisionmaking process will resemble that suggested by the economic model. In the absence of a programmatic framework, institutional goals are likely to influence resource allocation *only* if decisionmakers use them explicitly to direct choice.

The Budgetary Process

　　Rules:

The budgetary process is important because the decisions which shape it determine both who participates in resource allocation and what influence participant goals have. Participation in the process insures that a person's or group's goals are heard, not that they are realized. A set of rules determines who prepares the initial request for resources and what the constraints are. These rules also determine who reviews the requests and how choices among alternatives will be made. Rules are also likely to define how external-funder goals will be integrated into the organization.

Nothing inherent in the environment of most universities suggests that the parties to the resource allocation process will be the same parties who determine institutional goals. The former are usually department chairpersons, deans, and finance and budget people, while the latter are more likely to be planners, faculty, and administrators from the academic affairs office. Links between the two groups may occur, however, if senior management commits to a resource allocation process that directly integrates institutional goals into the budget process. But an explicit effort must be made to relate the rules of the budget process to goals if such links are to be achieved. In the absence of such an effort, institutional goals may not have much impact.

Hierarchy:

Most universities introduce a number of steps into the budget review process. The number of steps is based both on tradition and on whether the institution is publicly or privately controlled. At each level, the goals of the participants come into play. The broader the consensus as to what the goals of a university should be, the less likely it is that hierarchy will cause alterations in institutional goals. To the extent that each level has its own idea of what a university should do, it is likely that the final allocation will differ from that likely to emerge if institutional goals affected the process. Particularly in a state institution, the goals of specific institutions may differ from those of the funding agent.

The Nature of the Goals

Several insights arise out of the analysis of institutional goals presented earlier. Specifically, these goals: (1) will have more impact if they are well defined and broadly held than if they are a product of ad hoc efforts by a small group; (2) are more likely to have an impact if they are stable than if they constantly change; (3) are more likely to play a role in resource allocation when the economic, political, and social environment is stable than when it is unstable; (4) will have more of an impact if they are widely perceived as valid than if they are viewed as narrow and self-serving; (5) will be unlikely to guide the resource allocation process if they are the product of a weak compromise or are the product of sharp conflicts; (6) will be stable if they conform to the preferences of those who actually allocate resources; and (7) are more likely to guide resource allocation if they are stated in specific than in general terms.

A Linkage Model

The analysis presented above provides an understanding of what it would take for an institution to insure that institutional goals guide budgetary decisions. The following items are key to the success of this type of effort:

- A set of institutional goals which are well defined, specific, widely held, and stable.
- A set of budget categories which reflect the major goals of the institution and which are defined in terms of outputs which have meaning to the decisionmaker.
- A set of rules for the budget process that reflect institutional goals and that provide for the input of participants who use these goals in establishing priorities.

- A review process which incorporates institutional goals into the rules and which insures that external reviewers will be thoroughly acquainted with what the university is trying to accomplish.

To achieve these objectives a university must be willing to undertake a major education effort. Broad-based involvement is necessary at every step if the participants in the process are not to view this as just one more ill-fated attempt to restructure the budgetary process. Whether the benefits of such an effort will outweigh the costs cannot be determined based on information currently available in the literature. At present, while some universities claim that they have achieved a connection between budgeting and institutional goals, we know of no studies which have attempted to quantify the efficiencies which are achieved under these circumstances. It is likely that more universities will have to embrace this approach to budgeting before quantitative conclusions can be drawn on the value of goal-linked budgeting. In the interim, this will remain one of the many approaches that universities can consider in exploring alternatives to their existing budgeting schemes.

Conclusion and Summary

In conclusion, we believe that institutional goals can be formulated, albeit imperfectly, to reflect the goals of participant groups with an interest in the direction of a university. We also believe that these goals can play a role in resource allocation but their importance will depend on how the budget process is structured. The nature of an institution's budget categories, of its institutional goals, of its rules for resource allocation, and of its budget hierarchy help to determine the importance of institutional goals in the resource allocation process.

The economic model represents an ideal for efficient resource allocation against which alternative budgeting approaches can be judged. Unfortunately, our analysis does not provide an optimistic picture for the practical application of this model by universities, except perhaps where a single decisionmaker allocates resources based on a broad awareness of the outputs of the institution and their effects. Both the comprehensive nature of the outputs of a university and their intangible and often controversial nature place limits on the ability of decisionmakers to fulfill the conditions required for the economic model to work.

Among the alternative budgeting approaches, program budgeting comes the closest to meeting the ideal defined by the economic model. However, management by objectives and zero-based budgeting approaches may also provide good second-best solutions if they are based on programmatic rather than management categories. An institution can create a link between institutional goals and the budget process if it is willing to: (1) build support for this connection, (2) take the time to define carefully its goals, budget categories and budgetary rules, and (3) work with participants in the budget hierarchy to gain consensus on the process. Such output-based budgets have the potential to provide a meaningful second-best alternative to the economic model. Finally, while a rich literature exists on what the goals of institutions of higher education are and how they differ, more work is needed to explore how institutional goals are used in practice by universities. This chapter makes a first step toward addressing this significant gap in the literature.

CHAPTER 4

Decision Processes and Priorities in Higher Education

ESTELLE JAMES

This chapter surveys what economists know about decision processes and priorities at American colleges and universities. My conclusion after reviewing the literature is that economists have some theoretical models, a few testable and tested hypotheses, but relatively little empirical evidence about the resource allocation process at institutions of higher learning (IHLs).

This, after all, is not surprising because we customarily do not pay much attention to what goes on *inside* institutions. Instead, we usually assume that profit maximizing is the only objective or, at least, the major argument in the firm's objective function, that all team players share this goal, and if they don't act accordingly the organization will either go out of business in a competitive environment or will be a prime target for takeover in an oligopolistic environment. Furthermore, although a substantial literature has developed recently about informational and monitoring problems, mainstream microeconomic theory still assumes that a firm has enough information about and control over its own production function to operate efficiently. The decision process can therefore be bypassed, the priorities are assumed ex ante, and the (price and quantity) outcomes simply depend on factor costs, available technology and demand. Most economic analyses have focused on these variables.

More recently, some work has begun to question whether these assumptions hold for large-scale economic organizations (see Baumol, 1967 and Williamson, 1964 and 1975). And for colleges and universities, the subject of this paper, they clearly do not hold. First of all, rather than being profit-maximizing enterprises most IHLs are nonprofit organizations (NPOs). Some are private nonprofits and others are public nonprofits, with different revenue sources and constraints, but for all, distribution of monetary profits is not an option; there are no stockholders anxiously awaiting dividends or capital gains. Instead, all revenues must be used within the organization for current or future production; and all utility derived by IHL managers (beyond their fixed salaries) must come from organizational, not personal, expenditures. Their object, then, is to choose a set of activities for the college or university that maximizes their utility, subject to the constraint that revenues must cover costs.

The fact that colleges and universities are nonprofit rather than profit-maximizing leads to a number of behavioral implications, including the presumption that objectives (tastes) of managers matter in determining outputs, that cost-minimizing factor combinations may not be chosen, and that cross-subsidization plays an important role. Basically, the IHL carries out profitable activities that society is willing to pay for (e.g. the teaching of undergraduates in large classes) in order to obtain the resources for costly utility-maximizing activities that society will not fully finance directly (e.g., graduate training and research). In Part 1 I discuss in greater detail exactly how this process of cross-subsidization works.

The complexity of the decision process is compounded by a second major characteristic, imperfect information and ambiguous goals. Reaching widely endorsed decisions and monitoring the results is made difficult by the unobservability of many inputs (such as faculty effort), by the absence of a consensus on the educational production function (including the marginal productivity of different factors), by the inability to quantify educational outputs (especially the quality dimension) and by the fact that student consumers are also major inputs determining these outputs. There is no readily available measure of total performance, such as profits provide in a conventional enterprise. Moreover, consumer valuations of different outputs, which are generally used elsewhere in the economy, are difficult to infer because of the prevalence of nonprice rationing in higher education (which means that relative prices do not inform us of relative marginal utilities). Besides, many (faculty) producers would distrust these valuations, believing that consumers do not place correct values on different educational products. Instead, various proxies for or indirect indicators of outputs are used, these often measure gross output rather than value added, and if proxies that faculty members consider credible are not available (as for quality of undergraduate teaching) the output tends to be overlooked.

The fact that different actors have different information at their disposal is a major reason for a third major characteristic of IHL's: decentralization of decisionmaking among multiple actors, a characteristic which led Cohen and March (1974) to describe academia as "organized anarchy." Administrators, students, alumni, donors, and legislators all participate in this process but a key group of workers, the faculty, invariably plays a major role. In this sense, the IHL is a labor-managed enterprise.

While decentralization may solve the informational problem, it creates a host of other problems since the goals of these decisionmakers may differ and, in fact, conflict. Decisions made by one sub-unit may not take into account benefits and costs thereby generated for others. Moreover, decisions made at one level may be implemented at a different level in quite a different way from the original intent. For example, the central administration may allocate to a dean a faculty line with a particular department in mind; the Dean may give it to a different department for teaching purposes; the department may use it to give a faculty member released time for writing a grant proposal; and the faculty member may, in fact, use the extra time to do nonsponsored research. To control the ultimate use of the line, the administration would have to be able to predict the behavior at each level—when each level would have an incentive to distort this information. Obviously, the central-planning and principal-agent literature on incentives, monitoring, and strategic behavior is relevant here.

In the pages which follow I review the theoretical predictions regarding the implications of these characteristics as well as the empirical observations of IHL behavior which test these predictions. Wherever appropriate and feasible, I distinguish between colleges and universities, public and private institutions. Part 1 sets forth models of nonprofit behavior which assume that all decisionmakers at the IHL have common objectives and are affected in similar ways by all outputs. When utility is maximized for one (subject to the nonprofit constraint), it is maximized for all. Cross-subsidization is an important outcome. Part 2 moves on to consider the impact on decisionmaking processes and priorities of differing (often conflicting) objectives, spillover effects, imperfect information about production functions, unobservable inputs, and nonmeasurable outputs. Socialization, selection, incentives, and regulations are considered as alternative ways of resolving these problems. The conclusion raises policy issues and, given the paucity of analytically based empirical work on this topic, outlines some unanswered questions that might be illuminated by future research.

1. Decisionmaking under a Team-Objective Function in a Nonprofit University

Key Decisions and Decisionmakers

Who are the key actors at the IHL and what are the major allocation decisions to be made? IHL behavior depends on revenues and revenues depend on consumer demand—from students, legislatures, research-funding agencies, and donors. An important part of the revenue decision concerns how many students to enroll and what price to charge, which in turn determines student quality and total revenues from teaching. The revenues are then allocated among the major (academic and nonacademic) units within the IHL, thus determining the disciplinary product mix of the institution and the intermediate inputs (support services) into these final products. These decisions are made by the trustees and administrators in private colleges and universities, but they are strongly influenced by the legislature in public institutions.

A whole set of key decisions—whom to hire and recommend for promotion and tenure, what teaching loads should be, which courses to teach, how many graduate students to enroll, etc.—are made by departments. These are particularly crucial decisions at a university since they determine the teaching/research, undergraduate/graduate mix of institutional outputs. As a result, the departments are likely to perceive the administration as making the major decisions (on size of budget) while the administration is likely to view the departments as exercising major control (on how to spend it). Departments are, in some cases, run by an autocratic head but are more often faculty collectives. We may therefore assume that their decisions are made to maximize the utility of faculty within the department.

Yet another crucial group of decisions is made by the individual faculty member—how to divide time and effort between work and leisure, teaching versus research (T vs. R), and which topics to research (see Becker, 1979; Doi, 1974). While classroom and office hours can be assigned and observed, research time is particularly difficult to monitor; hence faculty discretion will be greater at universities than at colleges. Faculty-time-allocation surveys indicate that the research/teaching mix of time inputs at universities has grown substantially during the post-World War II period, and is now about 2/1 (James, 1978, 1986, and Dornbusch, 1979).

But faculty members do not make these decisions in a vacuum. Instead, external forces, particularly the labor market dominated by the national disciplines, play a major role in setting both pecuniary and nonpecuniary rewards. Furthermore, for some research topics, outside funding is necessary in order to cover essential supplies and equipment. Decisions about who should get research grants are made by funding agencies with peer review by members of the national disciplines. In this way outside groups ultimately decide what topics get investigated, which units get internal support and who gets tenure at the university.

We move on now to discuss how the internal actors make their input and output choices. Managers of nonprofit organizations (NPOs) can be assumed to maximize an objective function subject to a break-even constraint. (For a survey of the NPO literature see James and Rose-Ackerman, 1986.) It is essential, then, to consider what are the arguments in the IHL objective function. In this section I assume that everyone at the college or university has an identical team-objective function (which can therefore be termed the institution's objective) and, moreover, that everyone is affected in similar ways by its arguments. The group then collapses to a single decisionmaking entity. In Part 2 I relax these stringent assumptions.

Objectives

Our knowledge of IHL objectives comes from studies which have assumed a plausible utility function and derived testable hypotheses that have been confirmed by empirical data. Most of this literature deals with universities so we know very little about colleges and even less about community colleges, although I will draw some inferences below.

Breneman (1970) assumes prestige maximization to be the major goal at universities and shows that evidence of graduate student admission, retention, and placement decisions is consistent with this assumption. Garvin (1980) similarly assumes that the university's utility is a function of prestige and cites a number of other studies which agree (Jencks and Reisman, 1968; Caplow and McGee, 1958; Brown, 1967; Vladeck, 1976; Mayhew, 1970; Ben-David, 1971). Student quality and sometimes quantity also enter into Garvin's utility function. He derives and tests a number of propositions about university behavior that are consistent with these objectives, including the gain in relative prestige and enrollments of public universities during the 1960s.

James (1978, 1986) assumes that research (R), graduate training (G), student quality ($QUAL$), and small, advanced classes enter into the university's objective function while colleges care more about undergraduates (U). Evidence about undergraduate and graduate tuition and costs at colleges and universities are shown to be consistent with this assumption. Decisions about teaching loads (TL) at different institution types and changes in teaching loads through time also give evidence of the increasingly heavy weight given to research, especially at universities. Numerous studies of faculty reward (salary, promotion, and tenure) structures show that research productivity is the prime ingredient at universities and teaching is relatively unimportant (see Katz, 1973; Siegfried and White, 1973; Tuckman et al., 1977; Tuckman, 1979; Dornbusch, 1979; Lewis and Becker, 1979; McKenzie, 1979). On the other hand, I am not aware of any such studies for colleges. That IHLs care about student quality is obvious from the elaborate nonprice selection procedures used in many of them, particularly in the private sector.

These findings are all consistent with the prestige-maximization hypothesis, since prestige depends primarily on R, G, and $QUAL$. Indeed, variables such as research funding, rankings of graduate departments and undergraduate selectivity are often used as proxies for prestige, which is difficult to measure directly. The same findings are consistent with the view that the IHL is essentially a labor-managed firm which cannot distribute a monetary residual to its workers because of the nonprofit constraint so instead spends potential profits for on-the-job consumption of goods they prefer, such as $QUAL$, low TL and small graduate classes (see James and Neuberger, 1981). In the rest of this chapter, I take prestige and faculty-worker satisfaction as the underlying goals while U, G, $QUAL$, R, TL and teaching technology are the intermediate objectives used to achieve these goals. Because the following analysis depends heavily on these intermediate objectives, I expand on them briefly below:

Research and low teaching loads:

Faculty may enjoy spending their time on research, asking questions and proceeding to answer them. Moreover, research enhances institutional and individual visibility, status and prestige. Research grants, further, increase the resources available to the institution, particularly through indirect cost recovery and faculty time-buyouts. More altruistically, universities may regard themselves as responsible for expanding society's stock of knowledge, and this is the stated goal of the research university, which has grown overwhelmingly in importance over the last half-century. Research appears to count in the more selective colleges as well, although to a lesser extent, because of shared values reinforced by norms set by national disciplinary groups. Research (quantity and quality) is difficult to measure, but books, articles in refereed journals, citations, ability to secure grants, and subjective assessment of experts have all been used as proxies, both in hiring and promotion decisions and in econometric studies of salary determination. The measurement of teaching quality is even more problematic. The relative availability of quantity-quality indicators for research may be another reason for its importance as an output goal and employment criterion.

Quantity of undergraduate (U) and graduate (G) students:

Number of student credit hours or degrees, weighted by field, may also enter into the objective function, as they do, for example, in a study of university costs by Verry and Davies (1976). This item will have a positive sign if faculty enjoy teaching their subject or if they use students as research inputs (*G* are more likely to play this role than *U*, and are therefore more likely to appear in the utility function with a positive sign). Student quantity will, on the other hand, have a negative sign in the objective function if large numbers are an unwelcome distraction from research.

Quality of students:

The better the student input the more fun it is to teach them and the more they teach each other. The gross output of an IHL will be greater with a brighter student body, even if the value added is less. Moreover, student selectivity (as measured by SAT or GRE scores, GPAs, required for admission, etc.) is often a prime determinant of prestige, especially for colleges, where research is less important than for universities (see Hagstrom, 1971). Thus, the IHL undoubtedly derives utility from higher quality students. (See Ehrenberg and Sherman, 1984, for a model in which the university cares about "quality units" of different categories of students, with categories differentiated by race, sex, ethnic status, etc.) The institution faces a quantity-quality tradeoff for any given applicant pool, and must choose the optimum combination of these two attributes, where quantity brings revenue and quality brings prestige. One IHL priority will be to shift the constraint outward by enlarging the pool in order to increase both the quantity and the quality of their students by aggressive recruitment and retention techniques.

Input mix and class size:

In the case of the IHL, unlike conventional models of the firm, the production function is still largely unknown, cost minimization need not be pursued or achieved, and there is no technologically determined marginal cost for many outputs. Instead, technology may enter into the objective function of faculty and administrators (much as it does in Williamson's [1964] expense preference firm). This probably accounts for the large variation in costs and input-output ratios found in higher education (see Balderston, 1974 and O'Donoghue, 1971).

The choice of technology may also be viewed as a choice of product quality. For example, an additional student may be absorbed into existing classes at no apparent increase in cost, but perhaps with a decrease in quality. There is no clear evidence that more is learned in small classes, but many of us believe this is so. Furthermore, small classes are preferred by student-consumers, and may therefore enlarge the applicant pool. James (1978, 1986) argues that faculty have a preference for teaching small classes at more advanced levels, and this is balanced by a concentration of large classes at the lower-division level. A small-class technology may also be given a heavier weight at colleges than at universities, where other objectives such as R and G are more important.

Teaching quality:

It is noteworthy that none of the models surveyed include as objectives a direct measure of teaching quality or its consequences, the incremental value added to learning increased or future earning power of students. In addition, consistent with this theory, none of the analyses of faculty-reward structures indicate that teaching quality is an important determinant of salaries (see references above). Dornbusch (1979) showed that Stanford faculty were dissatisfied with the evaluation of teaching quality, thought it should be more influential in determining salaries but, given the current reward structure, wanted to spend less time on teaching (T), more on R. Similarly a study of sixty-eight universities by Gross and Grambusch (1968 and 1974) showed student-related goals to rank low, research to rank high. These studies typically do not cover colleges, which may be more concerned with teaching, but the same results are obtained over and over again for universities.

Part of the disregard for teaching quality probably comes from the extreme measurement problems (see Doyle, 1979, for a survey of methods and problems in measuring teaching quality). Faculty members interact with students to produce teaching quality, the final product depends on student inputs at least as much as faculty inputs, and different professors may have greater value added for different types of students. However, the fact that more systematic evaluative techniques have not been developed, as they have been for research, suggests that more basic forces are at work. I suggest that IHLs do not reward quality of teaching and apparently do not include it in their objective functions because it is not a source of prestige. Research produces wide visibility while teaching is appreciated locally, at best. In addition, the ability to conduct publishable research is a scarcer skill than the ability to teach, hence it is more highly rewarded, both in dollars and in prestige. In a society where half the secondary school graduates go on to higher education, there must be many acceptable professors; but the contributors to exclusive refereed journals are relatively small in number. Moreover, research grants increase the institution's resources while there are no equivalent external teaching-quality grants. (Teaching quantity, on the other hand, is highly rewarded in the form of tuition fees or the equivalent from state legislatures.) The low value placed on quality of teaching may therefore reflect a broader societal value, which is why it persists.

Summary of objectives:

In sum, the IHL probably wishes to maximize an objective function which depends positively on research, student quantity and quality, and small class size, particularly at advanced levels. To do so it must choose its optimal enrollment levels of U and G, which in turn determine its feasible tuition fee and student-quality combination (price and nonprice rationing). For any given tuition fee, a higher number of students means lower quality but more resources for research. It must also determine its optimal teaching load (TL), which determines class size and time left over for research; a lower TL means more R but larger classes. The following mathematical formulation sets forth, for those who are interested, the first order conditions which depict the equilibrium level of these decision variables, where utility is maximized subject to the break-even constraint that resources generated are exactly used up by teaching and research.

Suppose the IHL wishes to maximize an objective function such as

$$W = W_1 \; (PRES, FACSATIS)$$

$$= W_2 \; [U, QUALU(U), G, QUALG(G), R(F, TL, RGR),$$
$$U/TL_U(F), G/TL_G(F)]$$

subject to the break-even constraint that:

$$P_U U + (P_G - Ta) \, G + D(A) - A + RGR = (S+K)F$$

where:

$PRES$ = prestige
$FACSATIS$ = other sources of faculty (or managerial satisfaction)
U = number of undergraduate students
G = number of graduate students
$QUALU$ and $QUALG$ = quality of undergraduate and graduates, respectively
$R \; (F, TL)$ = research, a function of F and TL
F = number of faculty
TL = teaching load = $TL_U + TL_G$
TL_G and TL_G = average undergraduate and graduate teaching loads
P_U and P_G = additional revenue from each U and G

RGR = research grants
Ta = average graduate student support
D = donations that are not directly contingent on output
A = administrative expenditures
S = average faculty salary
K = support services per faculty member (supplies, secretaries, equipment)
$U/TL_U(F) = ACS_U$ = average undergraduate class size
$G/TL_G(F) = ACS_G$ = average graduate class size

If we assume that P_U and P_G are given by the external market (or the state legislature), the IHL must choose its optimal U and G, which in turn determines $QUALU$ and $QUALG$: in general, for any given P, a higher U or G means a lower $QUAL$, possibly a larger ACS, but more F to do R. The IHL must also choose its optimal TL_U and TL_G which, together with the above, determine R and average class size; a lower TL means more R but larger classes. Furthermore, the IHL must decide how to divide total resources between F and A; in this simple model, where A is used only to raise D, all net resources generated by U and G are used for F. In a multi-period model savings and dissavings would also have to be determined, but I abstract from this question here. The equilibrium conditions are summed up below:

(1) $dW/dU = \partial W/\partial U + (\partial W/\partial QUALU)(\partial QUALU/\partial U) + (\partial W/\partial R)(\partial R/\partial F) P_U/(S+K) + (\partial W/\partial ACS_U)[F-UP_U/(S+K)]/TL_UF^2 + (\partial W/\partial ACS_G)[-G.P_U/(S+K)/TL_GF^2] = 0$

(2) $dW/dG = \partial W/\partial G + (\partial W/\partial QUALG)(\partial QUALG\partial G) + (\partial W/\partial R)(\partial R/\partial F)(P_G-Ta)/(S+K) + (\partial W/\partial ACS_U)[-U(P_G-Ta)/(S+K)/TL_UF^2 + (\partial W/\partial ACS_G)[F-G(P_G-Ta)/(S+K)]/TL_GF^2 = 0$

(3) $dW/dTL_U = (\partial W/\partial R)(\partial R/\partial TL) - (\partial W/\partial ACS_U)[U/TL^2_U(F)] = 0$

(4) $dW/dTL_G = (\partial W/\partial R)(\partial R/\partial TL) - (\partial W/\partial ACS_G)[G/TL^2_G(F)] = 0$

(5) $(\partial W/\partial ACS_U)(U/TL^2_U) = (\partial W/\partial ACS_G)(G/TL^2_G)$

(6) $dD/dA = 1$

Equation (1) tells us that undergraduates will be admitted so long as the utility from increased numbers $(\partial W/\partial U)$ and revenues for the cross-subsidization of R $[(\partial W/\partial R)(\partial R/\partial F) P_U/(S+K)]$ are greater than the corresponding decline in student quality $[(\partial W/\partial QUALU)(\partial QUALU/\partial U)]$ and larger class size implied $[\partial W/\partial ACS_U][F - U(P_U)/(S+K)]/TL_U F^2 + [\partial W/\partial ACS_G][- G(P_U)/(S+K)]/TL_G F^2$.

Equation (2) gives a similar condition regarding graduate enrollments, and shows that increases in G are further limited by the cost of graduate student support *(Ta)*, which detract from the increment to *F*.

Equation (3), (4) and (5) indicate that *TL* is lowered so long as the utility from marginal research $[(\partial W/\partial R)(\partial R/\partial TL)]$ exceeds the disutility from larger class size $[\partial W/\partial ACS)(U/TL_U^2 F)]$ or $[(\partial W/\partial ACS)(G/TL_G^2 F)]$.

Finally, equation (6) tells us that resources can be used to increase *A* so long as $dD > dA$.

This specification assumes a precision which does not exist in reality. That is, faculty and administrators are probably not able to describe their exact objective function. However, if their actions are purposeful they must be based on a rough estimate of these goals. Hopkins and Massy (1981) describe a sophisticated attempt by model-builders and administrators at Stanford University to specify managerial preferences more precisely and to create a method for searching systematically among the budget-balancing input and output combinations for the mix that maximizes institutional utility. Such computerized models have been used increasingly in higher education as an aid to managerial decisionmaking.

Cross-Subsidization

Given this simple model, what are the priorities of the IHL? Its first priority must be to stay alive, to discover some mix of activities for which revenues cover the costs. In recent years a number of colleges, unable to find a break-even product mix, have closed and more may do so over the next decade.

However, this break-even constraint need not apply to each product taken separately. As I have shown in other papers, cross-subsidization is an essential characteristic of IHLs and other NPOs. These institutions carry out a set of profitable activities that do not yield utility per se to derive revenues they can then spend on utility-maximizing activities that do not cover their own costs. The former subsidize the latter. For example, the legislature may give the university the same number of dollars per undergraduate and graduate student, but the university may actually spend more on graduate students by teaching them in small classes while undergraduates are taught in large classes. Similarly, the administration may base its allocation to departments on enrollments, but departments may assign low teaching loads thereby allocating much of their resources to research (see James, 1978, 1986; James and Neuberger, 1981; Hoenack, et al., 1986).

Thus, the survival priority of the IHL requires it to find a set of profitable activities which attract a clientele and which the faculty are willing to carry out using a low-cost technology. Activities which have played this role are: vocationally oriented programs such as education, management, and law, evening programs utilizing cheap, part-time faculty, and, to a large extent, lower-division undergraduate teaching as a whole. Applied contract research often falls into a similar profit-making category. Because of the disutility and low status attached to some of these activities, faculty are sometimes unwilling to give them a high priority or even to include them in the institution's offerings. However, as budgets get tighter the need to find profitable activities increases and the priority accorded activities whose revenues exceed their costs increases, because without those profits other utility-yielding projects cannot be funded.

While profitable activities are essential to the flourishing IHL, utility-yielding activities are, after all, the faculty's reason for existence and these will be carried out even if they don't pay their own way. The number of such programs is limited, however, by the fact that their losses must be covered by profits made elsewhere. Consequently, an important managerial decision concerns the choice of top priority loss-making activities; the success of academic managers often hinges on this choice. One important decision concerns the relative emphasis to be put on U, G and R. It is not surprising that these choices turn out to be different for colleges and universities, and for public versus private institutions. Another type of decision concerns which departments or disciplines to cross-subsidize; this will be discussed in the following section.

Differences between colleges and universities:

In the case of colleges, G is ruled out as an option so faculty and administrators who prefer graduate training will congregate in universities, while those who prefer teaching undergraduates will be concentrated in colleges. If R and G are complementary, those with a high preference for R will also flock to universities. As a result of these different options and preferences, we would expect undergraduate teaching to be more faculty-intensive, expensive, and subsidized at colleges. At universities, however, where G and R are supported as loss-making activities, undergraduate teaching will use less faculty time and will therefore be profitable. Similarly, TL will be lower at universities and disproportionately allocated to graduate courses, making faculty time available as a major input into G and R. From this perspective, undergraduate students are inputs that generate the faculty for G and R, which are the primary output objectives at the university.

Available data support these hypotheses about the profitability of U (for example, see Hopkins and Massy, 1981). Longitudinal data also show that this tendency to cross-subsidize increased through the 1960s; both undergraduate tuition and enrollments rose while the real resource input into teaching, per student, fell at universities as R and G became increasingly important sources of prestige (James, 1978 and 1986). The pressure for growth in enrollments and class size should be much smaller in colleges where research is valued less and faculty-student interaction are valued more. Indeed, we observe that in colleges, enrollments and class size have grown at a much slower rate.

Differences between public and private IHLs:

Next to the college-university distinction, the private-public distinction is probably the most important because these depend on different sources of funds and therefore have different abilities to earn a profit on U. Also, different administrative labor markets, which foster different objectives, may operate to some extent for public and private institutions. Ability to get along with boards of directors and donors may be more important for private schools, while the ability to work with political bureaucracy is essential for public institutions. Studies of principals of public and private secondary schools indicate that different skills and values are found in administrators of these two types of institutions; the same may be true in higher education (Chubb and Moe, 1985).

Although public universities, like privates, have multiple revenue sources, one source dominates all others and that is the state. This concentration of funding power means that public IHLs lose some of their autonomy; state legislatures and executives, having monopsonistic power, may specify certain inputs and outputs that must be met, as part of an all-or-nothing package. For example, the state may determine the tuition that can be charged, so the institution does not have the option of raising its fees to provide higher-quality education. Similarly, the state often determines enrollment targets, so the campus does not have the option of admitting fewer students in order to raise student quality. Thus, state universities face fewer decision variables and more constraints.

They may also face greater uncertainty about revenues and incentives, if political demand functions are less stable than market-oriented demand functions of students and donors (see Hopkins and Massy, 1981). Elections may bring about abrupt discontinuities. Moreover, by the law of large numbers, it is generally harder to predict the actions of a small number of actors (as in the political arena) than the average action of many actors (as in a competitive marketplace).

Nevertheless, despite this uncertainty, public universities must try to estimate these political demand functions, which will determine their future revenues. What, then, do members of the legislature care about, what are their priorities? If politicians want to maximize their votes, we may deduce that they care about the quantity of undergraduate students, increasing which provides a direct service to their constituents. For this reason, the funding of public IHLs is tied to undergraduate enrollments under funding formulae used in many states (see Hoenack and Pierro, 1990). Garvin (1980) shows that during the period of higher education expansion in the 1960s, public universities improved their position through enrollment growth while elite private institutions grew less but raised $QUAL$ more. However, according to Leslie and Ramey (1986) the funding-enrollment connection has been weakened during the past decade, particularly in states that do not use workload formula budgeting. Perhaps such ties are more tenuous when some institutions are experiencing enrollment declines while others are still growing; downward adjustments are difficult, and this in turn may retard upward adjustments.

Secondly, legislators probably care about vocational programs and applied research, which benefit politically influential firms. For documentation that public institutions engage in these activities more than privates see Peltzman (1976), Garvin (1980), and Gross and Grambusch (1968).

Hoenack and Pierro (1985) show that legislatures in some states are not willing to pay a higher price for G than for U, despite G's higher costs; graduate students are not a more potent interest group than are undergraduates. However, because of their price advantage, public universities are able to attract U while using a low-cost technology to teach them, so their universities' revenue per student exceeds the students' average cost, thereby allowing the university to earn a profit which they spend on G and R. Apparently academic departments 'charge' the administration more than they actually spend per U and the administration in turn 'charges' the legislature more than it pays departments (Hoenack, et al., 1986).

Why does the legislature allow this profit to remain? Hoenack and Pierro (1990) maintain that the surplus is due to imperfect information; state governments cannot eliminate the profit and the cross-subsidization because of difficulties in monitoring university behavior. An alternative interpretation of their data is that legislatures also care about prestige and are willing to spend more per G, but know that universities have an even stronger preference for G. Consequently, legislatures choose to set uniform implicit prices and to forgo monitoring, with the knowledge that faculties will then shift resources to G. By paying for G (partially) through U, legislatures dampen the G/U cost disparity and simultaneously create an incentive for the teaching of U. Government thereby achieves the product and cost mix it wants through the use of incentives rather than regulation.

The small group of prestigious private universities behave quite differently. They can select their own tuition-quality and quantity-quality combination which often leads to great selectivity. Their students are willing to pay high tuition for prestige even if classes are large, so undergraduate tuition exceeds real costs, and these profits can be maintained and used to cross-subsidize G and R.

The nonprestigious private universities are in between these two extremes. They receive most of their funds from tuition revenues, so enrollment is also important to them, as it is to the publics. However, to attract students in competition with cheaper public institutions, they must offer inducements such as lower S/F ratios, smaller classes, and more personalized attention, all of which are costly (James, 1978, 1986). Competition with public institutions also limits the tuition they can charge as well as the profits they can earn on U to subsidize G and R. We would therefore expect the majority of nonprestigious private universities to spend most of their revenues on U and to carry on relatively little G and R, except for part-time professional Masters' programs which cover their own costs. Evidence from international research is consistent with this expectation: Private universities rarely engage in expensive, loss-making activities such as G and R unless these activities are publicly funded or recipients of donations—and large donations are very limited outside the U. S. (James and Benjamin, 1988; Levy, 1986).

Within the U. S., the prestigious universities are also the heaviest recipients of donations from alumni, corporations, and other sources. Just as the public institutions must respond to the objectives of state legislatures, the privates must respond to donors, and this becomes one of their top priorities. Donors are probably more interested in quality and visibility than in quantity of students. Donations also serve as a substitute for U in generating funds for G and R. Unrestricted endowment income, also larger in the private sector, is truly discretionary and can be used to enhance the utility of faculty and administrators with few strings attached. For all these reasons, enrollments are less important as a source of revenue and administrators have greater discretion in the prestigious privates; they use this discretion to choose a higher ratio of G and R to U than either the nonprestigious privates or the public institutions (James, 1978). This, in turn, enables them to be more selective in their admissions of U, thereby retaining their prestige.

Both private donations and profits from undergraduates provide resources for research at the prestigious private universities. This head-start enables them to garner a disproportionate share of federally funded grants, which cover some of the direct and indirect costs of research, especially in the sciences (Garvin, 1980). The higher are research grants, the more research will be done, both because of a price effect and an income effect: A high rate of grantsmanship makes research less of a loss-maker and also makes the university wealthier, able to afford more of its preferred activities. It also brings about a shift in power from administrators to faculty-entrepreneurs who generate the grants. In any event, once again prestige leads to funding which enables research which helps these institutions retain their prestige.

The impact of demographic decline:

The prevalence of cross-subsidization means that the ultimate impact of a cut in revenues may be quite different from the initial incidence of funding cuts or the intent of the funding source. In the case of nonprofit organizations, unlike profit-maximizing enterprises, income effects as well as substitution effects must be taken into account, and these two effects may move in opposite directions, producing unexpected results.

For example, this analysis suggests that G and R will be hurt as U declines due to demographic change. Both colleges and universities are currently competing for U by enhanced recruitment efforts and by offering smaller classes and other personalized services that make student life more attractive. These efforts may increase the proportion of high school graduates going on to college and may produce happier students. However, such efforts are also costly. Thus, U has probably become less profitable in the 1980s, just as it became more profitable in the 1960s. More has been spent on administration (to attract U), leaving less for G and R. This situation has been exacerbated as state legislators have fewer constituents with college-age children and therefore feel less pressure to support state universities. Funding for G and R which produce intangible or chronologically distant benefits, has therefore been cut by this demographic decline, not because of technological interdependencies between U and G or R, but because of the joint funding mechanism that is used.

At the same time, universities have been induced to increase other profitable activities such as the teaching of part-time adult students. Also, applied contract research, which is funded by corporations rather than government and was less preferred before, has now become more common. Thus, not only has the total amount of research declined, but its basic nature has changed as well. These trends will be accelerated as ability to raise funds becomes an increasingly important hiring criterion, changing the skill mix at the IHL. People tend to value activities in which they perform well. Thus as hiring criteria change, the objective function of IHL decisionmakers will also change and this may have the most important future consequences on its decisionmaking structure.

Allocation Among Departments

An important part of the product mix at IHLs is determined by allocations to academic disciplines. The U, G, and R terms in the IHLs objective function given earlier are really vectors denoting outputs of different departments, which depend on the inputs they have been assigned by the administration. This allocation process obviously sets the stage for conflict among departments about their claims to resources. However, at this point we are still assuming that everyone has a common objective of maximizing institutional prestige and has the same information about how to accomplish this. In Part 2 we discuss the mechanisms for resolving conflicts that arise when different faculty members have different information or are mainly interested in the prestige of their own departments and are trying to extract the maximum amount of resources to accomplish this.

If the university's object is to maximize prestige for the institution as a whole, faculty lines will be allocated so that, in equilibrium, the marginal prestige added by the last dollar spent is equalized across departments, taking into account both the direct impact on prestige and the indirect impact via 'profits' generated (e.g., tuition in excess of costs from instructional workload). Tenure and other long-term contracts may prevent this equilibrium from being reached for a long period of time when the external environment changes and total budgets are stable or contracting. However, the movement would always be in this direction.

Referring back to the basic objective function given earlier, this implies that all other things being equal, departments with heavier workloads, a better graduate applicant pool, or the potential for hiring faculty with greater research productivity will have greater access to faculty lines because this will maximize institutional profits and, ultimately, prestige. In order to continue satisfying and attracting students—the major source of revenues—enrollments must enter into the allocation process. However, this effect is limited if undergraduate enrollments are unresponsive to departmental allocations and depend instead on other factors such as the general support facilities, ambience and reputation of the campus. Also, undergraduate tastes among departments may shift from year to year while many departmental resources (e.g. tenured faculty) are committed on a long-term basis. For these reasons, we would expect graduate enrollments, which are department-specific as well as a direct source of prestige, to be given a heavier weight in the allocation process.

In fact, empirical evidence demonstrates that enrollments influence departmental budgets, with G earning a higher reward than U. Along similar lines, departments with strong graduate and research programs are less likely to lose resources when their enrollments decline (see Pfeffer and Salancik, 1974; Pfeffer and Moore, 1980; Hoenack, 1986 et al.). Departments that can attract scholars who will add to the institution's research grants will also have a claim on faculty lines and dollars, since they will help expand the school's budget constraint (see Salancik and Pfeffer, 1974). That is, external funding seems to have a complementary rather than a substitutive relationship with internal funding. In this way, decisions by government agencies about how to allocate research funds will also influence the allocation of university resources across academic disciplines, but should have much less impact in teaching-oriented colleges. Given the influence of external funds on internal resource allocation, it is not surprising that faculty salaries are higher and teaching loads lower in the sciences, which get most grants, than in the humanities, which get least.

Academic disciplines may be arranged in a heirarchy, with high-status fields bringing greater prestige to the IHL than low-status fields (see Alpert, 1985). In general administrations will tend to favor departments where status weights are large. These higher-status disciplines include core departments which are central to the mission of most universities, as well as departments in which the job market for graduate students is strong. Departments with strong paradigms may also be high-status departments. A study of resource allocation by Pfeffer and Moore (1980) showed paradigmic development to be significantly related to departmental budgets. While these status weights vary by department they are constant across universities and constitute an important force leading toward uniform priorities. If they are an accurate approximation of the relative social importance of different disciplines, this is an effective allocation system; if not, it leads us away from an optimal mix.

Suppose that each university sets as a priority maintaining its own strong departments and improving a few high-status fields. Since many universities are then competing for the best faculty members in the high-status fields, this depresses the chance of success, hence the expected faculty productivity in these fields. Some universities might then shift their emphasis to fields that rank lower in the status hierarchy, which they can more easily dominate. They may try to carve out a reputation or market niche in these less-competitive fields. Again, in equilibrium the expected gain in university prestige from the marginal faculty line should be the same for all departments; the higher status of disciplines at the top of the pecking order should be counterbalanced by the lesser competition, hence the higher probability of success of those lower down, and each IHL must decide which strategic plan it will follow.

In sum, to make decisions about allocations among departments, the administration needs information regarding the additional U, G, $QUAL$, R and R grants, stemming from an incremental faculty member in each field. It also needs information about the status of different disciplines. It gets this information from periodic reputational rankings, from assessment of graduate applicant pools and faculty appointments, from external review committees, from past records of publications and grants. However, much of this information is outdated and some of it is asymmetrical: The department is more likely than the administration to have it and it may be in the interest of a department to select or distort the information which it passes on. This brings us to Part 2, where problems stemming from conflicting objectives and imperfect information are discussed.

2. Decisionmaking Under Conflicting Goals

Until now we have assumed that everyone has the same objective function and there are no conflicts over its implementation. Actually, conflicts abound and these stem from three sources: first, the zero-sum nature of the allocation process across departments (and fields within a department); second, spillover effects across departments, which make many production decisions; and third, differences in faculty and administrative preferences among U, G, R, and the other activities of the institution.

Even if faculty members all cared about the same activities (e.g. cared primarily about prestige and research), they might weight their own welfare or the welfare of their own departments above that of the institution as a whole. In addition, some people at a university (for example those less interested in mobility) may believe that the institution should place greater weight on educating students than on building prestige. On the other hand, some college professors who would have preferred a university environment may advocate a higher research/teaching ratio than espoused by the college. Differences among administrative preferences is documented in a case study of Stanford University (Hopkins and Massy, 1981). the fact that different parties have access to dif-

ferent information may also lead them to different evaluations of benefits and costs, even when their underlying objectives are similar. This
creates intransitivity and implementation problems for group decisionmaking, makes it difficult to speak of a prime objective function of the
IHL, and implies that the outcome depends strongly on the decision
structure (see March and Olsen, 1976).

If differences in objective functions are very great in an organization
that features collective decisionmaking, it will face difficulties in making consistent, binding decisions on which to base its actions. Therefore,
academic organizations have certain mechanisms for assuring a considerable degree of uniformity. Some of these are internal mechanisms and
others stem from the external labor market, a kind of protection for the
system as a whole. These are discussed in the next section (see James
and Neuberger, 1981, for a fuller discussion of these mechanisms).

Nevertheless, as anyone familiar with academia will realize, many
differences in preferences remain, often leading to extensive argumen-
tation and sometimes to organizational paralysis. In the following sections
I analyze conflicts stemming from the process of allocating resources
among departments, and the use of incentives, regulations, and committees to exchange information and resolve differences in goals. Although
public universities may be constrained by rules imposed by the state
legislature, and some decisions may be taken out of their hands, I focus
here on choices and processes that are found in both the public and
private sectors.

Homogeneity Mechanisms

Economists usually do not deal with the formation of preferences or
their grouping across firms. If preferences were exogenous and randomly
distributed, we might find a wide variety of utility functions at each IHL.
I believe, in contrast, that a systematic process of preference formation
takes place in academia which, together with the selection and self-
selection of faculty and administrators for jobs, assures considerable
homogeneity.

The indoctrination process begins in graduate school, where student protégés emulate the values of their faculty mentors (see Colander
and Klamer, 1987). Since all G training is done at universities, we would
expect these values to be tilted toward G and R, which may help explain
why even some colleges have a strong research component in their objective functions.

When graduate students enter the labor market, the academic department takes into account the expected research and teaching value of job

candidates and candidates self-select themselves into departments with compatible preferences. For example, those interested primarily in T will go to colleges while those interested in R will try to get jobs at universities. Socialization then takes place during the probationary pretenure period; the tenure process serves as the opportunity for weeding out those who have not absorbed and demonstrated the right values. This sequence of indoctrination, selection, self-selection, socialization, and weeding out is especially important in academia because of the group decision process and because effort cannot readily be monitored. It is important to identify people for whom academic work is an innate source of satisfaction.

Further sorting occurs when faculty members voluntarily move to other, preferred institutions later in life. Since research is a more general, observable, and transferable activity than teaching, research output facilitates mobility and researchers of similar productivity tend to be clustered together by the labor market. Moreover, competition with external labor markets forces internal wage structures to reward researchers if the institution wants to keep them. This helps explain the repeated finding that research productivity is the most highly rewarded activity at universities. According to cognitive dissonance theory, beliefs often follow behavior, in other words, people develop values consistent with their actions. Consequently, faculty who do research because this is encouraged by the labor market will also internalize research into their objective functions. (Of course, faculty who have no intention of moving may develop different values and this is one of the sources of conflict I shall discuss later.) These values are reinforced by the national disciplinary organizations, which are research-oriented (see Alpert, 1985, for a matrix diagram depicting cross-cutting campus and disciplinary loyalties).

Administrators, too, undergo a process of indoctrination and labor market pressures which lead them to have similar objectives. First of all, many of them have originally been faculty members at their own or a similar institution and have therefore been socialized as described above. Second, since faculty members often sit on search committees, this leads to a congruence between the values of the administrators who are chosen and the faculty members who help choose them. Third, after becoming administrators they may attend regular national or regional meetings where deans, provosts, presidents, etc. share ideas and reach a consensus. Finally, the external labor market plays an important role here too. If administrators have any potential interest in moving, they must rate high by the success indicators of their profession-success in attracting funds, hiring academic stars, building top-rated departments, starting new programs, improving quality of incoming students, etc. Higher-level administrators (presidents, provosts) try to select lower-level administrators (deans, departmental chairs) who will help them achieve these goals. While administrators may try to indulge their own programmatic likes and dislikes on an individual basis, the opportunities for doing so are limited by the scarcity of discretionary funds and the need to meet the success indicators of the marketplace. Thus while the focus on utility rather than profits in NPOs permits heterogeneity, pressures from the labor market would lead one to predict considerable homogeneity in behavior among administrators, and this homogeneity should increase as budgets tighten.

Conflicts Due to Zero-Sum Allocations and Departmental Preferences

Nevertheless, despite these homogeneity mechanisms, conflicts abound in academia. Even if everyone at the IHL cares about prestige, there is considerable reason to believe that faculty members care mainly about maximizing the prestige of their own departments and only secondarily about general institutional prestige (see Alpert, 1985). Thus, each department wants more faculty lines (F) to increase R and G, but the total number F must be parcelled out among departments in a zero-sum game—a clear source of conflict, especially in a stable or declining resource environment. This allocation is probably the most political and divisive decision at most IHLs and a model based on bargaining or organization theory might be more appropriate than a maximizing model to describe the process (see, for example, March and Olsen, 1976; Baldridge, 1971a and 1971b; Richman and Farmer, 1974).

We may imagine that each department tries to extract the maximum possible resources from the adminsitration with a combination of promises and threats. The promises come from its ability to increase U, R, G, and $QUAL$, as already described. The threats—implicit or explicit—come from faculty members who may reduce their work effort (e.g. their teaching) and ultimately leave if their departments do not receive what they consider adequate resources. In this bargaining process departments try to convey favorable information about their productivity and status. They also convey their intensity of feeling about their needs, since this itself has implications for morale and work effort. External review committees are one device used for channeling information, both by departments and administrators.

According to this bargaining view of the IHL, the job of the administration is to find the set of allocations that keeps the unhappiness of each department below some minimum threshold, thereby minimizing the probable loss. The fact that much of the relevant information (e.g.

on whether the threats are really credible) is uncertain and asymmetrical adds to the bargaining indeterminacy. However, a few generalizations can be made.

First of all, the threat of leaving is a particularly effective bargaining lever for the most productive faculty members who have the greatest opportunities elsewhere and whose departure would result in the greatest loss of institutional prestige and resources from grants and overhead. This group may constitute a 'replacement coalition' which helped to select the current administrators and whose support the administrators need in order to stay in office (Hoenack, et al., 1986). By imposing the threat of disaffection and resignation, these faculty members and the departments which contain them are likely to have substantial power over university decisions and may be able to shift the balance of university resources and utility toward themselves. In a study by Pfeffer and Salancik (1974, and Salancik and Pfeffer, 1974), political power (e.g. membership on key committees) and ability to attract outside funding were shown to have a significant and sizeable effect on departmental budgets. This is particularly the case in situations characterized by uncertainty, secret information, and great resource scarcity (Pfeffer and Moore, 1980).

It follows that strong departments are usually at an advantage in this bargaining process and may be able to secure more internal resources than the prestige-maximizing equilibrium described in Part 1. Since these departments already have the most visible and productive faculty members, the mobility threat is most credible and the prestige loss to the institution would be high if they left. Consequently, departments that start out strong are likely to get the resources that will keep them strong. As a corollary, weak departments may be left with so few resources that their most productive members may leave. Bargaining forces thus accentuate the polarization between strong and weak departments which comes out of the prestige-maximization process described in Part 1. They also help explain why university resources may be concentrated and why departmental size and priorities vary from one university to another.

Another general outcome is that if we compare the revenues and costs generated by each department and school we will undoubtedly find that some make profits and others make losses, reminiscent of the process of cross-subsidization discussed in part 1. Here the imbalance is partially due to differing technologies or demand conditions in different disciplines and partially due to their differential bargaining power. A strong or high-status profitable unit is more likely to be able to retain and reinvest much of its profits, while a powerful loss-making unit is more likely to be able to justify these losses and subsidies as necessitated by technology and justified by the prestige it buys for the institution. If we observe a policy of 'each tub on its own bottom' being enforced on a loss-making unit we may infer that it is weak, low status, and thereby deemed not worthy of cross-subsidization.

Nevertheless, despite the differential bargaining ability and profitability of departments, the administration must try to convince the major internal and external constituencies of the IHL that its strategy is fair, in the institution's best interest, and therefore does not warrant retaliation. The desire of the administration to appear equitable and to minimize internal conflict that will be destructive to the institution is stressed by Garvin (1980) and Cootner (1974). This desire mitigates the willingness of the administration to accede to the demands of strong departments. Another mitigating factor is that, if the bargaining allocation should deviate too much from the optimal allocation described in part 1, the resulting gradual loss of utility (prestige) from misallocation exceeds the potential immediate loss due to faculty departure. it is obviously in departments' interests to keep their demands within feasible limits. Skillful chairpersons and adminsitrators will usually convey to each other the information needed to reach a solution within these limits. However, in occasional cases, particularly where other institutions are willing and able to offer more resources, the minimum demands of mobile faculty members and the maximum amounts the administration is willing to supply do not overlap, and departments break up.

In some cases the desire to avoid conflict and appear fair leads the administration away from the optimal plan instead of toward it. When sudden budget adjustments are necessary, administrations often resort to practices such as across-the-board cuts, hiring freezes, attrition, and the using up of capital through deferred maintenance (see Balderston, 1983, for a discussion of these practices). These techniques may be the only possible response to short-run emergencies and may give the institution breathing space to reevaluate its priorities at a time when budgetary conditions are changing. However, they are obviously not optimal in the long run, since the resulting allocations tend to be random rather than rational. While such universities may survive, particularly if state-supported, they will tend to lose their best faculty and departments because high productivity is not being rewarded, and they will end up concentrated at the lower end of the prestige hierarchy of institutions.

Conflicts Due to Differing Information or Preferences

As outlined at the beginning of this paper, decisionmaking at IHLs is very decentralized because the locus of relevant information is decentralized. But if there are important spillover effects in a decentralized system some method of internalizing the externalities must be devised or the result will be inefficient. Such spillover and free-rider effects abound at universities. A faculty member may prefer to play golf rather than do research, although he benefits from the prestige generated by the collective output of others in his department. A department may use poor judgement in its hiring or promotion decisions, thereby hurting the prestige of the entire university. One department whose courses are prerequisites for many other fields may set up its curriculum without taking into account the needs of other disciplines. Another department may prefer not to teach any undergraduate courses at all, leaving more of that task for other departments. Events may be scheduled in ways that conflict, even when these conflicts could be avoided by a cooperative exchange of information. This section describes two important control mechanisms for incentives and regulations—used by colleges and universities for resolving free-rider and principal-agent problems, as well as the final resort to moral suasion when all else fails.

Incentives:

A major mechanism for getting subunits to act in the interest of the institution is the use of incentives. I have already described the role of U, G, and R in the budget allocation process, when institutional and departmental goals coincide. Tying budgets to these activities also provides an incentive for departments to carry them out when these goals diverge. For example, departments may be induced to teach large undergraduate service courses if their workload entitles them to additional faculty lines. To illustrate how this incentive works, one study showed that departments vary their curriculum in order to attract more students (and resources), especially during periods of tight budgets; but this effect is weaker in departments with higher national reputational ratings for their graduate and research programs. Apparently the more prestigious departments consider themselves somewhat immune from budget cuts that hinge on undergraduate workloads and are therefore less responsive to enrollment incentives (Manns and March, 1978).

Similarly, faculty members are induced to do research by the possibility of promotion or job mobility, by privileged access to secretaries, travel funds, and equipment for the most productive. While salary differentials in academia are limited relative to those in private industry, some reliance on wage incentives still exists at most institutions. As noted earlier, empirical studies have shown that research productivity is the main determinant of salary and promotion at universities (see Katz, 1973; Siegfried and White, 1973; Tuckman et al., 1977; Tuckman, 1979; Dornbusch, 1979; McKenzie, 1979).

Teaching, on the other hand, is usually controlled via regulation rather than incentives. That is, faculty members are encouraged to maximize their research subject to a minimum teaching constraint, usually specified in terms of courses and hours. This difference in approach toward T and R may stem from the fact that teaching inputs and research outputs are more easily observed and measured than teaching outputs and research inputs. In addition, the institution needs greater certainty about teaching loads and course schedules, which only regulation can provide. Whereas uncertainty is inherent in the research process, and incentives are deemed likely to induce the greatest effort. However, it does appear that teaching quality falls between the cracks in this system.

Hoenack (1977), Hoenack and Norman (1974), and Hoenack and Berg (1980) advocate the increased use of incentives to minimize conflicts, avoid hidden subsidies, encourage efficiency, and reward teaching quality (also see Cootner, 1974). Under their scheme, a set of internal prices would be established for each teaching activity, and the allocation of resources among departments would then depend on their responsiveness to these incentives, instead of being a separate political decision. Similarly, departments (and faculty) would be charged for their use of general university facilities. Departments would then take into account all the real costs of an activity, since they would be bearing these costs and would keep their own 'profits.' This is in contrast to the present system where costs are often borne in one place and profits diverted elsewhere. Since enrollments would be explicitly rewarded, departments would have an incentive to attract large numbers of students and to reward faculty members for doing so; quality of teaching might begin to matter.

As economists we can hardly quarrel with the recommendation for greater reliance on incentives in the interest of efficiency. However, we are also aware of the pitfalls. First of all, this is efficient only if consumers have enough information to act intelligently in their own self-interest; many faculty members believe this characterization does not hold true for students. Second, an explicit incentive system would pose the well-known central planning problem: Departments would tend to substitute out of unobservable activities that are not specifically rewarded (e.g. informal advising, intangible, quality components of teaching and grading that may not be appreciated by students) in favor of activities that are rewarded (e.g. teaching large numbers). If the unobservables are also important, this will not be an efficient improvement. Ambiguity in allocation criteria serves a useful function here: It allows these nonmeasurable activities to matter, in a very loose, uncertain, subjective way, and therefore keeps some departmental interest alive.

In addition, I do not believe that an explicit incentive system will avoid conflict. Rather, it will simply shift the arena for conflict. Instead of arguing over allocations to departments, faculty will now argue over the correct weights to be given to *U, G,* and *R,* the proper rewards for spillovers, the price to be charged for various support services, and the way in which the differing technologies of each discipline should be taken into account. Given the difficulties in measuring the quality components of these terms and given the fact that different weighting schemes will help some departments and hurt others, I believe that agreement on incentives is just as unlikely as agreement on direct allocations.

Some universities (the University of Pennsylvania is one) have implemented a weaker variant of this incentive system, known as responsibility center management (see Zemsky, Porter, and Oedel, 1978). The basic idea here is that each school or responsibility center gets a budget based on the tuition generated by its teaching activities, the income from its grants and gifts, and a lump-sum subsidy from the university in some cases. The unit must then cover its own costs, including a share of general institutional expenses. As expected, much argument takes place over size of subsidy and share of costs. This kind of experiment seems even more rare at public institutions, which face the additional problems of not wishing to reveal to legislatures the internal importance of and subsidies given to various activities and the possibility that any surplus generated by enhanced efficiency would be taken away by the state. Perhaps these reasons explain why, despite much discussion and some experimentation at private universities, such explicit incentive schemes have not been widely used in academia. But they would be worth a try and worth a research project to follow up.

Committees and regulations:

The presence of multiple objectives, imperfect information and spillover effects explains a central fact of academic life—the proliferation of committees. (For a discussion of the overabundance of committees see McKenzie, 1979.) In fact, committees and regulations issuing therefrom are probably used more than incentives as a means for influencing departmental actions.

In some cases, departmental committees are set up because different people have different intensities about their preferences for different IHL activities. People with similar preferences may be grouped together and allowed to have prime influence over specified inputs or outputs which they care about most. For example, those concerned primarily with undergraduate education sit on a committee which controls the undergraduate major; computing facilities are overseen by a user group, etc. This partitioning of decision responsibility has the advantage that it gives faculty members power in the very areas where they have the greatest information and intensity of preference. Also, by grouping together people with similar concerns it reduces the time cost and indeterminacy of the decision process itself. The corresponding disadvantage is that trade-offs with other activities may not be considered. For example, a committee establishing small class sizes for undergraduate education may not take into account the opportunity cost this implies for the other activities of the department or the university.

Another set of committees is organized to control the spillover effects which cut across departments. For example, college-wide curriculum committees and personnel committees are designed to exchange information and review departmental actions that might, if unchecked, damage the rest of the institution. The corresponding disadvantage is that they themselves use up faculty time and may result in decisions made by those who do not have the most information. One of the major reasons for decentralization to departments, after all, is that they have the best information about the discipline and its labor market.

Committees may also be set up to provide a flow of information to the administration, particularly with respect to such activities as the establishment of budget priorities and other general university policies. In these cases, instead of decisionmaking flowing down to lower levels, information flows up to higher levels through a committee structure. Middle management positions such as deans and department chairs serve a similar purpose. The upper administration may use this information in the process of resource allocation and may also use it to establish standards designed to eliminate negative spillover effects—e.g., standards governing minimum teaching loads, maximum or minimum class sizes, course scheduling, etc. The problem here is that a wrong standard may be selected, or a uniform standard imposed which is right for some departments but wrong for others.

Moral suasion:

A final method for resolving conflicts is moral suasion—using logic to convince others to act in a certain way. For example, administrators may try to persuade the faculty to pay more attention to undergraduates in order to boost enrollments as the pool of applicants in the relevant age group declines. They may point out that such contributions of effort should be perceived as a repeated game in which each faculty member's contribution also induces others to participate. This argument can be used most effectively to support a change which moves the institution from an interior point to the efficiency frontier or one which expands the frontier; e.g. to get concurrence on undertaking a clearly profitable activity, from which all parties can ultimately benefit. Such persuasion will probably not be very effective, however, for cases where most parties believe the compensation principle will not be followed, so there will be winners and losers, and where movement along the efficiency frontier is involved (e.g. reallocating a stable budget among departments), inevitably enriching one party at the expense of another. A majoritarian or dictatorial decision may then be reached and implemented, but part of the cost will be the disagreement and possible effort loss or exit of the dissenting group.

Conclusion

I want to conclude by raising a few normative and positive questions that emerge out of this literature survey. The most important normative issues relate to the emphasis on prestige maximization and cross-subsidization discussed in Part 1. Is prestige maximization a socially worthwhile goal and does it encourage higher education to concentrate on the most socially worthwhile activities? Should we view this desire to be best as a competitive mechanism which rewards those who maximize the social value of output and weeds out the others, much as the profit motive does under Adam Smith's "invisible hand"? Does this competition entice more productive people into the academic arena and create incentives for greater effort and productivity? Is the status of different disciplines a reasonable approximation of their relative social value, so that when IHLs weight each discipline's output by its status, this produces an efficient departmental mix? Can we presume that positive externalities are greatest for R and G so that cross-subsidization of these activities by universities is desirable? Do we have the right mix of teaching and research for the system as a whole? If the answers to these questions are yes, prestige maximization may also be maximizing social product, especially in the long run. If the answers are no, then the competition for prestige, which is essentially a relative concept, may be a zero-sum game in the short run and may be leading us to produce the wrong output mix, or to produce it inefficiently, in the long run.

However, these questions are hard to address because we have no firm way to measure the relative social value of research, graduate training and undergraduate teaching, of different disciplines and of different teaching technologies. Indeed, this lack of agreement on value, combined with informational asymmetries, is probably a major reason why we decentralize so much decisionmaking in higher education—to institutions, departments, and individual faculty members, who are supposed to have the greatest expertise. But expertise does not necessarily give us the right or the ability to determine values.

In addition to these normative questions several positive questions have also emerged, most of them related to the use of decentralized decision structures and incentives, discussed in part 2. Does degree of centralization vary systematically with variables such as the type of decision at hand, budgetary conditions (expansionary versus contractionary), public versus private legal status, or the size of the institution? What control devices and incentives are used in decentralized systems to resolve conflicts, take account of spillover effects and assure that faculty and departments are acting in accordance with institution-wide interests? What are the differences between public and private institutions in objectives, processes, and behavior? How does the greater autonomy in the private sector affect its input and output mix? its costs and efficiency? its reliance on centralized versus decentralized decisionmaking? Along similar lines, to what degree do state legislatures use regulations versus incentives to control resource allocation? Do they pay uniform or varying amounts for different fields and levels of education? Do they fund research directly? Are there large differences in funding systems from state to state and what are the consequences for economic efficiency? Finally, we would like to know what factors determine the hiring and remuneration of top administrators since this, ultimately, determines their objective function in making allocation decisions. Is there a division between the public and private sectors, between colleges and universities, in the labor market for administrators? Have hiring criteria changed over the last decade; if so, will this change the objective functions of decisionmakers and hence the choices they make to adapt to any given environment?

Hopefully, a few years from now we will have answers to some of these questions and therefore more empirical information to accompany our theoretical models and normative assessment of decision processes and priorities in higher education.

CHAPTER 5

Higher Education Cost Functions

PAUL T. BRINKMAN

This chapter summarizes what is known about certain elements of cost behavior in higher education, insofar as that knowledge has been set down in the literature. Studies of the behavior of average and marginal costs are given particular attention. Specific empirical issues addressed include the marginal and average costs of instruction, evidence for economies of scale for research universities and other four-year institutions, economies of scope, and unit costs by level of instruction or student. This review will indicate where answers have been forthcoming and where work remains to be done.

The literature reviewed included published articles and books, dissertations, unpublished material in the Educational Resources Information Center collection, agency reports, and other unpublished material. Pertinent literature came primarily from economics and education administration.

Evidence from empirical investigations is useful to the extent that it is understood and interpreted properly. Accordingly, the context for interpretation is also a major focus in this chapter. It will be taken up first, followed by a review of the cost studies. A concluding section summarizes what the studies indicate about the factors that influence average and marginal costs in higher education.

Analytical Context

This section includes a discussion of the cost function concept, its applicability to higher education institutions, and an overview of various types of cost studies.

Cost Function Concepts

The total cost of a production process can be written as:

107

(1) $$C = \Sigma \, p_i x_i$$

where p_i is the price and x_i is the quantity of the ith input. Henderson and Quandt (1971) refer to equation (1) as the cost equation. The total cost of a production process can also be written as:

(2) $$C = C(q,p)$$

where q is a vector of output quantities and p is a vector of input (or factor) prices. When $C(q,p)$ minimizes $\Sigma p_i x_i$ subject to the production frontier $F(q,x) = o$, where x is a vector of input quantities corresponding to p, then equation (2) is a cost function within the framework of economic theory. The production frontier, more commonly known as the production function, specifies the maximum output obtainable from every possible input combination. The cost function relates the production function and input prices in such a way as to specify the minimum cost for a given level of output. In other words, cost minimization and an explicit mathematical relationship with the production function are part of the definition of the term *cost function*. Indeed, it has been shown that the total cost function is dual to the production function (Shepard, 1953), i.e., the two functions are different but equivalent ways of looking at the production phenomenon.

The average total cost function is found by dividing each term in the total cost function by the output level. The marginal cost function is found by taking the first derivative of the total cost function with respect to output. Economists, in their theoretical presentations, usually assume that average cost and marginal cost are second-degree curves which first decline and then increase as output is expanded. While that may be true for some extreme range of output, the empirical evidence of the past several decades indicates that actual cost curves in various industries typically decline initially, as output increases, and are then flat-bottomed over the remainder of the observed range of output (Scherer, 1980).

The total cost function can be extended so that equation (2) may be written as:

(3) $$C = c(q,p;t)$$

which solves

$$min \, \Sigma \, p_i x_i$$

subject to

$$F(q,x;t) = 0$$

where t is a vector that summarizes technological conditions important to the production process (McFadden, 1978). The higher education cost functions that will be examined later take the form of either equation (2) or equation (3).

The cost function is a relatively old, even classical concept in economics; for example, most of the early statistical estimates of economies of scale, such as those conducted by Dean in the 1930s, were based on the estimation of cost functions (Dean, 1976). New functional forms, such as the translog cost function developed by Christensen, Jorgenson, and Lau (1973) or the flexible fixed cost quadratic function developed by Mayo (1984), continue to appear in the literature. Yet there are problems —gray areas, at least—in the empirical application of cost function theory.

Cost Function Applicability

The first difficulty in the empirical application of the cost function concept stems from the fact that the form of the production function is seldom known a priori. As a result, instead of being able to derive a cost function mathematically from an explicit production function, a researcher has little choice but to rely to some extent on statistical curve-fitting techniques in attempting to find an appropriate functional form (Cohn, 1979). Nor is the proper specification of the cost function a trivial matter, as marginal cost estimates in particular are very sensitive to functional form (Lave and Lave, 1970). This combination of circumstances reduces the likelihood that a variety of estimated cost functions will lead to consistent results and makes comparisons among studies more tenuous.

Another source of potential difficulty is the assumption that organizations minimize their costs. This assumption must be plausible if the estimated cost function is to be given a technical rather than a merely behavioral interpretation (Pauly, 1978). To put it another way, this assumption is the basis for viewing the organizations under investigation as being bound to the cost curve by the technical aspects of their production activities.

The conventional wisdom is that higher education institutions do not minimize costs. They have no fundamental, abiding interest in minimizing costs, at least not in the sense of the expenditures that almost all cost studies examine. Those who work in higher education, especially the faculty, are concerned primarily about creating and transmitting knowledge. At times, cutting costs can have utility for them, but never in the direct manner in which cost savings benefit a profit-seeking venture. Furthermore, even if the motive were present they would still find it difficult to minimize costs because of a lack of knowledge about the production process. Outcomes in higher education typically are ill-specified, poorly measured, and only loosely connected to inputs (Bowen, 1980). If proof of the unwillingness or inability to minimize costs is needed, Carlson's (1972) production frontier analysis of various types of higher education institutions demonstrates that most of those institutions were operating well off the frontier, at least given his output measurements.

Some observers are even willing to suggest that the operating principle of colleges and universities might better be thought of as cost maximization. This notion is implicit in the proposition that higher education institutions raise all the money they can and then spend all that they raise, which in turn is a cornerstone of the so-called revenue theory of cost elaborated by Howard Bowen (1980). Essentially, Bowen argues that in the short run costs are a function of revenue. Institutions that are more successful in raising revenue on a unit basis (e.g., per student) will have higher unit costs.

While there is more than a grain of truth in this theory, it is an overstatement if taken literally and without qualification. It is not true that all institutions raise as much revenue as they can. Many elite private institutions, for instance, certainly could charge higher tuitions than they do and not lose enrollment. Nor is it true that all institutions spend all the revenue they raise. For example, private institutions fortunate enough to have a substantial income from endowment seldom spend all of that income. Less well known is the fact that many private institutions lacking a substantial endowment work hard to increase such funds by not spending a portion of their current operating budget and then transferring the unspent portion to quasi-endowment (a reserve account). Public institutions that are not allowed to roll over funds from one year to the next can generally be counted on to spend all of their budgeted funds for the year. But when these institutions are given a chance to roll over funds into the next year, experience shows that at least some of them will take the opportunity to reduce expenditures and create reserves.

The truth lies somewhere between the extremes. Higher education institutions neither minimize nor maximize costs; instead, they operate within a range of accepted norms for production relationships, such as student-faculty ratios or lab space per student for instruction. Typically, institutions that are relatively successful in raising revenues will operate at the opposite end of those ranges from institutions that are relatively unsuccessful in raising revenue. We must agree, then, with Cohn's (1979) conclusion that estimated cost functions in higher education should be interpreted as being approximate rather than actual representations of the minimization principles embedded in cost function theory.

Finally, applying the cost function concept to higher education is complicated because colleges and especially universities produce more than one 'product' or service—including instruction, separately budgeted research, and public service—and because some of the products and services are produced jointly. In addition, the instructional activity itself often yields distinguishable 'products' in several senses, such as graduate versus undergraduate degrees, or degrees in one field versus another, or even in the sense of knowledge versus skills versus attitudes. In these latter examples, joint production is commonplace.

The allocation of costs between goods and services that are jointly produced is arbitrary. Institutions occasionally go to considerable lengths, using detailed faculty activity analyses, to determine appropriate cost allocations, but the arbitrariness remains, although it is possible, as we will see, to estimate statistically the costs of jointly produced goods and services.

Types of Cost Analyses

The earliest recorded cost analyses in higher education date from the late nineteenth century (Witmer, 1972). Stevens and Elliot (1925), who undertook an early, wide-ranging analysis of higher education financing, are credited with being the first to note the difference between marginal and average costs in the higher education context (Adams, Hankins, and Schroeder, 1978). In a landmark study of costs at forty-four small colleges, Russell and Reeves (1935) analyzed for the first time some of the fundamental relationships between unit costs and size, quality, and program breadth. They used data aggregated at the institutional level. By contrast, the *California and Western Conference Cost and Statistical Study* (Middlebrook, 1955) is often cited for its detailed analysis at the departmental level, focusing on technical relationships in the instructional process at twelve research universities. Statistically estimated cost functions appear in the literature beginning in the late 1960s.

Most higher education cost studies undertaken in this century feature straightforward calculations of average historical costs. A typical calculation done in most institutions is the division of a budget center's direct costs by some measure of that center's activity. A budget center can be anything from an administrative office to an academic department to one or all of the functions (instruction, academic support services, and so on) in the current fund. For example, the direct costs of an academic department may be divided by the number of credit hours generated by faculty in that department to yield an average direct cost per credit hour. Similarly, all direct expenditures for instruction may be divided by the number of full-time equivalent students to yield the average direct cost per student for all instructional activities combined. Average full costs (direct plus indirect) are calculated less often. Even more rare are studies where full cost includes the cost of capital (a recent example is Health Resources and Services Administration, 1986). Institutions will occasionally calculate average costs by level of student, using allocation algorithms that are based primarily on the distribution of faculty effort. They will sometimes calculate average incremental costs as a substitute for true marginal costs; the latter normally cannot be calculated directly (Allen and Brinkman, 1983).

Statistical estimates of average or marginal costs comprise a second type of higher education cost study. These studies contain explicit estimates of the cost function as defined above, as well as comparisons of average and marginal costs. As noted earlier, it is generally not possible to derive the proper functional form for a cost function. Thus, in higher education as in other industries a variety of functional forms have been used. The models typically are estimated by some form of regression procedure.

Because higher education institutions do not minimize costs, those statistically estimated cost functions are in effect generating data on average behavior. On a few occasions, higher education cost studies have focused on the most efficient behavior. They usually employ linear programming techniques or other procedures to compute a convex hull, as in Carlson's analysis (1972; 1975) at the institutional level and Gray and Weldon's (1978) at the departmental level. When employing these techniques, it is nesessary to make substantive assumptions about the thoroughness with which output can be measured within the estimation model. That and the complexity of the procedures may explain why only a few researchers have pursued this line of inquiry as a way of examining costs in higher education.

There are few published accounts of what might be called "engineering" cost studies in higher education. In a well-known example of this third form of cost analysis, Bowen and Douglass (1971) considered for liberal arts colleges the impact on costs of rearranging the basic production relationships (class sizes, modes of instruction, and so on). Costs in medical education have been looked at in similar fashion (Gonyea, 1978), as have costs in a variety of disciplines in a European university (Bottomley, 1972). While insights regarding cost behavior can no doubt be gained using this approach, the softness of production relationships in higher education effectively makes such an analysis a hypothetical one. Less is learned about actual cost behavior than about potential cost behavior.

Most cost analyses in higher education focus on two kinds of costs: educational and general (E&G) and instructional. In statistical studies of E&G costs (i.e., the direct costs of the three final activities, instruction, research, and public service, plus all of the costs of support activities such as general administration and operation of the physical plant), authors will occasionally develop a model that includes both enrollment and research as outputs (for example, Cohn, Rhine and Santos, 1989). Enrollment is used often as a proxy for the output of instructional activities, as are credit hours. Research dollars in the form of either revenues or expenditures are used as proxies for research output. Sometimes the number of faculty publications or a citation index is used instead. Apparently, no statistical estimates of E&G cost behavior have included public service as well as enrollment and research as independent variables; and some E&G studies have included only enrollment as an output. A particular strategy for dealing with the multiproduct nature of higher education may or may not be appropriate depending on the type of institution analyzed, i.e., some institutions actually engage in only one or two of the three primary activities.

In studies of instructional costs, there are variations in the number of levels of instruction included in the models. Sometimes students (or credit hours) at all levels are treated as being equivalent, as if there were only one instructional product or service. In other models, graduate enrollment is distinguished from undergraduate enrollment, and on occasion undergraduate instruction is broken down into upper and lower divisions.

When joint production has been analyzed in statistically estimated cost functions, it customarily has been done by incorporating separate terms (variables) for each of the products and their interactions (see, for example, Verry and Davies, 1976). Baumol, Panzar, and Willig (1982) recently developed new theoretical tools to examine costs in multiproduct firms, with respect to both economies of scale (overall and for particular products) and economies of scope (the extent to which joint production is efficient). Only one study was found (Cohn, Rhine and Santos, 1989) that examined higher education costs within this new framework.

On occasion, instructional cost models will contain variables that measure curricular, or programmatic emphasis (for example, Smith, 1980; Brinkman, 1981b). This is much the same strategy as that used, for instance, by Pauly (1978) in his incorporation of "case mix" variables when estimating cost functions for hospitals. The case mix and curricular variables are proxies for the technological conditions in equation (3) above.

In most cost estimation models, if a variable for input prices is included it is either average full-time faculty salaries or average full-time faculty compensation (salary plus benefits). Other input prices such as salaries for clerical staff are often ignored, although location variables, such as region of the country or urban versus rural, sometimes afford a measure of control over nonfaculty prices.

Studies of instructional costs usually ignore the fact that the expenditure category *instruction* as it is used nationally includes the activity known as departmental research, i.e., research and scholarly activities that are not separately budgeted but for which faculty are often given release time from teaching duties. The variables used in attempting to explain or predict instructional expenditures usually represent only the amount of teaching activity, such as credit hours produced or the number of students enrolled. Departmental research is not acknowledged as a distinct activity with possible consequences for costs. In an important exception to this rule, James (1978) not only acknowledges this dimension of so-called instructional costs, but shows that ignoring it can lead to misleading results. An obvious example of potential trouble is a study in which instructional cost at an institution with a considerable amount of departmental research activity is compared to instructional cost at an institution with little such activity.

Cost Function Results

The bulk of this part of the paper is devoted to economies of scale, i.e., the relationship between unit costs and organizational size. There are two additional sections dealing with the behavior of average costs. The first concerns the possibility for economies of scope, i.e., whether there are cost advantages in producing multiple outputs. The second looks at differences in average costs by level of instruction and level of student.

Economies of Scale

The relationship between size, or scale, and unit costs has been of considerable interest to cost analysts in higher education. A few cost studies deal with the issue by estimating the ratio between marginal and average costs (MC:AC); whenever the ratio is less than one, scale economies are present. They will be examined first. Most studies look for evidence of economies of scale in the form of average or marginal costs that decline as size increases. These studies will be addressed in three sections. The first examines economies of scale from the perspective of research universities, the second looks at the same issue from the perspective of other four-year (essentially teaching) institutions, and third examines economies of scale from the perspective of studies that ignore institutional type.

Ratio of marginal to average costs:

The discussion of MC:AC ratios could have been folded into the subsequent sections on economies of scale. The underlying issues are identical. The ratio studies were kept separate because the way in which their results are presented provides a particular insight into the behavior of unit costs. Rather than leaving the relationship between average and marginal costs to be inferred, as most studies do, they provide an explicit numerical estimate of that relationship.

The number of estimates of MC:AC in higher education is small, and most of the estimates are at the department or other subinstitutional level. In a study of departmental costs at private liberal arts colleges, Tierney (1980) found that MC:AC averaged only .38 across seven departments. There was considerable difference by department: English had the highest estimate at .54, biology had the lowest at .16. Of the departments analyzed, the two in the natural sciences had considerably lower ratios than the two in the social sciences. The former departments also had higher average costs. The study, a pooled cross section of forty institutions over four years, was meant to be an analysis of long-run cost behavior. Assuming a correct specification of the estimating equation, the rather low ratios suggest perhaps that the results are more a reflection of short-run costs. That is, the homogeneity of the sample and the (presumably) limited extent of enrollment variation may mean that the ratios represent a good deal of underutilized capacity at a given scale, rather than cost behavior related to differences in scale. The low MC:AC estimates may also be reflective of the type of institution analyzed.

Brovender (1974) used two models to analyze MC:AC at a large public research university. In the first model, he regressed instructional expenditures in aggregate enrollment; the second model was the same as the first except that the independent variable was disaggregated into graduate and undergraduate enrollment. In both models, the unit of analysis was expenditures and enrollments by groups of academic programs. For the natural sciences, MC:AC was estimated to be .53 using model one, and .66 using model two. The corresponding results for the social sciences were .72 and .81, and for the humanities, .49 and .66, respectively. One way of interpreting the comparative results in Brovender's study is to assume that they reflect short-run cost behavior. His data are for the late 1960s, a time when enrollment in the social sciences was high. Those high enrollments may have resulted in the social sciences having less unused capacity than did the other areas, which would have lead to relatively high MC:AC in the short run.

Razin and Campbell (1972) used a statistically estimated cost function to examine instructional expenditures at six undergraduate colleges within a large public research university. The average value for MC:AC across the six colleges was .58. The authors speculated that the variation in scale effects among the colleges was due to better utilization of courses in some colleges.

While this review is limited for the most part to studies of American higher education, some of the results of the major study done by Verry and Davies (1976) of universities in Great Britain deserve mention. Of the six types of departments examined, MC:AC was lowest for mathematics, .44, and highest for engineering, .67. The ratio for the social sciences was .54, slightly below the mean of .58 for the six departmental types. These results were based on a multiplicative cost function in which the independent variable was a composite enrollment variable that weighted enrollments by level of student.

It is difficult to draw definitive conclusions on the basis of so few data points. In all instances, however, the ratios were less than one, giving a clear signal that scale economies were present. The ratios were particularly low at small, elite private colleges, which is perhaps not surprising. In addition, for the research universities studied there was a concentration of values in the .5 to .7 range for MC:AC, suggesting that the available scale economies were quite substantial for those institutions too.

In two studies (Brinkman 1981b; 1984) in which MC:AC is estimated for instruction as a whole, the samples analyzed included mostly nonelite four-year colleges. The estimated MC:AC was .81 in both studies, for both public and private institutions. Apparently, these institutions, while they still had opportunities for achieving scale economies, were operating closer to the point at which the cost of additional students would be the same as the average cost per student of current students.

Cost curves at research universities:

Broomall et al. (1978) found no evidence for economies of scale in a sample of twenty-two major public universities, regressing expenditures in various categories on total full-time equivalent (FTE) enrollment, with no controls in the estimating equation. Controlling for the proportion of graduate students, curriculum complexity, and sponsored research emphasis, Brinkman (1981a) also found no evidence for economies of scale in instructional costs among twenty-five public research universities, but he did find considerable evidence for such economies in a combined sample of fifty public and private universities. Among the reasons cited for this latter finding were that the private institutions, which without exception were smaller in size, had lower student-faculty and student-staff ratios and paid higher faculty salaries. In a recent study of land-grant institutions, many of which are research universities, Stommel (1985) reports that current fund expenditures per student were twenty-one percent lower at institutions with 22,850 FTE students compared to those with one-fourth as many students (5,700), when controlling for the number of academic specialities, the proportion of research expenditures, and the proportion of graduate students.

In another study in the same vein, Smith (1978) used a regression model to analyze instructional costs at Michigan's public colleges and universities, two of which are research universities. He examined six discipline areas at four student levels and found a mixture of size and interaction effects. Overall, he found considerable evidence for economies of scale at the undergraduate levels and for both economies and diseconomies of scale at the graduate levels. Size effects were more dramatic at lower enrollment ranges. Evaluated at mean enrollment, marginal costs were less than average costs in seventeen out of twenty-four instances. Variables representing the interactions between student levels were significant in all disciplines except engineering. Similarly, in a time series analysis of cost behavior at the University of Oregon, Siegel (1967) found that size effects could be detected at three levels of instruction in each of the curricular areas he examined. In the great majority of instances, larger size resulted in lower unit costs.

Cohn, Rhine and Santos (1989) found evidence for economies of scale in a study of 121 large universities (public and private), the majority of which would qualify as research universities. They regressed E&G expenditures on enrollment and a research variable (alternatively, revenues for sponsored research and number of publications). Generally, overall economies of scale existed for all but the highest enrollment levels (about fifty thousand students). No statistically significant, product-specific economies of scale for instruction were found. Economies of scale for research varied slightly depending on the specification of the cost function, but typically they existed for the entire range of the data. The authors concluded that the most efficient institution is one in which enrollment is close to thirty thousand FTE students and research grants amount to roughly $80 to $100 million (as measured in 1981-82). Only a handful of the very largest public research universities fit this description.

In a regression study of instructional costs at research universities, Brinkman (1981b) found that changes in marginal costs were negligible over most of the enrollment range, provided that the proportion of students by level remained constant. There were substantial scale-related economies available at the graduate and upper-division levels, provided those enrollments were allowed to increase independently. Somewhat similar results were reported by Verry and Davies (1976) in their study of British universities. On the basis of cost functions in which total expenditures were regressed on graduate and undergraduate enrollment, their overall conclusion was that marginal costs for both graduate and undergraduate students were generally constant. However, they found considerable evidence for a variety of curves when marginal costs were estimated using allocated cost functions. An example of the latter would be faculty salaries that are allocated to undergraduate instruction and then regressed on undergraduate enrollment. There was considerable variation in the shape of the cost curves from one department to another and from one level of instruction to another.

Evidence in regard to the overall shape of marginal cost curves at American research universities is ambiguous. Razin and Campbell (1972) found that marginal costs declined at a decreasing rate in their study of six colleges in a large public research university. Sengupta (1975), using a logarithmic function with a composite enrollment variable, obtained results that show increasing marginal costs for a small group of public research universities. Brinkman (1981b) estimated a variety of functional forms in examining marginal costs of instruction at various types of public colleges. Little evidence was found that unit costs were higher at relatively large research universities.

A number of studies examine cost behavior by comparing average costs calculated at various enrollment intervals. If average costs are lower at large institutions than at small institutions, then, other things being equal, economies of scale are present. Although synthesis of these studies is difficult, they appear to indicate that economies of scale typically will be experienced by a representative group of private research universities of varying sizes but not by public research universities. In a Carnegie Commission study (1972), instructional costs per student at private research universities in the 3,000 to 4,999 FTE enrollment interval were twenty-five percent higher than costs at comparable institutions with 7,000 to 9,999 students. For the same range, but using a weighted student count (each graduate student multiplied by three), the difference in cost was twenty percent. However, in that same Carnegie study the data also suggest that the average-cost curve for private research universities is saw-toothed. The very small institutions and those with enrollments in the 10,000 to 15,000 range experienced the highest costs. Similarly, Corrallo (1970) found that the lowest unit costs were achieved by research universities, public and private, at enrollment levels of 6,000 to 10,000 and 14,000 to 18,000. Lyell (1979) found that over a twenty-three-year period a public research university experienced increasing costs per student in growing from 10,000 to nearly 16,000 students and then nearly flat costs thereafter in growing to just over 20,000 students. Bowen's (1980) analysis of educational costs (a broader category than instruction, but narrower than E&G) also indicates an uneven pattern. Using an enrollment range divided into quintiles, the public institutions show very modest differences, with the smallest, middle-sized, and largest institutions having the highest educational costs per weighted student (by level). The private institutions show large differences. with the smallest and next to largest institutions having the highest costs.

Additional insight into size-related cost behavior at research universities can be obtained from several studies that examine instructional costs for different-sized departments, programs, or colleges within universities. In every instance where cost differences were found, the larger operating unit had the lower unit costs. Borgmann and Bartram (1969) examined costs at engineering schools at fourteen institutions in the western United States and found that a 4-fold difference in enrollment was associated with a 29 percent difference in average cost per student. The corresponding cost differential for mineral engineering programs only was 45 percent. In a study of nineteen engineering schools, Terman (1969) found that a 3.5-fold difference in enrollment was associated with a 29-percent difference in average cost per student. Gibson (1968) examined departmental expenditures at a single public research university and found that a 3-fold difference in enrollment was associated with difference in average cost per credit hour of 40, 36, and 30 percent respectively for lower-division, upper-division, and graduate-level instruction. In Brovender's (1974) study of expenditures by instructional division in a public research university, a 3-fold difference in credit hour production was associated with difference in average cost per credit hour of 29, 28, and 19 percent respectively for the humanities, natural sciences, and social sciences. In a study that attempted to capture the full costs of producing doctoral degrees, Butter (1966) found that a 3-fold difference in enrollment in physics and sociology was accompanied by differences in average costs per degree of 62 and 69 percent, respectively; by contrast, no differences in costs related to departmental size were found for English and zoology.

Buckles (1978) examined departmental full costs (direct plus allocated indirect costs) at a private research university and found that a 3-fold increase in enrollment was accompanied by a 28-percent decrease in average costs per credit hour. This result is higher than might be expected, given that both average class size and faculty course load were held constant in the estimating equation. The author suggested that increases in scale over the six years analyzed might not have been the reason for the decline in average costs. The decline could have been due to departments with low levels of output operating below capacity (resulting in high average costs), while departments with high levels of output were operating at or near capacity (resulting in low average costs). In this case, the data would represent movement along a short-run cost curve rather than along a long-run curve. Unfortunately, it is impossible to determine which of several explanations for the observed change in the cost-size relationship is the correct one. This typifies the difficulties researchers have in coming to definitive conclusions about the reasons for cost behavior in higher education.

On the basis of a linear programming analysis, Carlson (1972) reported that the marginal costs at efficient institutions are lower for institutions below the average level of enrollment than for those with above-average enrollments. This relationship held for various levels of enrollment at various types of institutions including research universities.

Overall, the various studies of cost-size relationships at research universities indicate that modest economies of scale are prevalent. This is especially true at the level of departments and schools within these institutions. Differences in average cost typically are on the order of twenty to forty percent comparing large to small organizational entities (where the large entities are three to four times as big as the small entities). The evidence with respect to costs for all of instruction or for all of the E&G functions combined is less compelling. Very small research-oriented institutions are quite likely to have higher unit costs than their medium or large counterparts with the same mission. Beyond that, the studies give a conflicting picture of the cost-size relationship. It is conceivable that an institution's expansion path typically includes points at which an increase in size is likely to trigger an institutional response that tends to drive up unit costs. For example, it may be that when institutions reach a certain size they tend to expand their offerings at the doctoral level or broaden the variety of research they are willing to undertake. These kinds of developments are probably beyond our capabilities to discern with much precision given the multitude of factors that can affect unit costs.

Cost curves at other four-year institutions:

In an integrative review of studies of cost behavior at baccalaureate and comprehensive institutions, Brinkman and Leslie (1986) found strong evidence for modest economies of scale for several types of expenditures.

Aggregating nineteen data points from thirteen studies, they found that institutions with roughly two thousand FTE students had lower unit costs than did institutions with five to six hundred students. That three- to four-fold difference in size was associated with the following mean percentage differences in average costs per student: E&G, 23 percent; instruction, 16 percent; administration, 34 percent; operation and maintenance of the plant, 26 percent; and library, 20 percent. These results are plausible comparing one to another. For instance, because the administrative functions are generally thought to have a relatively high proportion of fixed costs, economies of scale should be greater in those functions than in other areas such as instruction or student services.

An analysis of 17 California state colleges (California Coordinating Council for Higher Education, 1969) indicated that total expenditures per student at an institution with twelve thousand FTE students could be expected to be 22 percent lower than at an institution with four thousand students. In a study of 145 private liberal arts colleges, Calkins (1963) found that E&G revenues per student declined about 28 percent in conjunction with a three-fold increase in enrollment. Since institutions usually spend most of their E&G revenue, this finding would likely be approximately the same if the dependent variable had been expenditures instead of revenues.

For these less complex institutions (they seldom engage in significant research or public service), the evidence is inconclusive regarding the shape of average-cost curves—apart from declining costs in the low enrollment range. There is some reason to think that baccalaureate colleges typically achieve most of their scale-related economies by the time enrollment reaches two thousand FTE students (Brinkman, 1981b; Corrallo, 1970), or even a little sooner (Carnegie Commission on Higher Education, 1972). The comparable range for more comprehensive (master's-oriented) colleges is probably three to four thousand students (Brinkman, 1981b, California Coordinating Council for Higher Education, 1969; Maynard, 1971). Maynard's findings suggest that relatively large four-year (nonuniversity) institutions experience higher unit costs than mid-sized institutions, or in other words, that the cost curve is U-shaped. He estimated that minimum average costs were reached at just over five thousand FTE students.

Other studies such as Brinkman (1981b; 1984), California Coordinating Council for Higher Education (1969), Carlson (1972), and Metz (1964) suggest that after its initial decline the average-cost curve tends to remain essentially flat as four-year colleges become very large. In the Carnegie Commission study (1972), the largest colleges typically did not have the lowest costs per student across the various expenditure categories, but there was no clear size-cost relationship evident for size levels beyond the middle ranges. Similarly, Bowen (1980) found that among liberal arts colleges and public comprehensive (non-doctorate-granting) institutions the interval containing the second-largest institutions recorded the lowest educational costs per student, while for private comprehensive institutions the largest institutions experienced the lowest unit costs.

Cost curves across institutional types:

Cost studies in higher education, like those discussed above, almost always address a particular type of institution. Two studies were found that include essentially all four-year institutions. A subsample within Cohn, Rhine and Santos' (1989) study was discussed earlier in connection with research universities. Their full sample contained 1,887 four-year schools. They estimated several E&G cost functions. Of interest is a quadratic form with two outputs, enrollment and research.The results suggest that overall economies of scale exist up to about five thousand FTE students for institutions that do little research, and up to about twenty-five thousand FTE students for institutions that do a large amount of research. No product-specific economies of scale were found for instruction. Such economies did exist for research; the results suggest a level of about $5 million in research must be reached before substantial economies are obtained. They also estimated a three-output model, in which graduate and undergraduate enrollment were treated as separate outputs. No product-specific economies of scale were found for undergraduate instruction, but such economies were found for graduate instruction.

McLaughlin et al. (1980) used path analysis to analyze cost and production activities for all four-year institutions with enrollments from two hundred to forty thousand FTE students, excluding a variety of special institutions such as U.S. service academies. They found that enrollment size does have a direct effect on average instructional cost per student. However, the estimated magnitude of the effect was small and easily eclipsed by a strong correlation between increases in curriculum complexity and increases in unit costs. They defined curriculum complexity in terms of the number of majors offered at three levels of instruction.

The findings of these two studies with respect to instruction are open to question because the studies ignore the proportion of faculty effort going into departmental research. This strategy is not likely to cause problems when analyzing institutions of the same type, but it can cause problems when very different institutions are being compared. If the proportion of faculty time spent on departmental research were correlated with the size of the institution—a distinct possibility—the effect would be to distort estimates of economies of scale.

Economies of Scope

Very little research has been done on the question of whether the multiproduct nature of higher education leads to production economies. As discussed earlier, several higher education services are produced jointly including instruction and research as well as undergraduate and graduate instruction. There is evidence that average costs for lower-division students at research universities are less than average costs at two-year colleges (James 1978) and that the same relationship holds for marginal costs (Brinkman 1981b). Furthermore, the study by Cohn, Rhine and Santos (1989) indicates that economies of scope exist for instruction and research, i.e., that the cost of producing these goods together is less than the cost of producing them separately. But there is much that we do not understand, mostly because we cannot arrive at definitive interpretations of available data.

For example, while it is suggestive, the presence of higher average costs at two-year colleges actually proves little. These institutions may employ different technologies, use different resources, educate different types of students, and achieve different outcomes than do research universities in their lower-division instruction. Or consider what should be a straightforward approach to establishing the presence of joint supply, namely, regressing expenditures on multiple outputs and output interaction terms (quantity of product one times quantity of product two, and so on). A significant, negative coefficient on an interaction term would indicate that the two goods were being produced less expensively together than separately. Yet, as Verry and Davies (1976) point out, the absence of a negative coefficient on an interaction term would not be a conclusive refutation of the joint supply hypothesis because joint supply effects could be qualitative. More fundamentally, James (1978) argues that this type of interaction term, whatever its sign, may not be used to infer joint supply in higher education. Her argument is that the joint supply inference would follow only if the interactions were due to technological imperatives, whereas, in higher education the interactions are likely to be the result of deliberate choice. In the same vein, Cohn, Rhine and Santos' finding of economies of scope between instruction and research probably tells us more about administrative and faculty decisions than about technology. However, the same could be said for much of what we know about cost behavior in higher education. Furthermore, it would be appropriate for those who are more interested in cost containment per se than in understanding the reasons behind cost behavior to take note of negative coefficients on interaction terms and the Cohn, Rhine and Santos results.

Costs by Level of Instruction

A simpler, but related, issue is the relative unit cost of instruction by level of instruction or by level of student. These costs can be important for comparisons over time or among institutions. For example, cost ratios by level of student play an important role in O'Neill's (1971) landmark study of higher education productivity over four decades. The validity of cross-sectional analyses, such as Bowen's (1980) or the Carnegie Commission's (1972), that use a weighted enrollment figure depends on the weights used to reflect relative costs by level of student. Also, various funding formulas for public colleges and universities acknowledge variations in costs by level of student or instruction.

On occasion, just two levels, undergraduate and graduate, are recognized, but more often relative weights are assigned to lower-division, upper-division, masters, doctorate, and sometimes even first-professional students or instruction. Most available data that might help establish the proper weights are the result of cost allocation activities rather than statistical estimates and they concern average rather than marginal costs.

Differences in costs by level vary by type of institution and discipline. For analytical purposes, researchers tend to ignore those differences and use a single set of weights. Those used by Bowen (1980) for average full costs by level of student are as follows: lower division, 1; upper division, 1.5; masters, 2.1; first professional, 2.5; and "beyond first year" graduate students, 3. He used the weights to calculate average costs per lower-division student unit, which allows for a meaningful comparison of unit costs between two-year and four-year institutions and between four-year institutions with varying emphasis on graduate education. Bowen's figures were derived from fifteen or so studies of costs by level of student.

In an integrative review of available literature, Brinkman (1985) assembled more than two hundred data points on direct and full costs per credit hour by level of instruction. For universities, direct costs per credit hour for advanced graduate instruction were, on average, 8 to 9 times as high, masters-level 4 to 5 times as high, and upper division 1.6 to 1.8 as high as costs at the lower-division level. The range around these mean values was considerable, which is typical for cost data in higher education. The cost ratios did not appear to differ by sector, but few private institutions, were represented in the sample. Across all types of institutions, cost differentials by level of instruction tended to be greatest among the natural and social science disciplines and least among the fine arts and professional disciplines such as education, business, and engineering.

A few estimates are available for marginal costs by level of student. In Cohn, Rhine and Santos' (1989) study of all four-year institutions, the ratio of graduate to undergraduate E&G costs was estimated to be 4:1. In Brinkman's (1981b) study of public institutions, the instructional cost ratios for graduate to lower-division students were 11:1, 4:1 and 1.5:1, for research, doctoral, and comprehensive institutions, respectively.

It is clear from these studies that substantial differences exist in unit costs by level of instruction or by level of student. These differences need to be kept in mind when making interinstitutional cost comparisons or cost comparisions over time for the same institution or set of institutions. With respect to configuring appropriate higher education cost functions, these differences provide some justification for dealing with instruction as if it resulted in a set of different outputs (i.e., lower-division credits, upper-division credits, and so on).

Conclusion: Factors That Determine Marginal and Average Costs

The cost studies reviewed above contain much of what has been learned about how costs actually behave in higher education institutions. In this concluding section, the focus shifts slightly from how costs behave to the reasons for that behavior. Of course, the reasons are at least implicit in much of what has already been discussed, so part of what follows is something of a summary.

The behavior of marginal and average costs in higher education can be associated with the following dimensions:

- size (quantity of activity or output)
- scope of services offered
- level of instruction or student (for instructional costs)
- discipline (for instructional costs)
- revenues

Each dimension has both independent effects on costs and interrelated effects with one or more of the other dimensions. The extent to which the influence of these dimensions is a matter of technology versus one of faculty or administrative norms varies considerably but is not always apparent.

In the main, size clearly does affect both marginal and average costs in both the short and long run. For E&G expenditures, fixed costs associated with administrative overhead, plant operation and maintenance, and so on, are reasons why higher levels of output are accompanied by lower average costs. For instructional expenditures, norms regarding a core faculty create a type of fixed-cost situation, as does faculty tenure in some circumstances. The effects of size are seldom seen in isolation, however. Intervening variables include funding or resource allocation formulas, relationships between size and input prices (for example, larger institutions generally pay higher salaries to their administrators), and differences in available revenues.

Another intervening variable with respect to instructional costs and related E&G expenditures is the rate of change in enrollment. Institutional resources typically are neither acquired nor relinquished at the same rate as variations in student demand. This lag pushes average costs down in periods of enrollment growth and up in periods of enrollment decline.

It is also true that changes in resources, in response to changes in demand, can occur in large increments thereby leading to major swings in both marginal and average costs but especially the former. In instruction, however, given that capital costs are handled separately, the only sizeable increment typically is an increase or decrease in the number of faculty, and a faculty member is a sizeable increment only if the unit of analysis is at a micro level, such as a small to medium-sized department. The more macro the unit of analysis, the more likely it is that the relationship between faculty resources and output will behave like a continuous function.

The effects of scope seem to run two ways. On the one hand, it seems to be less expensive on a unit basis to do instruction and research jointly than separately; likewise for graduate and undergraduate instruction. On the other hand, there is evidence to suggest that greater scope in the form of expansion in the number of programs offered often leads to, or is at least accompanied by, higher unit costs, perhaps because it tends to spread out demand and to require additional departmental set-up costs. In both instances, it is not clear whether observed differences in costs are due to technological aspects of the production process, which would be required to have economies of scope in the proper sense of the term, or whether those differences are primarily the result of decisions that have little if anything to do with technological imperatives. Additional research needs to be done on the question of economies of scope before any definitive conclusions can be reached.

With few exceptions, the higher the level of instruction or student, the higher the average cost. This is true because norms regarding resource utilization differ by level, because student demand often differs by level (usually the higher the level the lower the demand, especially relative to the set of courses offered by level), and because the resources required (particulary the type of faculty and the type of equipment) can also differ by level.

While differences in cost by discipline were not a focus of the cost studies reviewed for this paper, there is ample evidence that costs do indeed differ by discipline, sometimes substantially. There are three major reasons why this is so: 1) the price of inputs, 2) input requirements, and 3) utilization of inputs. Supply and demand relationships for faculty differ greatly by discipline, resulting in substantial differences in salaries by discipline. Some disciplines require resources, such as lab facilities, that add to unit costs. Some resource utilization 'requirements,' such as student-faculty ratios, vary by discipline, with considerable effect on costs.

A particular level of resource utilization can sometimes be required in the form of an accreditation standard. Beyond that, utilization is generally a function of three factors: disciplinary norms, institutional norms, and student demand. Disciplinary norms, which can differ widely—consider a writing course versus introductory social science versus a nursing practicum—usually serve to put an upper limit on resource utilization rates. They do not exist in isolation, however, in that they are modulated by institutional circumstances and traditions. The typical difference in average class sizes between an elite private institution and a regional state university is an example of the institutional factor. Institutional norms serve to establish both upper and lower limits on resource use. Student demand is often an exogenous factor. Relatively few institutions and relatively few departments within institutions can either dictate or know in advance precisely the extent of student demand.

Some of the differential in average costs among institutions of the same type apparently can be explained only by differences in the revenues (per student) available at those institutions. More affluent institutions tend to spend more per student. They pay higher prices for their faculty inputs and they have a lower utilization rate for many of the resources. It may be that as a result of the increased expenditures they turn out a higher quality product, which would invalidate, or at least change the meaning of, comparisons with less affluent institutions. A definitive answer to this problem may never be forthcoming given the difficulty of dealing with the outcome of higher education.

Finally, during the past several years, Stephen Hoenack and his colleagues at the University of Minnesota have provided new insights into cost behavior at a public research university (Hoenack, et al., 1986). In brief, they have shown how instructional costs differ depending on whether the perspective is that of legislators, administrators, or faculty. Legislative demand for higher education (at least in one state) is shown to be undifferentiated by level of instruction, i.e., the legislature will pay the same amount for educating students regardless of their level, while the administration is willing to pay much more for graduate than undergraduate instruction. Instructional costs for individual faculty members vary with their interests, but typically the marginal costs associated with additional classroom enrollments are modest while marginal costs for advising are high. The latter costs can be offset if the quality of the additional students is high. The concept of opportunity cost, which underlies this type of analysis, is not new, of course, yet it offers a relatively new line of research, given the widespread preoccupation up to now with expenditure analyses conducted from an administrative perspective.

CHAPTER 6

An Economist's Perspective on Costs Within Higher Education Institutions

STEPHEN A. HOENACK

The ready availability of data on expenditures in colleges and universities has enabled these institutions to respond to funders' desires for accountability with a proliferation of cost measures. Internal records on enrollments, faculty workloads, and the uses of support services have been employed to allocate institutional expenditures in order to calculate the costs of instructional programs. However, these measures of costs can in some contexts seriously misinform decisionmakers.

This paper examines how economics can improve the conceptual basis for cost analysis. We shall focus on large research universities and consider the costs appropriate to a variety of decisionmaking situations, including institutional management, state legislative financing, and federally sponsored funding.

Economic Analysis of Costs within Higher Education Institutions

Economic Concepts of Costs

Two economic concepts are useful in the consideration of higher education costs. The first concept is the familiar one of opportunity cost. The cost of accomplishing a particular educational outcome, based on this concept, is the value of the alternative outcomes that, as a result, are not accomplished. The idea is that scarce resources are allocated to one function at the expense of others. Often, this valuation cannot be quantified precisely. For example, the cost of an instructional outcome might be the sacrifice of a research activity that is highly valued but not assigned a specific dollar value. One can readily see that opportunity costs often differ from accounting costs; an added student in a class may represent little opportunity cost for the instructor while the student's accounting cost would include his or her pro-rated share of the

129

instructor's salary. The marginal opportunity cost of an educational outcome is that which can be identified with a particular planned increase in the provision of it.

The second economic concept is that a supplier of a good or service may be able to charge clients more than his or her own cost. This concept is most familiar in the context of a private firm. It is less familiar—but nonetheless applicable—to the analysis of nonprofit enterprises such as colleges and universities. Most studies of higher education costs are based on the implicit assumption that the costs of instruction, for example, are the same for the faculty members supplying this activity, for the administrators who provide budgets in response to departmental instructional outcomes, for legislators who similarly allocate budgets to public institutions, and for the students receiving this service. However, academic departments may be able, for example, to receive budgetary rewards for instruction and other services that exceed faculty members' opportunity costs of supplying them.

The Relationships of Resource Uses and Costs to Production Functions

The economist's concept of a production function is useful in considering a faculty member's opportunity costs of carrying out instructional activities. Most economists believe that there is typically a wide range of alternative methods of making a given set of productive contributions, and production functions represent the available information about technological production possibilities. Economic behavior vis-à-vis production functions comes into play via the incentives both to learn about production possibilities and to select among them. In higher education there is a significant degree of diversity in the possible methods to carry out instruction and research. Even more variety would be observed if academic personnel had more incentive to learn about and test new methods. Hence, the production function concept applies in this sector of the economy.

Production functions are a helpful conceptual tool for the economic analysis of costs in colleges and universities. For example, a faculty member's opportunity costs in terms of foregone research to produce more instruction are determined by the production possibilities indicating the utilizations of resources to produce instruction that would be otherwise useful for research. To the extent that the same resources jointly produce instruction and research, the faculty member's opportunity costs would be lowered. That production functions can assist in the analysis of costs does not necessarily imply that researchers can overcome the measurement problems involved in estimating their parameters.

Why Costs are Lower for Suppliers of an Outcome

Elsewhere (Hoenack, 1983) I have suggested that employees are given discretion over part of the production functions for an organization's intermediate and final outputs. On-the-job learning gives them cost advantages in obtaining the information needed to find more efficient production possibilities. Unless constraints are imposed requiring them to do so, employees will not necessarily supply outputs at their own costs. Because the expense of the information necessary to monitor and influence academic activities is high, the constraints on faculty and other university suppliers of education and other support services are loose. As a result, the observed budgets that universities and their subunits receive for instructional services more than compensate the opportunity costs incurred by faculty and other employees. Hence, a university's instructional budget is larger than an aggregation of these costs.

The excess of an institution's instructional funding over the opportunity costs directly facing its employees gives these personnel a degree of discretion over resources that can be used for purposes independent of the demands of the institution's clients. The most important use of such discretion by faculty is the performance of research. This includes (1) basic research which is often incompletely compensated by government agencies and other funders who usually have an applied purpose when contracting for research; and (2) preliminary research underlying sponsored research contracts.

Academic departments can use discretionary resources for such purposes as providing departmental aid to the highest-quality graduate students. Administrators can also use these discretionary resources for financial aid, supporting high-cost programs, and investing in facilities and support services that help faculty attract sponsored research funding. Discretion over resources could even be used to support leisurely life styles. However, since each individual's productivity affects the institution's overall reputation, members of a research-oriented faculty often devote effort to helping ensure that the institution's internal governance provides incentives for scholarly accomplishment.

Measurement Issues

It would be difficult, if not impossible, to measure the cash equivalent values of the time and other resource costs of instruction and research directly facing individual faculty. What we can readily observe are the departmental instructional funds allocated by administrators and the instructional funds paid by students, legislatures, and donors. Because of internal discretion over resources, these budgeted costs support many other activities than those for which the purchasers of departmental services would be willing to pay if given a choice. Nonetheless, they are the opportunity costs faced by these clients for outcomes that they demand. These costs, however, are not derivable from the production possibilities and opportunity costs directly facing faculty. The same argument holds for the relationship between the budgets for the institution's administrative and support services and the economic costs facing the personnel in these units.

The opportunity costs faced by clients are often determined by the constraints facing academic personnel. However, such constraints could be loose enough not to have a binding effect on clients' costs. In this case, the revenues received by the institution for its instructional and research outcomes would be constrained only by clients' willingness to pay, i.e., their demands for its service flows. One of the most interesting commentaries on what is known about costs in higher education is provided by the eminent economist of higher education, Howard Bowen. He argues (1980, p. 18) that: "On the whole, unit cost is determined neither by the rigid technological requirements of delivering educational services nor by some abstract standard of need. It is determined rather by the revenue available for education that can be raised per student unit. Technology and need affect unit cost only as they influence those who control revenues and enrollments."

Implications of Faculty Facing Lower Costs than Their Institutions

The hypothesis that employees within universities do not necessarily supply their productive contributions at the opportunity costs directly facing them has a number of implications. One of these is that data on institutional expenditures cannot be used to make inferences about the opportunity costs directly facing faculty. An understanding of these costs requires observation of how academic personnel carry out varying workloads. While such analysis holds the promise of greatly improving understanding of production behavior in higher education, it is unlikely to result in useful estimates of dollar equivalents of instructional costs because of the difficulty of attaching values to individual faculty members' forgone outcomes.

In order to infer the opportunity costs that clients must pay from institutional expenditure data, it is necessary to distinguish the underlying supply behavior within the university from demand. That is, the supplies of academic units must be identifiable in the context of an implicit market for instruction. In such a market, demand derives not only from the external instructional demands facing the institution, but also from the internal demands for academic activities. These latter demands reflect the budgetary and other rewards for academic activities as established by the institution's internal governance. An institution's supply behavior, representing opportunity costs faced by its external constituencies, must be inferred separately from those external and internal demands.

Another implication is that separate inferences about fixed and variable opportunity costs cannot generally be made by regressing institutional or departmental expenditures against enrollments as in the studies to be discussed later. For example, observed variations in a university's total funding with respect to enrollments depends not only on resource uses within the institution but also on the demands of students, donors, and legislatures of public institutions along with the amounts these clients can be made to pay.[1]

One of the most important economic aspects of management in higher education is dealing with variable funding from clients to cover costs which are fixed over budgetary periods. Institutions require major investments in buildings, equipment, and support staff, while the quality of research and instruction in their academic departments depends on core faculties covering the various specialties of their disciplines.

We now turn to the literature about costs in higher education.

Literature on the Direct Costs of Instruction and Research

There is a vast literature on instructional costs in higher education, and the costs dealt with in many studies are not readily interpretable as opportunity costs. In the literature a distinction is usually made between direct and indirect costs. Direct costs are derived from the expenditures by those units, mostly academic departments, that are considered to be directly involved in instruction. Indirect costs are based on the expenditures of administrative and support service units.

This section focuses on studies of the direct costs of instruction and aims to point out approaches to the measurement and analysis of costs and the economic meaning of their results. We emphasize costs in research universities. Although the discussion deals with the direct costs of instruction and research, many of the studies considered include indirect costs, which will be examined more thoroughly in the following section.

We first discuss descriptive studies that measure unit instructional costs in higher education institutions. Such measures are based on allocations of expenditure data to categories of students or credit hours.

Unit costs are derived by dividing the numbers of students or credit hours into the appropriate cost pools. Most of the descriptive studies that measure unit instructional costs include allocations of academic salaries to individual courses or categories of courses according to the proportion of faculty time in the classroom each course takes. The result is a set of unit course costs. These in turn can be converted to costs per credit hour via the use of course credit and enrollment data.

With additional data on the patterns of students' course selections, the credit hour cost data can be used to calculate costs per student. For example, by taking the distribution of courses in all departments carried by the undergraduate majors in a given department, it is possible to calculate the total cost and cost per student of these majors. Historical data on students' course choices are frequently used to calculate induced course loads. That is, given an increase in a category of enrollments such as majors in a field, it is possible to calculate the impact on course enrollments throughout the institution.[2] The cost implications of these enrollments can be calculated by using the unit-cost data for each course.

Unit-cost measures are widely used both for internal institutional planning and budgeting and in the legislative funding requests of public universities. The application of comparisons between institutions and disciplines has recently expanded in the seventeen public institutions that provide cost data by discipline to the Association of American Universities Data Exchange. In spite of the popularity of these cost measures, from an economic perspective they have serious limitations. They represent at best the opportunity costs faced at administrative levels of institutions, not those directly faced by faculty. As such they tell more about the institution's internal demands for instruction at various levels and its procedures for imposing constraints on departments than about production possibilities and faculty behavior. They also reflect average (rather than marginal) costs over the entire range of enrollments.

Another important limitation of unit-cost measures is that advising, which we have found to be the single most resource-absorbing activity in many graduate programs at the University of Minnesota (Hoenack, et al., 1986), is usually completely ignored. Depending on the offsetting factor of reciprocal benefits of advising to faculty, the relative opportunity costs of graduate education are understated, perhaps by a large margin. It is interesting to speculate whether faculty advising activities are budgetarily rewarded at all. Many public institutions are externally funded based on credit hours of classroom instruction. Even when there is recognition that the institution's reputation may depend on the quality of advising and when faculty interested in advising are influential in the university's internal budgetary governance, advising time is difficult to measure—it is usually not part of institutional records and thus requires self-reporting—and it is probably impossible to assess its quality. As a result, it may be that graduate advising represents one of the discretionary resource uses that result from departmental instructional income in excess of the costs to faculty members' for classroom instruction.

Universities will undoubtedly continue to make calculations of unit instructional costs because they provide a degree of accountability, especially for public institutions. Such measures provide a readily understood interpretation of how a university's instructionally related revenues are allocated to instructional purposes. However, because they do not capture opportunity costs, these calculations have limited usefulness for internal planning and budgeting and, if used seriously, would create perverse incentives.[3] For example, a department can reduce its cost per student by placing regular faculty on sponsored research contracts or encouraging them to go on leave and then substituting graduate teaching assistants. Another well-known means to reduce per student costs is to raise course enrollments by imposing additional requirements on majors.

Perhaps the most undesirable incentive created by misuse of unit-cost measures is to devote more resources to enrollment numbers than to the activities (e.g., advising) that may contribute to students' learning and completion of their degree requirements. A similar perverse incentive was noted in a discussion by Peter Blau (1963) of an employment agency. The manager of this group initially collected data on personnel contacts with clients. Even though the data were not explicitly used for a management purpose, client contacts rose, but there was a drop in clients' success rate in finding employment. When additional data on placement rates were collected, this rate rose but there was a fall in successful employment, as measured by the proportion of placed individuals still in the same job six months later. The implication is that personnel may treat information collected by administrators as incentives even if this is not the manager's intent, and that incentives should reward all economically important characteristics of employees' contributions. There are many other excellent illustrations of these points in Berliner's (1957) study of enterprises in the Soviet economy.

We now turn to a number of studies of costs carried out by economists. Most of these studies do not make use of administrative calculations of unit costs but rather are based directly on institutions' financial records. All of these studies deal in one way or another with the joint production of research and instruction.[4]

Studies of Costs of Joint Production

The funds provided by universities to their academic departments for instruction and departmental research are, of course, not separately allocated according to the amounts provided for instruction at the undergraduate and at the graduate levels and for nonsponsored research. In a 1978 study, Estelle James made such allocations by using faculty responses to questionnaires about their uses of time. Data obtained by different researchers and for different institutions showed consistent results. The total time spent on all teaching activities in research universities dropped from around seventy percent in the early sixties to somewhat less than fifty percent, even though the time spent on graduate education rose five to ten percentage points. The time spent on research rose from somewhat less than twenty percent to the neighborhood of thirty percent. Another increase was the time spent on departmental administration and "other."

Using these data to allocate departmental expenditure data to the two levels of instruction and to nonsponsored research,[5] the author showed that the recalculated costs of undergraduate instruction were about thirty-two percent less than would be shown otherwise in measures of costs adapted from June O'Neill's (1971) study of historical trends in measures of costs and productivity in higher education. James interpreted these results in the context of her theory of nonprofit organizations (applied to academic departments by James and Neuberger, 1981) in which some activities operate at a profit to subsidize others, depending on the preference of personnel regarding the quality and quantity of each.

James is one of the first authors to suggest that faculty research is funded with instructional revenues. (Verry and Davies, 1976, pp. 142-3, provided evidence based on regression equations relating measures of research—articles and self-reported time devoted to this activity—to instructional expenditures.) James also noted that what might appear to be joint production of instruction and research could result from "a deliberate and interdependent choice of product mix and factor mix" (James, 1978, p. 162).

Economies of Scale in Higher Education

There have been many regression analyses that have attempted to test the hypothesis of economies of scale in higher education institutions. For example, numerous studies use cross-section financial data for different colleges and universities and regress direct instructional funding (or a total value including funding of support services) against enrollments by level. Brinkman and Leslie (1986) provide a survey of these studies. Generally, two-year and four-year institutions exhibit economies of scale while the results are mixed for research universities.

We shall examine four studies of economies of scale that are of particular interest to economists. In many ways the most ambitious and carefully executed econometric study is Verry and Davies' (1976) study of costs within British colleges and universities. In order to control for the costs of research activities, the authors used data both on self-reported allocations of time by faculty and on counts of articles. A unique feature of the study is an attempt to control for the quality of instruction via graduation rates and crude measures of value added based on labor market and test data. The major data source was the financial information provided by all British institutions in 1968-69 to the British Government's University Grants Committee. However, the authors omitted data from the most prestigious research institutions: Oxford, Cambridge, and the Institutes of London University. A brief summary of some of this study's main results cannot capture the authors' craftsmanship and thoroughness nor the immense detail of their work. The reader with limited time should definitely include this among a sample of works to read.

One finding by Verry and Davies is that the economies of scale found in regression studies that relate expenditures to enrollments are modest and often not statistically significant. When the authors entered variables for research activity (reported time and counts of articles) in equations that express departmental instructional expenditures as functions of undergraduate counts, they did not obtain higher estimates of scale economies. They note (p. 119) that "the cause of this unexpected pattern is that, contrary to what is often supposed, the ratio of research to teaching falls, rather than rises, as departments get larger."

The weak findings of economies of scale could also result from the estimated equations reflecting demands for and supplies of departmental instructional services, rather than the opportunity costs directly facing faculty. Observed expenditure data (whether for the institution as a whole or for units within it) are generated by the interaction of demands (largely for instruction) and supplies which can be independent of the costs directly facing faculty and other personnel. Although faculty personnel may face substantial economies of scale in the opportunity costs of instruction directly facing them, these economies may not be revealed by regressing departmental budgets, which instead reflect the opportunity costs of instruction faced by administrators, against enrollments.

Although equations that relate departmental expenditures to enrollments and other institutional variables do not permit inferences about the opportunity costs of instruction directly facing faculty members, it may be possible to use such equations to infer about administrative demand behavior and faculty supply behavior, provided that separate demand and supply equations can be identified. In any event, since regression equations relating departmental expenditures to enrollments reflect demand behavior, supply behavior, or some combination of the two, it is not surprising that studies based on this methodology frequently do not find economies of scale in research universities.[6]

Interestingly, however, Verry and Davies tested the hypotheses that the quality of teaching is positively related to scale by entering their measures of graduation rates and of value added. For departments in arts and engineering and in the biological sciences, they found that "the estimates offer some tentative evidence that the omission of any qualitative dimension of undergraduate teaching output ... causes economies of scale to be underestimated" (p. 139). An alternative hypothesis is that departments having measures of greater teaching quality may face somewhat larger budgetary rewards. That is, instructional demands facing these departments may be higher.[7]

Verry and Davies also found (p. 130) that interaction terms between levels of graduate and undergraduate instruction and between levels of graduate instruction and measures of research activity were usually statistically insignificant and often positive. As James (1978) noted, statistically significant negative coefficients could result from faculty choices to combine activities for purposes of cross-funding, rather than from economies of joint production. Nevertheless, the absence of such coefficients should not be interpreted as evidence against either hypothesis because the estimated equations could be more representative of demands facing departments and their supply behavior, rather than the costs directly facing faculty.

In a section titled "The Effect of Departmental Finance on Departmental Outputs," Verry and Davies explicitly address the issue of departmental supply behavior. They state (1976, p. 141) that "educational planners may not be able to direct or induce university departments to do more teaching without at the same time permitting them to do more research." However, they appear to interpret their cost functions as representing opportunity costs directly facing faculty. Actually, these functions are hybrids. The use of expenditure data suggests inferences about administrative demand and departmental supply, while the research activity variables in these equations may be controlling for an underdemanded output supplied by faculty with discretionary resources.

Two especially interesting studies of costs in American institutions were carried out by Brinkman (1981b) and Cohn, Rhine and Santos (1989). Both are based on data from the Higher Education General Information Survey (HEGIS) on institutional expenditures and enrollments. Brinkman separately analyzed expenditure data in each major category of institutions, and we shall consider his results for 50 public institutions classified as research universities by the National Center for Higher Education Management Systems (NCHEMS). Cohn, Rhine and Santos examined a sample of 1,887 institutions of all types, representing most of those responding to the HEGIS survey.

Brinkman regressed instructional expenditures against enrollments by level (lower-division undergraduate, upper-division undergraduate, and graduate) and sponsored research funding. He attempted a variety of alternative functional specifications and interaction terms. Although multicollinearity caused his results to vary somewhat from equation to equation, he generally found economies of scale. In another study (1981a) he regressed data on expenditure per student against enrollments and other variables to be described below. Here, economies of scale did not appear to be present in a subsample of twenty-five public research universities but were present in a larger sample of fifty public and private universities.

In the 1981b study of fifty public research universities, Brinkman found very low marginal expenditure effects of lower-division undergraduate instruction (Table 14, p. 83) and an absence of statistically significant interactions between the sponsored research variable and enrollments at any level (Table 13, p. 81). In contrast, significant interactions of research and upper-division and graduate enrollments were found in a sample of "doctoral" institutions which carry out less sponsored research than those classified as "research" universities.

The Cohn, Rhine and Santos study is an important advance because it separately estimates three types of scale economies (see Baumol, Panzar, and Willig, 1982): ray economies (due to the expansion of all outputs); product-specific economies; and economies of scope (due to complementarities among outputs). In their large sample of diverse institutions where three separate outputs—undergraduate and graduate enrollments and sponsored research funding—were considered, they found that there were product-specific economies of scale for graduate, but not for undergraduate enrollments. For institutions engaging in small amounts of research the authors found ray scale economies up to only about five thousand students while they found that institutions having very large values of the research variable had ray scale economies up to about twenty-five thousand students. There were substantial economies of scope among all outputs.

Cohn, Rhine and Santos reestimated their model with a smaller sample of 121 institutions for which they obtained data from the National

Academy of Sciences on faculty publications. The results were similar (using either the publications or research-funding variable) for ray economies of scale. However, there were no product-specific economies of scale for all enrollments taken together in this smaller sample when they used the research-funding variable. Economies of scope generally existed, but not in certain ranges of the data. The authors concluded from both samples that the most efficient institutions are the major public research universities that have both large enrollments and substantial research enterprises.

In his 1981a article, Brinkman provided estimates of two alternatively specified data functions relating expenditures and enrollments for a sample of fifty public and private institutions. In one equation, he expressed unit costs as a function of variables intended to control for inputs: the faculty student ratio, average faculty compensation, the institution's staff-student ratio, and average incomes in the county where the institution is located, which could control for staff wages. The other equation explains unit costs as a function of what could be interpreted as outcomes: total full-time-equivalent (FTE) enrollments, the graduate student proportion, and measures of curriculum diversity and of research emphasis.

These equations represent a first step toward a simultaneous-equations model of university costs and outputs. The unit cost equation is essentially an accounting of the institution's costs, although it does not provide a separate analysis of costs facing faculty (nor could any equation based on expenditures). The outcomes equation could be interpreted as a hybrid of demand and institutional supply. The variable for the graduate student proportion may be an internal demand variable (i.e., the institution may have a higher demand for graduate than undergraduate students), and this variable may also reflect the revenues the institution can command because of greater complexity and thus also be a supply variable. The same possibilities hold for the variables controlling for curriculum diversity and research emphasis.

Research at the University of Minnesota

My colleagues and I at the University of Minnesota have been studying the opportunity costs directly facing our faculty as they carry out their instructional and research activities as well as the costs to administrators, students, and legislators of eliciting these service flows. As noted, faculty costs depend on the underlying production relationships for instruction and research along with the individual characteristics and preferences of faculty members and the incentives facing them, none of which is readily quantified. Costs to administrators, students, and legislators are expenditure responses to instructional outcomes and depend largely on the institution's internal governance and its relationships with clients. These costs can be quantified, but require an identified structural model of the relevant internal demand-and-supply behavior.

Our study of both types of costs (Hoenack, Weiler, Goodman and Pierro, 1986) first analyzes opportunity costs directly facing faculty and the institution's internal markets for instruction. We collected historical data on eight academic departments and spent about a year and a half closely following these units' activities. One department is in an engineering field, three are in the laboratory sciences, one is in agriculture, two are among the social sciences, and one is a foreign-language department. We focused particularly on graduate education, and each of these units provided access to its records on advising assignments. We had many detailed discussions with faculty and administrators in these units. We also employed data from the central administration's records on each unit's course, class enrollments, credit hours, and expenditures.

Although the opportunity costs facing individual faculty members differ according to their interests and capabilities and are difficult to measure, it was apparent that well-staffed departments already teaching a large variety of courses face modest opportunity costs of additional classroom enrollments. We found, for example, that new sections are rarely added in response to higher levels of graduate enrollments and that many faculty feel that their graduate courses are underenrolled. This result holds for both short and relatively long time periods. This is in contrast to what has been proposed by Mark Blaug (1981), one of the few economists to address the opportunity costs of enrollments in the short run versus the long run. While he argued that increased enrollments will be accommodated by higher faculty workloads in relatively short periods, he suggested that over longer time periods faculty numbers will be roughly proportional to enrollments.

We found that, in general, faculty members' opportunity costs of advising graduate students are high. Nonetheless, advising has offsetting benefits that vary greatly with the quality of the student. The costs and benefits of advising are especially large in the laboratory sciences, and the technology of graduate education is different from others in these fields. Advising loads can cause numbers of faculty to vary with enrollments, and yet we observed considerable variation in these loads for the same individuals over time. There is usually a willingness to take on additional high-quality advisees, and in the laboratory sciences, funding for students often appears to be the limiting constraint on the sizes of graduate programs.

The marginal instructional opportunity costs faced at administrative levels are the increases in departmental expenditures that occur in response to higher instructional workloads. We developed a theory of the university's internal markets for instruction based on Hoenack (1983), and estimated an econometric model of these markets that has some similarities to the structural model proposed by Sherwin Rosen (1974). Our estimated administrative demand equations exhibit much larger rewards to academic departments for graduate than undergraduate instruction.

The result is of interest in the context of our econometric model of the University of Minnesota's legislative funding (Hoenack and Pierro, 1990). This model contains separate equations representing legislative demand for instruction, institutional supply (instructional costs faced by the legislature), and enrollment-demand behavior. The specification of the equation representing legislative behavior is based on an application of consumer demand theory to derive legislative demand functions (Hoenack, 1983, Chapter 6). Aside from price and income variables, the size and strength of beneficiary and competing interest groups influence legislative demand. Although it is widely believed by personnel in public research universities that legislatures are willing to provide higher funding per student for graduate and professional enrollments than for undergraduates, this would occur within our framework only if the graduate and professional students and other direct beneficiaries form stronger interest groups. This is unlikely because a larger proportion of undergraduates originate in Minnesota and thus have long-term parental ties to the state's political processes.

We tested the hypothesis that legislative demand is affected by the mix of the university's enrollments at different levels and rejected it. It was found that this mix affects the opportunity costs faced by the legislature through its influence on the complexity of the institution, in turn making it more difficult and expensive to impose constraints on the university. However, these costs can be constrained by legislative demand. In F tests for the correctness of overidentifying restrictions in each of the model's equations, all equations passed. However, while the legislative demand and enrollment functions had F statistics well below five percent, the critical value at which one would reject this hypothesis, the institutional supply-cost function's F statistic was very close to this critical value. This result suggests some support for Bowen's (1980) revenue theory of costs.

The contrast between the finding that legislative funding is not differentiated by the mix of enrollments and the finding that departments receive much larger fiscal rewards for graduate than undergraduate enrollments implies an internal budgetary governance that operates independently of legislative preferences. From the estimated equations, we calculated the discretionary funds that accrue to the administration as a result of the university's major role in undergraduate instruction and specified an equation that explains graduate and professional enrollments as a function of these revenues. We found that discretionary funds strongly influence these enrollments with a very small standard error.

In summary, our studies at Minnesota provide support for the hypothesis that the opportunity costs of instruction for faculty directly involved differ from those faced at administrative levels. In turn administrative costs differ from those faced by the institution's legislature. The opportunity costs faced by one state legislature may be bindingly constrained by its demand function for public university enrollments. There is also support for the hypothesis that one institution uses the opportunity-cost differences faced by it and its legislature to produce discretionary funds that in turn are employed in the support of graduate and professional programs.

A problem limiting the managerial usefulness of any measures of instructional opportunity costs is that the value added by costed activities in higher education is often unmeasurable or highly ambiguous. (The elusive value-added measures are somewhat inaccurately referred to as the 'output' or 'outcomes' measurement problem by many researchers.) For example, differences in direct instructional costs can result from variations in class sizes and academic salaries. Class sizes can affect students' learning experiences as can a faculty's research orientation, which in turn can affect salaries. In other words, students can gain from more complete and well-staffed libraries, well-designed buildings, and better equipment. The value-added problem can be noted from many public institutions' practice of presenting to legislatures data on costs per student at the same time they present comparative data showing their legislatures that other institutions provide higher salaries, smaller class sizes and more equipment such as computers for student use. There is essentially the same issue with calculations of indirect costs for sponsored research. Without the right measures of benefits it is not possible to determine whether a lower set of indirect costs reflects correspondingly less valuable services to those working on sponsored research projects. We now turn to the literature on these costs.

Literature on the Indirect Costs of Instruction and Research

If little is known about the direct opportunity costs of instruction, much less is known about indirect opportunity costs. These include the resources that universities devote to the purchase, operation, and maintenance of plant and equipment, to libraries and other academic support services, to student services, and to business and accounting operations along with the other components of general administration. An institution's expenditures on these items can nearly equal its direct expenditures for instruction and departmental research (see table, p. 7 in Bowen, 1980).

Universities are usually 'functionally' organized in that their support services are centralized and managed directly by their administrations rather than by academic units. The budgets of support units are determined by central administrators, and these units' services are usually supplied without stated cost to academic units, students, researchers on sponsored projects, and to other support units. One result is that institutional records provide incomplete information about the amounts, qualities, and economic costs of services allocable to each recipient.

Each support unit responds to administrative demands for services it provides to decentralized units throughout the university. This does not imply, however, that support units are not responsible to their clients. The influence of a university's academic and other units on the institution's internal governance greatly constrains administrators' discretion over the budgets they directly control and helps shape administrative demands for the services of academic and support units (see Hoenack, et al., 1986). Evidence has already been cited that one institution's internal rewards for graduate versus undergraduate instruction are highly differentiated in contrast to its undifferentiated legislative funding for these activities. This is the result of the influence of faculty on the priorities reflected in the administrative demands for departmental instruction. One can expect similar influence on administrative demands for the services of support units.

With a highly political internal governance, administrators can gain from the absence of readily available information about the relative benefits that different academic units receive from support units. For example, if central administrators wish to allocate part of the growth in available funds to support services that improve their institution's ability to attract and maintain sponsored research funding, the absence of information can greatly reduce internal opposition to this strategy. The benefiting academic units similarly gain. Of course, some expenses such as general administration are inherently difficult to allocate to beneficiaries in an economically meaningful way.

These gains from incomplete and ambiguous information also help explain why universities do not make more use of independent suppliers for support services. Another reason relates to the accounting for use of capital facilities. External suppliers would charge for interest, risk and depreciation and, if explicit, these charges would worsen the stated financial condition of most institutions. This point is developed in Jenny (1981).

One suspects that the lack of information about internal allocations of services and the absence of external competition are accompanied by loose constraints facing the support units that supply these services. Unlike the case where an institution's internal governance provides strong incentives for faculties to use discretionary resources to enhance their research productivity, there may not be similar incentives for support units to use the discretionary resources available to them in ways that serve institutional objectives.

In spite of the absence of knowledge about opportunity costs of support services, there has been a great deal of effort to provide accounting costs measures, starting in the beginning decades of this century. Much of the early work dealt with ways of organizing the financial records of income and expenditures in higher education institutions so as to improve comparability and provide information useful to managers. This work, which included early efforts to measure instructional costs, is surveyed by John Dale Russell (1954), one of the pioneers in this field.

The most important impetus to the measurement of support costs in higher education has been the growth of sponsored research funding. Federal guidelines (the famous Circular A-21, Executive Office, 1982) allow institutions to add charges for their indirect costs associated with sponsored research. These charges are based on accounting rules for allocating various categories of expenditures (e.g., for physical plant) to federally sponsored research (e.g., on the basis of assignable square feet).

The National Association of College and University Business Officers (NACUBO) provides manuals and monographs on cost allocation procedures and serves as a forum for discussions regarding the validity of comparisons of institutional data. The table reproduced from a NACUBO monograph written by James Hyatt (1983, p. 19) illustrates procedures in use to allocate support costs. The rows in this table show categories of support costs to be allocated, and the columns with x's show the alternative formulas frequently used by institutions to allocate these costs. Circular A-21 allows choices of allocation formulas provided they are justified. For example, plant maintenance can be alternatively allocated by users according to measures of the costs of tasks actually carried out, and each user's budget and assignable square feet. The first measure has the potential of approximating opportunity costs. However, such measures are usually wide of the mark. For example, fixed and variable costs are often not distinguished, and marginal costs are rarely measured. The

TABLE 1
Alternative Bases for Allocating Support Costs

Support Activities	Alternative Allocation Bases								Cost Objectives Receiving Support Cost
	Actual Usage Data: - job orders processed - purchase orders - requests for service - voucher	Total Direct Costs	Assign Square Feet	Total Comp.	Instr./ Res./ Public Service Comp.*	Student Head-quarters	Total Hours of Use	Student Credit Hours	
Academic Support									
Libraries	X	X			X		X	X	Instructions, Research, and Public Service
Museums and Galleries		X					X		Instruction and Public Service
Audiovisual Services	X				X				Instruction
Ancillary Support	X	X							Instructions, Research, and Public Service
Academic Admin. and Personnel Dev.	X	X							Instructions, Research, and Public Service
Academic Computing	X	X							Instructions, Research, and Public Service
Course and Curriculum Dev.		X			X				Instruction

		Instruction	Instruction	Instruction	Instruction	Instruction	Instruction	All cost objectives eligible to receive support costs
Student Services	Student Services Administration	X						X
	Social and Cultural Activities	X						X
	Counseling and Career Guidance	X	X	X				X
	Financial Aid Admin.	X			X			X
	Student Admissions and Records	X			X			X
	Health and Infirmary Services		X		X			X
Institutional Support	Executive Mgt..					X		X
	Fiscal Operations					X		X
	General Administrative Services					X		X
	Logistical Services							X
	Community Relations						X	X
Plant Operation and Maintenance	Physical Plant Admin.							X
	Building and Equip. Maintenance							X
	Custodial Services							X
	Utilities							X
	Landscape and Grounds Maint.							X
	Major Repairs and Renovations							X

* Compensation of individuals, such as faculty, involved in the areas of instruction, research, and public service.

Source: Hyatt (1983). Reprinted by permission of the National Association of College and University Business Officers, *A Cost Accounting Handbook for Colleges and Universities*, December 1983.

commonly used expenditure and square foot measures can result in widely inaccurate measures of opportunity costs.

Support expenditures can be allocated according to the 'direct' or 'step-down' methods. The direct method allocates each support cost directly to instructional, research, and public service activities while step-down allocation recognizes that a given support activity provides service to other support activities. In his 1983 NACUBO monograph, Hyatt notes (p. 18) that "a necessary requirement of the step-down method is to identify and order all support activities according to the sequence in which allocations should occur. Those support activities assumed to provide the broadest support (such as plant operation and maintenance) are allocated first; those that provide the next broadest support are allocated second, and so on." The right column in the table shows the cost objectives that receive support costs: the support activities in the left column within the categories "Institutional Support" and "Plant Operation and Maintenance" are allocated in the step-down method to all activities, including support services.

Among the most important issues in the determination of indirect costs are the expenses associated with the depreciation and the opportunity cost of funds devoted to plant and equipment. Circular A-21 allows for depreciation, but not opportunity costs. Allowed are annual use charges equivalent to a straight line depreciation of fifty years for buildings and fifteen years for equipment. (A good discussion of related accounting issues in higher education is provided in Robinson, 1986.) Based on a search of literature on capital and equipment costs in higher education, there appear to be no empirical studies at all of the *actual* rates of depreciation and obsolescence of plant and equipment. This is a major lack of information because indirect costs cannot be calculated accurately without it. However, there has been work on audits of the condition of capital facilities, which in turn have formed the basis of state legislative requests for capital maintenance budgets. (see Albright, 1982).

Because of the lack of reliable information, there is widespread dissatisfaction about federal cost reimbursement for sponsored research projects, in spite of the elaborate allocations used to measure indirect costs. Many institutions suspect that they are inadequately compensated by the federal government. (Woodrow, 1972, remains one of the most thoughtful discussions of this issue.) Many federal officials feel that universities receive excessive reimbursement, and those officials who are sympathetic have little hard contrary evidence.

There has been some work by economists on indirect costs. Powell and Lamson (1972) employed an input-output framework to illustrate the interdependencies among support units, although they provided no estimates of the economic values of the relevant coefficients. Nonetheless, their work provides valuable insights for possible improvements of step-down allocation procedures. Irene Butter (1966) pioneered in the use of rental values of capital facilities to allocate capital costs to instruction. My colleague, Rebecca Goodman (1985) has evaluated a number of the opportunity costs of sponsored research that are not included or are inadequately accounted for in calculations of indirect costs. These include the faculty and administrative opportunity costs associated with conforming to regulations and the disposal of hazardous materials. O'Neill (1971) provided historical data on capital costs in higher education, while a 1986 study by Charles River Associates also makes imaginative use of limited data (including unavailable empirical data on depreciation and obsolescence) to calculate for several separate fields the equipment stocks per scientist.

Some of the most interesting work by economists on support expenditures has been carried out by Verry and Davies (1976). Using their enormous data base on British universities, they regressed components of administrative support expenditures against undergraduate and graduate enrollments in arts and in science programs. Among their findings are that science enrollments have larger effects on plant costs while library expenses are more influenced by arts students. It will be suggested in the next section that a similar approach holds the promise of providing inferences about the relative impacts of sponsored research and enrollments on support expenditures in American universities.

In spite of these high-quality efforts by economists, much remains to be learned about the opportunity costs of support services and of plant and equipment utilization in higher education.

Conclusion: Some Proposed Studies

This chapter has applied two economic concepts to the analysis of costs within higher education institutions. One is the opportunity-cost concept and the other is the idea that the buyers of good or service may have to pay more than the suppliers' cost of providing it.

Most of the current literature on costs in colleges and universities is based on the institutions' financial and other records used for budgeting and reporting purposes. Data from these records do not permit measures of all the important opportunity costs facing institutional decisionmakers, particularly faculty. Available studies also often lack the theoretical basis needed to model the internal supply and demand relationships that determine the opportunity costs facing decisionmakers at different levels of educational institutions. A few of the studies discussed in this chapter, however, provide first steps in dealing with the types of data needed and evolving the requisite theoretical basis.

There has been much less attention given to the costs of research activity and support services in universities than to the costs of instruction. The following are suggestions for three studies that could help provide inferences about the opportunity costs faced by the suppliers and clients of research and institutional support services.

1. Proposed Study on the Direct Costs of Departmental and Sponsored Research Facing Faculty

This study would involve close observation of faculty research activities in a selected group of departments both in the laboratory sciences and in other fields. The purpose is to improve understanding of the separate components of sponsored and nonsponsored research in different fields, and to explore each in terms of jointness with instructional outcomes, impacts on institutional resources and budgets, and perceptions (and measures, when available) of research outcomes. The few available discussions of the economics of research (e.g., Nerlove, 1972) treat this enterprise as an undifferentiated activity in spite of the fact that there are many separate functions: individual thinking, idea sharing, proposal writing, joint work with students and colleagues, gathering data, designing experiments, talking about results, writing them up, presenting them, etc.

These separate activities surely need not be carried out in fixed proportions. Institutional incentives and those created by research sponsors affect faculty choices of these activities, and since these incentives are not based on understanding of the research process and its interaction with instruction, it would be most surprising if faculty efforts devoted to various research activities had equal benefit-cost relationships for clients at the margin. A better understanding of the research process could be used by research sponsors and institutions to improve incentives.

The project would include discussing the separate research activities and the relevant incentives with faculty, students, and administrators in each department. In addition, data and qualitative evidence on research outcomes and advising and other instructional relationships would be obtained. As generalities become apparent, these would be carefully discussed with the interviewed personnel. Our similar study at the University of Minnesota that focuses on instruction (Hoenack, et al., 1986) suggests that departmental academic and administrative personnel are willing to spend considerable time with researchers and that much can be learned via this research methodology about the production relationships and costs directly facing personnel.

2. *Proposed Study on the University's Indirect Costs of Sponsored Research*

This study would estimate an econometric model of the relative influences of instructional activities and of sponsored research funding on institutional expenditures for support services and general administration. At present the only information about these relative budgetary effects is based on the allocation formulas currently in use in most universities (see Table 1, pp. 146-47).

The proposed study would provide inferences about actual relationships between sponsored research, instructional activities and the costs (faced at administrative levels) of support services. The econometric work would be carried out in two parts: a pooled time series cross section analysis of a large group of research universities, and a more intensive study of one or a small group of institutions.

Data on federally sponsored research funding by field of science are available in a National Science Foundation report titled *Federal Support to Universities, Colleges and Selected Non-Profit Institutions*. However, the HEGIS data on institutional expenditures have categories only for general administration and total support services. In the analysis of a large group of institutions, the estimated equations would explain these two categories of expenditure as functions of enrollments (total and proportions by level) and federally sponsored research (total and proportions by field of science). The intensive study of particular institutions would estimate similar equations, but would do so for each of their separately budgeted support units.

The estimated relationships would represent reduced forms of administrative demand and support units' supply. They would thus have limited usefulness for internal management. But they would greatly improve understanding of the relative effects of sponsored research and instruction on support costs. In turn, they would provide a step forward in our knowledge about the adequacy of federal indirect-cost reimbursement. Also, the more detailed results for the smaller group of institutions would point out the categories of support costs for which accounting costs may be especially divergent from those indicated by the regressions. These categories could then be analyzed in more detail.

The underlying structural supply-and-demand relationships for support services would require a much more ambitious study. The most difficult issues are: (1) modeling the influence of research-oriented faculty on university budgetary governance vis-à-vis the administrative demands for the support activities that serve sponsored research; and (2) specifying the supply behavior of these units. One outcome of the proposed estimation of reduced form equations would be insights into how to design such a model.

3. An Empirical Study of the Depreciation and Obsolescence of University Buildings and Equipment and of Induced Usages of These Resources

Buildings and equipment are the topic representing the single most serious gap in our knowledge about university costs. The main reason is that virtually nothing is known about the actually experienced depreciation and obsolescence of these resources. Also, little is known about what would be the actual capacities of buildings and equipment to accommodate alternative workloads of enrollments and research activities under incentives to utilize these facilities efficiently.

Universities typically maintain detailed data on the costs of maintaining and improving their buildings of varying ages and uses in order to calculate the expenses of federally sponsored research allowed by Circular A-21. The proposed study would utilize these data to estimate equations that explain these expenses for buildings as functions of their structural characteristics, previous maintenance and improvements, the ways in which the buildings are used, and their ages. Although such equations would not permit inferences about all aspects of the depreciation and obsolescence of buildings, they would substantially improve knowledge about the magnitudes of these costs. For example, it would be possible to learn about the effects of building age on maintenance and repair expenses, and about the costs of improvements that would renew older buildings.

Universities also maintain detailed data on equipment for the same purpose of capturing allowed charges for sponsored research. The proposed study would analyze equipment in separate categories for items having secondary markets (for which price data for items of varying age could be used); those not having secondary markets and which do not become obsolete quickly and are subject to regular repair and maintenance which could be analyzed in a manner similar to buildings; and those without secondary markets that are subject to rapid obsolescence. The analysis of last category of equipment would of necessity be, to some extent, subjective.

The part of the study dealing with induced usage of buildings and equipment would be based on equations explaining this usage on functions of enrollment variables and variables controlling for sponsored and departmental research activities. Although there are published standards that provide recommended space usage for various activities in higher education institutions (see Robinson, 1986), these usages are not necessarily economically efficient and, budgetary constraints can prevent these standards from being followed closely. The estimated equations would permit inferences about actual space usage implied by various activities, and accordingly, better information about the activities' space-related costs.

CHAPTER 7

The Demand for Higher Education

WILLIAM E. BECKER

The demand function for higher education can be defined in terms of many different services: undergraduate or graduate instruction, basic or applied research, certification, public service, or even entertainment.* Administrators and researchers in the area, however, tend to emphasize the enrollment aspects of higher education demand, giving little attention to the other products and services provided by individual institutions or by the industry as a whole.[1] Since tuition and fees account for 11% to 21% of public and 24% to 62% of private higher education institutional revenue, and instruction-related state, federal and private gifts account for most of the remaining revenue, the reason for this emphasis on enrollment can be appreciated (see Patton, 1981). What may be more difficult to appreciate are the different types of analysis that have been used to explain enrollment at the individual and industry levels. This chapter examines these different methods.

Demographics of Higher Education Enrollment

As represented by the work of Carter (1976), Peng (1977), Glenny (1980), and, most recently, Clowes, et al. (1986), the starting point for the study of the demand for higher education enrollments is a description of enrollment trends. Descriptions of enrollment trends concentrate on the rate at which graduating high school seniors enroll in higher education institutions in the year following their graduation. Enrollment projections are then based on observed trends.

Peng (1977) used Project Talent data on 1961 high school graduates and data from the National Longitudinal Study of the High School Class of 1972 to demonstrate a decline in postsecondary enrollment rates. Clowes, et al. have updated Peng's work by considering 1982 data from the High School and Beyond data set. As shown in Table 1, this work suggests that the proportion or overall rate of graduating high school

155

seniors matriculating to postsecondary education declined from 58.9% in 1961 to 53.8% in 1972 but then increased to 64.1% in 1982. Much of this increase was associated with the increased enrollment of females who had an overall participation rate of 66.5% in 1982. While enrollment proportions at two-year colleges or technical institutions rose throughout the 1961-82 period, when combined with the other vocational-technical category a dip in participation rates similar to that occurring at four-year colleges is discernable in 1972.[2]

Following a review of Table 1, Clowes, et al. conclude that "the fall-off of the 1972 cohort appears to be a deviation from the more general pattern of a slow increase and perhaps stabilization of the enrollment rate in

TABLE 1

Enrollment Rates in Postsecondary Education of Recent High School Graduates by Year of High School Graduation, Institution Type, and Sex of Enroller

	Enrollment					
	Female			Male		
Enrollment	1961	1972	1982	1961	1972	1982
Postsecondary education total	55.5	53.4	66.5	62.4	54.3	61.2
Four-year college or university	29.0	27.8	34.8	37.3	30.1	33.3
Two-year college or technical institute	7.1	13.7	20.9	8.2	15.1	18.7
Other vocational-technical institutions	19.4	11.8	10.8	16.9	9.1	9.2
Nonenrollment	44.5	46.6	34.4	37.6	45.7	38.8

	Enrollment Overall		
	1961	1972	1982
Postsecondary education total	58.9	53.8	64.1
Four-year college or university	33.1	29.0	34.1
Two-year college or technical institute	7.6	14.4	19.9
Other vocational-technical institutions	18.2	10.4	10.1
Nonenrollment	41.1	46.2	35.9

Source: Clowes, Hinkle, and Smart (1986). Reprinted by permission. ©1986 by the Ohio State University Press.

the 60-70 range" (p. 130). While Clowes et al. speculate on factors which might have affected the proportion of seniors who went on for postsecondary education (e.g. the Vietnam war, changes in preference by gender, ability level, and age), no attempt was made to model these changes via econometric techniques (see Iwai and Churchill, 1982, for a related discussion).

Frances (1984) presents information on percentage changes in enrollment and the college-age population that suggests that the demographics of the post-World War II baby boom may finally be catching up with enrollment rates (see Chart 1). Surprisingly, however, college enrollments are stable despite the bottoming out of the college-age population (see Chart 2). Based on her work with economic indicators, Frances identifies three trends to explain enrollment rates: First, higher education is counter-cyclical in relation to overall economic activity.[3] Second, colleges and universities are continuing to increase their services to older students. Third, students are borrowing to pay their costs. These explanations are addressed by many of the other authors considered later in this review.

In the middle 1970s, Dresch (1975) presented a view of higher education which suggests that higher education demand would experience severe cyclical swings during the period 1960-2000 as the demographics

CHART 1
Trends in College Enrollment
as Compared with Trends in College-Age Population

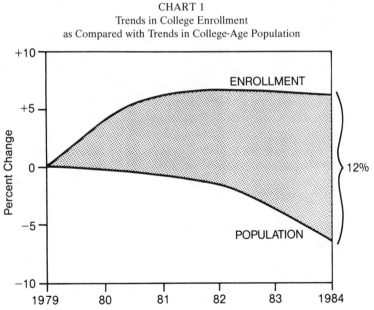

Source: Frances (1984).

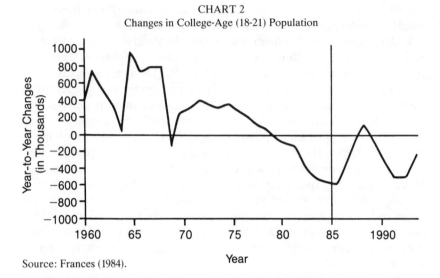

CHART 2
Changes in College-Age (18-21) Population

Source: Frances (1984).

of the population change.[4] Dresch argues that both demographics and market factors have influenced and changed the composition of the adult population since the 1930s. Saturation of the market by individuals born during the baby boom after World War II will lower the college graduate wage which in turn will work against college enrollments. (As reviewed later in this chapter, such a recursive scheme was also put forward by Freeman, 1971) in a model based on human capital considerations.)

Dresch projected a thirty-three-percent decline in college enrollments between 1970 and 2000. To date this decline has not materialized. Dresch's model did not capture the strength with which colleges have responded to threats of falling enrollments. As covered in the popular press, aggressive recruiting, prompted by the declining high school population, is one reason why enrollments have not fallen in the 1980s. In addition, wages of college graduates have not fallen relative to wages paid to non-college graduates. For example, between 1981 and 1986, the minimum wage of $3.35 per hour lost approximately twenty-six percent of its purchasing power to general price inflation while the starting salaries of college graduates tended to increase with inflation. The implications of this can be seen in Table 2, where the earnings of college graduates relative to the earnings of those who completed four years of high school or only some high school, have risen steadily in the 1980's after hitting lows in the 1970's. Murphy and Welch (1988) report similar patterns between the differences in the earnings of college and high school graduates; their work shows this difference to be larger now than it was thirty years ago. In addition, Howe (1988, p. 6) found that young college graduates had a relatively difficult time in the job market in the 1970's, compared with other college educated cohorts. Their labor market experience, however, has been better than young high school graduates.

TABLE 2

Median Income of Males with College Education and Males with 4 Years of High School, 25-34 Years Old, with Income in Selected Years 1964-1986

Year	College (4 and 5+ yrs) (1)	High School (4 yrs) (2)	Ratios (1)/(2) (3)
1964	$7,397	$5,933	1.25
1966	8,373	6,600	1.27
1968	9,264	7,402	1.25
1970	10,661	8,217	1.30
1972	11,751	9,316	1.26
1974	12,637	10,701	1.18
1976	13,965	11,416	1.22
1978	15,783	13,129	1.20
1979	17,345	14,280	1.21
1980	18,733	15,181	1.24
1981	20,589	15,393	1.34
1982	21,149	15,298	1.38
1983	21,988	15,789	1.39
1984	23,686	17,030	1.39
1985	26,174	16,981	1.54
1986	27,141	17,551	1.55

Source: U.S. Bureau of the Census. All values are in current dollars.

Ahlburg, et al. (1981) also provide enrollment projections to the year 2000 based on demographic and economic factors. They conclude: "The effect of cohort size on enrollment rates will be favorable over the next two decades, in contrast to recent experiences. . . . Only in the unlikely situation of low income growth combined with rising proportion of young females married do our projections show an enrollment drop for the period 1985 to 1995" (p. 226). This conclusion appears to contradict that of Dresch.

As already noted by Frances, the threat of falling enrollments has caused some institutions to increase their services for older students. It may also have tempted institutions to step up their recruiting of foreign students.[5] Although current foreign enrollment in the United States is only about 2% of all students in American institutions of higher education, the American Council on Education (ACE, 1982) warned that the foreign-student ratio may increase to as high as 10% by 1990. Using Box-Jenkins trend-analysis techniques, Chishti (1984) reanalyzed the ACE data set (*Open Doors*, 1980/81, Institute of International Education) and concluded that the ACE's projection was extremely high. Between the 1979-80 and 1988-89 school years the ACE's trend extrapolation suggested that foreign enrollment would grow by 181%; Chishti's extrapolations show an increase from only 69% to 88%. Because of the relatively small share of foreign enrollment, no additional consideration is given here to this source of demand (see Winkler, 1984, and Agarwal and Winkler, 1985).

Recently Baird (1984) provided descriptive information on the characteristics of a sample of SAT test takers who graduated from high school in 1981. His data suggest that at least some applicants from families of every income level generally obtain admission to college. Similarly, some applicants at every test-score level generally obtain admission to college; individuals with higher scores, however, tend to go to four-year and private colleges as full-time students. Family income seemed to have only a small influence on the type of college attended. The importance of these characteristics on the demand for higher education is considered in many of the statistical studies discussed below.

Models of Aggregate Student Enrollment Behavior

In the 1960s researchers began using econometric models to explain yearly changes in the aggregate proportion of the relevant age group enrolled in specific postsecondary institutions or in sets of institutions. Researchers also attempted to explain the number of persons who attended a given school or sets of schools in a given year relative to the number eligible to attend in that year. Both in time-series studies (data collected over time) and in cross-section studies (data collected at a point in time), explanations of the proportions attending tended to be based on ordinary-least-squares, multiple-regression estimation techniques. This section first presents a discussion of the variables considered in these time-series and cross-section regression analyses and then considers actual estimates of the enrollment effect resulting from changes in the cost of attending institutions of higher education.

Regression-Model Specification and Estimation

Throughout the 1970s the use of group data on the aggregate proportions attending a postsecondary institution or sets of institutions continued to be the primary enrollment variable to be explained in time-series and cross-section ordinary-least-squares analysis of the demand for places in higher education. As noted by Hoenack and Weiler (1979), most of the studies of attendance proportions were applied to sets of institutions rather than to individual institutions. More recent studies have emphasized enrollment at individual institutions. In these studies, for forecasting purposes, time-series studies have superseded cross-section studies, but the standard tool of analysis has continued to be least-squares, multiple regression.

The general explanatory variables used to explain attendance proportions at individual institutions typically include measures of tuition and fees at the institution, cash outlays to attend substitute institutions, labor market conditions, proximity of substitute institutions, financial aid at the institution, and other socioeconomic variables such as gender, income, and ability. The actual definition of explanatory variables differs depending on whether the study is based on time-series or cross-section data. For example, in a time-series sample, average aggregate ability of potential students will vary only slightly from year to year while in a cross-section study average ability of applicants may well vary greatly from school to school. Direct costs of attendance at each institution (e.g., tuition and fees) are the same for all individuals at a point in time and thus cannot be included as explanatory variables in some types of cross-section studies. Indirect costs (e.g., transportation costs), on the other hand, vary from individual to individual and thus may be included as explanatory variables in cross-section studies that are based on individual behavior, but such data are not always available. In time-series analysis, labor-market conditions (unemployment rates and wages) vary with the business cycle. However, business cycles cannot be captured in cross-section samples since data are collected at a point in time. Both direct and indirect costs vary over time since substitute institutions can open and close, transportation costs can change and other related costs can change. In time-series studies, however, tuition at substitute institutions will tend to be highly correlated so that it may not be possible to obtain separate estimates of the effect of own-versus cross-tuition effects.

Regardless of whether the demand study is based on grouped time-series or cross-section data, researchers have attempted to estimate an income effect and a cost effect. The income effect is a measure of how changes in applicant income affect college attendance. The cost effect is a measure of how changes in college costs affect attendance.

The income effect is typically given as an elasticity (i.e., the percentage change in the proportion of the eligible age group continuing schooling resulting from a one-percent change in an income measure). Unfortunately, there is less than total agreement as to the appropriate

measure of income to be included as an explanatory variable in an enrollment regression. For example, most studies use family income as the
relevant income variable in college decisions. Hearn and Longanecker
(1985) question the appropriateness of this income measure when growing numbers of students are claiming independence from their parents
and reliance on student loans is increasing.

As with the income effect, the cost effect is typically given as an
elasticity (i.e., the percentage change in the proportion of the eligible
age group attending college resulting from a one-percent change in the
cost of attending). The specification of the cost variable (tuition, fees,
transportation, etc.) as well as the specification of the equation system
itself depends on whether the institution under study is a private or public institution. The most prestigious private institutions typically have
more applicants than they wish to admit, yet they do not raise their
tuition to discourage this excess demand. Other private institutions may
have pricing policies which are more responsive to market forces (Mc-
Pherson, 1978). Public institutions, on the other hand, set tuition levels
in any one of three ways (Viehland, et al., 1982): Thirty states use an ad
hoc process (i.e., institutions have no formal process but consider inflation, tradition, enrollment changes, state appropriations, and other relevant factors). Another process is based on an index such as the Higher
Education Price Index, and the third is based on institutional costs.

Since private institutions are free to retain increased revenue from
higher tuition charges and higher enrollment, enrollment demand behavior must be estimated in a model that includes institutional supply behavior so that the interaction of both supply and demand are recognized as
jointly determining tuition and enrollment. As noted by Radner and
Miller (1975), estimation of an enrollment demand equation which is
part of a system of equations necessitates that the parameters of the
demand equation be identified (or over-identified) and estimated by
appropriate multistage techniques. Identification of a demand equation
requires that we know of variables that affect supply but do not influence demand. As discussed later in this chapter, economists have not
advanced a theory of supply that is fully adequate for this purpose. Identification of demand equations has tended to be ad hoc.

Public institutions typically are not free to retain revenues from
increased tuition charges. For example, Hoenack and Weiler (1979) note
that the Minnesota legislature requires the University of Minnesota to
set tuition charges at a specific fraction of its average cost per student.
The legislature then pays the remainder with certain university endowment income counted as part of the legislature's share. Thus, higher
tuition need not increase the university's willingness to supply more

admittance places. Furthermore, many public universities have open admittance policies by which all eligible students are always granted space. Based on such considerations, Hoenack and Weiler (1979) and more recently Weiler (1984) have argued that the identification of demand equations for public institutions need not be a problem and that ordinary-least-squares techniques can yield unbiased estimates of the parameters of the demand equation.

Estimates of Elasticity Using Grouped Data

As suggested by the above discussion, estimates of enrollment demand elasticity with respect to price or income are sensitive to the definition of other variables included as regressors and the type of data-base employed. They also depend on the functional form specification and the estimation techniques employed. Because of all these differences there is no unique basis for comparing elasticity estimates across studies, although Leslie and Brinkman (1987), McPherson (1978), and Jackson and Weathersby (1975) have proposed standards.[6] Nevertheless, as suggested by Cohn and Morgan's (1978) survey of the literature, a review of a large number of elasticity estimates from both time-series and cross-section studies will indicate the direction and possibly suggest the magnitude of expected percentage changes in enrollment participation rates resulting from a one-percent change in price or income (see also Hossler, 1984). Toward this end the following study summaries are provided.

Campbell and Siegel (1967) stimulated much of the empirical work on the estimation of higher education demand elasticities. They used a single-equation model to examine aggregate enrollment in four-year institutions (as a percentage of eighteen-to-twenty-four-year-old high school graduates not in the military) for data from the 1920s through the early 1960s. They reported income (real disposable income per household) and price (average real tuition) elasticities of 1.20 and −0.44. Galper and Dunn (1969) reanalyzed Campbell and Siegel's data using a distributed lag specification to estimate the short-run effect of the growth of the armed services. In addition to reporting on the effects of the armed services, they report an income elasticity of 0.69, which is close to that estimated by Campbell and Siegel.

Because of the aggregation of public and private schools in the Campbell and Siegel study, Hight (1970) postulated a four-equation supply-and-demand model for the two sectors of higher education. Using a time period similar to that in the Campbell and Siegel study, but employing a different price index to deflate tuition, Hight reported income elasticities (calculated about the mean values) of 0.977 for public schools and 1.701 for private. His price elasticities were -1.058 and -0.6414, respectively. It should be noted, however, that his elasticity estimates were not consistently significant across equations. Later Hight (1975) reported elasticity estimates suggesting that, if income is constant, equal percentage increases in public and private tuition will not affect the private-to-public enrollment ratio. (It is important to note in assessing this finding that Hight adjusted average tuition at selected institutions by subtracting the value of financial aid per student.)

Hoenack (1967) reports on his study of individual campus demand in the state of California. He estimated demand functions for each campus of the University of California (UC), including the option of attending private colleges, public state colleges or community colleges in California. Using 1965 cross-sectional data, Hoenack specified his dependent variable to be the proportion of eligible high school graduates who enroll at a particular UC campus. Independent variables were the cost to the student of attending various UC campuses, the cost to the student of attending the nearest state college or community college, average rate of unemployment and wages in each high school district, median family income in each district, and number of graduates from the high school. Since UC tuition was the same for all campuses, the cost to the student only included transportation costs and additional out-of-pocket costs. Hoenack found that a one-hundred-dollar increase in costs at UC decreased UC enrollment by three to six percentage points depending on family income and state-college-price changes. Average UC price (cost) elasticity was reported to be -0.85, varying from -1.12 for the lowest income bracket to -0.71 for the highest. (Although Hoenack did not report it, Radner and Miller (1975) calculated Hoenack's income elasticity to be 0.7.)

Hoenack's 1971 study extends his earlier work at the University of California and gives additional estimates of enrollment demand at the UC. He reports that a one-hundred-dollar increase in tuition decreases enrollment at UC by 0.60 percent. Most recently, a California Postsecondary Education Commission study (1980) reconfirms Hoenack's (1967 and 1971) findings that family income is inversely correlated with responsiveness to price. This commission estimates that lower-income students are approximately twice as price responsive as middle-income students and high-income students are about two-thirds as responsive as middle-income students.

Given the growth of community colleges over the last twenty years it may be of interest that in his early California studies Hoenack found that a one-hundred-dollar increase in junior college tuition reduced enrollment by about seven percent. Using this elasticity estimate, Tuckman and Ford (1972) stated that the existence of local community colleges in the Miami, Florida area could be responsible for forty percent of the enrollment in the area and that the close proximity of the junior colleges possibly played an important role in the postsecondary schooling choice of the marginal students.

The importance of the human-capital approach to estimating enrollment in highly specialized disciplines was brought to life by Freeman's (1971) estimation of the enrollment rates of freshman engineering students. The essence of human-capital theory is that individuals select training when the expected earnings exceed the expected cost of the training. For the 1943-1967 time period, Freeman's results suggested that students enroll in engineering programs on the basis of the earning experience of recent graduates. As starting salaries of graduating engineers rise, freshman enrollments in engineering follow. Rising enrollments in engineering implies a surplus of engineers in the future, which would in turn lower salaries and cause enrollments to fall; falling enrollments imply a shortage of engineers and higher wages in the future, and the cycle continues. While Freeman's empirical work does not cast light on the direct income and price elasticity of the demand curve for enrollment, he found the dynamics of his cobweb models to be consistent with oscillatory shortages and surpluses observed not only in engineering but in accounting, law, and other specialties as well, Freeman (1976a). (For other human-capital enrollment research, see Wish and Hamilton, 1980, Sloan, 1971, Scott, 1979, and Alexander and Frey, 1984.)

In 1972 Corrazzini et al. reported the results of their national study based on combined Project Talent data and Massachusetts data. In this study for the Massachusetts Area Planning Council they attempted to explain the proportion of high school graduates going on to higher education, as observed across states. The independent variables included father's education (as a measure of socioeconomic status), academic ability (as measured by standardized test scores), average income of production workers (as a proxy for the opportunity cost of postsecondary education), unemployment rates, and indices of tuition at community colleges, public four-year colleges, teachers colleges, and private four-year universities. Based on statewide averages, tuition at teachers colleges was not significant. Elasticities of percentage enrolled with respect to the statewide tuition averages were computed by Radner and Miller (1975) to be −0.09 for community college, −0.18 for four-year public universities, and −0.19 for four-year private universities. Feldman and Hoenack (1969) reported similar elasticity results in their Project Talent study.

Anderson, et al. (1972) report on two main data sources: the Wisconsin sample of ten thousand students used by Sewell and his associates (1967, 1968 and 1971) and the School to College Opportunities for Postsecondary Education (SCOPE) sample for California, Illinois, Massachusetts, and North Carolina. Using least-squares analysis, and in some cases logit analysis, the variables found to be highly related to college enrollment rates include student ability, parent education and income and high school program. With the exception of some low-income groups, college accessibility (proximity of college to student's home) is not a statistically significant factor in explaining enrollment rates.

Hu and Stromsdorfer (1973) develop a supply and demand model to simultaneously and recursively determine tuition and enrollment. Using a 1968 and 1972 sample of Massachusetts institutions (classified as public or private, two or four year) separate regressions were estimated. In the recursive specifications, where supply of places is rationed by the institutions via admission standards so that enrollment demand is determined with the level of tuition, they report significant tuition effects with elasticities of -0.46 and -0.77 for four-year and two-year institutions, respectively. The average family income elasticities obtained from the simultaneous equation model were reported to be 0.78, 4.32 and 13.19 for the public four-year, private two-year and public two-year institutions, respectively.

Hopkins (1974) used a cross-section of forty-nine states for 1963-1964 to analyze enrollment rates at public and private institutions. By comparing results Hopkins concluded that proximity to private institutions and high-income families are positively related to private enrollment but they do not influence total enrollment rates. This result supports the findings of Anderson, et al. (1972). In addition Hopkins found that tuition in public institutions does not have an effect on total enrollment but does have an effect on institutional choice (for comment on Hopkin's results, see Tannen, 1978). This result was confirmed by Tierney (1980) who found that as tuition differences between public and private schools increase, the probability of a student's attending a private school decreased.

Lehr and Newton (1978) use both time-series and cross-sectional data to analyze the demand response of different segments of the higher education market in the state of Oregon. Using time-series data they fit fall-term freshman enrollment to average real tuition, mean real per capita personal income, annual rates of unemployment, number of eighteen-to-twenty-one year olds in the armed forces, and a measure of the number of high school graduates as the eligible population. While their study is based only on state data, their estimates of the price and income elasticities (-0.6587 and 1.8822, respectively) in their log-linear specification were close to those of Campbell and Siegel. Based on cross-section data in linear discriminant analysis, where one variable measures the combined resources of a student (including own savings and current earnings, family support, and financial aid), Lehr and Newton concluded that financial constraints appear most severe for those who have chosen the low-cost community colleges while individuals with high resource availability in conjunction with high ability tend to choose the more expensive and prestigious private institutions. Exceptions to this conclusion may be students who attend sectarian schools. Enrollment demand estimates by institutional segments (two-year public, four-year public and four-year private) suggested that the enrollment of community college students was more sensitive to the existence of other alternatives or changes in the economic conditions. As they state, "the enrollment decision of community college students appears here to be a fragile one" (p. 420).

Cohn and Morgan (1978) examine two different measures of postsecondary demand of the eligible population (proportion of new freshmen entering versus proportion of persons admitted). As discussed later in this paper, these ratios imply different individual choices but Cohn and Morgan's models and data from 1970, for the state of South Carolina and for the United States do not lend themselves to the analysis of the sequencing of these choices. Using both the ratio and a logistic specification { Ln[Ratio/(1-Ratio)] } they find that in South Carolina county per capita income and young male unemployment rates are important explanatory variables, with income elasticities computed to be around 0.965, but their two models did not give consistent information. For the U.S. both models gave consistent information. They report that higher state aid per capita is associated with higher demand.

In Hoenack and Weiler (1975 and 1979), the demand for places at the University of Minnesota was considered. In the 1979 time-series study, Hoenack and Weiler take explicit account of labor-market values affected by business cycles. They report that a one-hundred-dollar increase in cost (tuition) of attending the University of Minnesota is associated with a decrease of 1.15 percent in enrollment. Their 1975 study (lacking labor-market variables) provided nearly identical time-series results and cross-sectional estimates of a 0.85 percent decrease in the University of Minnesota enrollment per one-hundred-dollar increase in cost. They concluded "the inclusion of labor-market variables does not substantially affect the magnitude of the estimated effects of tuition variables" (1979, p. 97).

Most recently Weiler (1984) reported that the cumulative work at Minnesota suggests that the enrollment elasticity with respect to tuition costs for lower-division students ranges from −0.5 to −1.0. For upper-division students the elasticity approximation is −0.25 and for graduate and professional enrollment it is zero. Thus, at institutions similar to the University of Minnesota it may be expected that lower-division enrollment will fall at least one half of the percentage by which the tuition rate rises.

In contrast to Hoenack and his associates' ongoing studies at the Universities of California and Minnesota is Spies (1973) work at Princeton University. In an attempt to explain demand for highly competitive private colleges, Spies specified different linear equations to describe three different individual decisions: the decision to apply to any school; the decision to apply for financial aid; and the decision to enroll once admitted. Contrary to the hopes of Bowen (1977) Spies was never able to capitalize fully on this implied decision tree although, as discussed below, researchers using discrete choice and random utility theories would. Nevertheless, an interesting finding by Spies is that a unit increase in the ratio of college cost to father's income made it 6.72 percentage points less likely that a prospective student would apply to college. Unfortunately, this finding cannot be generalized beyond the Princeton environment because Spies' sample has a family income that is on the average three thousand dollars higher than the average of family income of all college freshmen. In addition, Jackson and Weathersby (1975) warn against using the application response index which Spies employed as a measure of enrollment demand response since students from upper-income families are less sensitive to cost changes than those from lower-income families, and applications do not necessarily imply attendance.

Studies Based on Individual Behavior

The number of individuals attending college is a discrete whole number which is determined by individual choice. In the studies reviewed in the previous section, the actual choices made by each individual were lost when the continuous dependent variable was created by dividing the sum of individuals selecting postsecondary attendance by the total number eligible. The creation of this participation rate—and loss of information on individual choice—was dictated by the use of least-squares linear regression techniques, which requires a continuous dependent variable, and by the aggregate nature of the data.[7]

As an alternative to the least-squares estimation, Kohn et al. (1972) and Radner and Miller (1975) introduced analytical techniques which capture the discrete choice of individuals to attend or not attend a postsecondary institution. Maximum likelihood estimation techniques (in logit or probit models) enable the researcher to estimate the probability that an individual high school graduate will apply to certain schools, be accepted by the schools and choose to attend one of them.

The individual's demand for a four-year college, a two-year college, a vocational school, or no postsecondary education is then obtained from these probabilities. To obtain aggregate measures of attendance, the researcher must make predictions for each person in the sample, then add the results and divide by the number in the sample, giving the aggregate proportion in the sample predicted to choose each alternative.

The next section will demonstrate the maximum likelihood technique used in random utility analysis of individual choice. Following this introduction to the probit and logit maximum likelihood estimation procedures, recent findings from discrete choice studies will be presented. Once again emphasis is given to the enrollment effects of changes in attendance costs and changes in student income.

Random Utility Analysis and Discrete Choice Modeling

As a starting point assume that high school graduates have two alternatives: a college attendance option (c) or a work/unemployment option (w). If a student t chooses to go to college, then the benefit or utility from this option (y^*_{tc}) must be greater than the utility from its work/unemployment alternative (y^*_{tw}); i.e. $y^*_{tc} > y^*_{tw}$. If the student chooses not to go to college then y^*_{tc} must be less than y^*_{tw}. While utility is unobservable, the outcome of the student's choice is observable so utility can be inferred.

From the previous review of the literature, it seems reasonable to hypothesize that student utility depends on at least ability (a_t), family income (x_t), and the quality (q_t) and cost of the student's best college options (c_t) and other unknown chance factors (ϵ_{tc}). The utility of the work/unemployment option may depend on the student's potential wage (w_t) and chance of unemployment as well as other chance factors (ϵ_{tw}). For simplicity assume that the unobservable utilities are related linearly to their explanatory variables and chance factors,

$$y^*_{tc} = \beta_0 + \beta_1 x_t + \beta_2 c_t + \beta_3 a_t + \beta_4 q_t + \epsilon_{tc}$$

$$y^*_{tw} = \beta_5 + \beta_6 w_t + \epsilon_{tw}$$

where the β's are unknown parameters. Given observations on the outcome of student choices and observations on the explanatory variables and assuming that the chance factors have zero means, fixed variances, and follow a certain distribution (e.g. the normal), the revealed preference inequality

$$\beta_0 + \beta_1 x_t + \beta_2 c_t + \beta_3 a_t + \beta_4 q_t + \epsilon_{tc} > \beta_5 + \beta_6 w_t + \epsilon_{tw}$$

provides information on the β's. In particular we can write the probability that student t is observed to choose college enrollment as a function of the random variables ϵ_{tc} and ϵ_{tw}:

$$Prob \ (\beta_0 + \beta_1 x_t + \beta_2 c_t + \beta_3 a_t + \beta_4 q_t + \epsilon_{tc} > \beta_5 + \beta_6 w_t + \epsilon_{tw})$$

$$Prob \ (\epsilon_{tc} - \epsilon_{tw} > \beta_5 + \beta_6 w_t - \beta_0 - \beta_1 x_t - \beta_2 c_t - \beta_3 a_t - \beta_4 q_t)$$

The β's are estimated by selecting values that make the choice probabilities and observed choices in the sample most closely correspond. With estimates of the β's, the college/work decisions of students outside the sample can be predicted.

As a demonstration of estimation of the above random utility model consider the estimation of the probability that a student decides to attend college (see Becker and Waldman, 1987). (To avoid problems related to the college selection process it is assumed that the student has already been accepted by schools in the college option or that the schools have open admissions.) For pedagogical purposes assume a hypothetical data set where $y = 1$ if a student is observed enrolling and $y = 0$ if the student does not enroll. Assume also that for each student we have a continuous index of family income x, where $0 < x < 1$, and that students are alike on all other counts (i.e., "less than" the cost of attending and ability and are identical for all students).

For notational ease the student subscript t may be dropped so that y^*_t is the unobservable utility or benefit that a student expects to receive from enrolling. A student will enroll only if y^*_c is greater than the threshold value of $\beta_6 w + \epsilon_w$. For pedagogical convenience assume this threshold value is zero (the depths of a recession?). With the threshold value set at zero there is only one chance variable in the system, ϵ_c, which means we can now ignore its subscript as well as that on y^*_c. Assuming a probit specification implies that this ϵ follows the normal distribution. Assume that ϵ is standard normal.[8]

The expected value of y^* at any x is now given by $E(y^*|x) = \beta_0 + \beta_1 x$. This line together with the normality assumption form the basis of the maximum likelihood estimation method. In essence, this technique of estimation involves a search for the line that best describes the unknown y^* data given the relative frequency of $y = 1$ responses at each x value in the data set, and given the assumption that y^* is normally distributed.

Assembling the estimated coefficients gives the fitted line for y^*:

$$\tilde{y}^* = b_0 + b_1 x$$

To interpret the coefficient estimates in this equation consider the three-dimensional diagram in the lower part of Chart 3, drawn for a hypothetical example where $b_0 = -1.05$ and $b_1 = 2.69$. The density of the population error, $f(\epsilon)$, is measured on the vertical axis. The unknown y^* values and the known x values are measured on the horizontal plane. The $\bar{y}^*$ is graphed on this plane as the equation that estimates $\epsilon(y^*|x)$. At each x value there is a standard normal density which defines the probability of y^* values. Only two such densities are shown in the three-dimensional diagram, for $x = \bar{x} = 0.48$ in our example and $x = \bar{x} + s = 0.79$, where s is the sample standard deviation of x.

The calculation of the probability of $y^* > 0$ at the mean of the x values (i.e., the probability that a mean-family-income student goes to college) is seen in the three-dimensional diagram in Chart 3 as the area under the density for y^* values above zero. As shown, this area is identical to the height of the probability mass function at $y = 1$ in the top left-hand diagram in Chart 3, which is also the probability that a student from a family with mean income will attend college. Using the probability formulation given above, this area and mass are calculated as

$$Prob(y^* > 0) = Prob(y = 1)$$

$$= Prob(\beta_0 + \beta_1\bar{x} + \epsilon > 0) = Prob(\epsilon > -\beta_0 - \beta_1\bar{x})$$

$$= 1 - Prob(\epsilon < -\beta_0 - \beta_1\bar{x}) = 1 - F(1.05 - 2.69\bar{x})$$

$$= 1 - F(-0.241) = 0.60$$

where F is the standard normal probability distribution function.

The probability that y^* is greater than zero (hence $y = 1$) at $x = \bar{x} + s$, as shown in the three-dimensional diagram in Chart 3, is similarly calculated to be $1 - F(-1.086) = 0.86$. This value is shown in the mass function in the top right-hand diagram in Chart 3. For a one-standard-deviation increase in family income from the mean, the change in the probability that the student enrolls in a college is found to be 0.26.

In calculating changes in probability it is important to recognize that while x and $\epsilon(y|x)$ are linearly related, x and $P(y^* > 0|x)$ are not. Thus, the change in probability from $\bar{x}$ to $\bar{x} + s$ is not equal to the change in probability from $\bar{x} + s$ to $\bar{x} + 2s$. In addition, maximum likelihood techniques do not require the assumption of linearity between x and $E(y^*|x)$. Finally, while the above development is based on a utility-maximizing paradigm in which the value 0.241 can be interpreted as the utility of a mean-family-income student going to college, the calculation of probabilities does not require this utility interpretation. These probabilities are defined in terms of a normal random variable y^* regardless of

CHART 3

Probability of Choosing the College Option at Given Family Income Levels

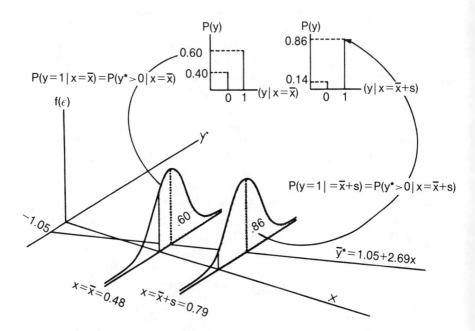

Source: Becker and Waldman (1987).

the name, definition, or interpretation given to this variable. Usually, however, y^* is defined and interpreted as utility and hence forth will be designated by the letter U.

Estimates of Enrollment Effects from Discrete Choice Models

The use of probit models to analyze the binary choice related to college enrollment is not new or uncommon. Christiansen, et al. (1975) used a probit model to analyze by gender enrollment rates of 400 high school graduates in Wisconsin for the year 1963. More recently Ehrenberg and Sherman (1982) used a probit model to analyze an admitted applicant's decision to enroll at Cornell University. They hypothesized that a decision to attend university s versus university o is based on a comparison of the net utility, U, that the admitted applicant would receive from each. The potential enrollee's utility depends on observed characteristics of the individual (X), the net cost to the enrollee of each option (N_s

and N_o), and other characteristics of the options (Z_s and Z_o), and the random variables (ϵ_{sk} and ϵ_{ok}). Hence the equations that describe utility are:

$$U_s = V(X, N_s, Z_s) + \epsilon_s$$

$$U_0 = V(X, N_o, Z_o) + \epsilon_o$$

where the ϵ's are assumed to be normally distributed and V's are linear in their arguments. With enrollment predictions from this probit model, Ehrenberg and Sherman consider the propositions studied by Hoenack (1971) regarding tuition, financial aid, and the desirability of certain types of students. Unlike Hoenack's model, however, their probit model distinguishes between the school's acceptance of an applicant and the admitted applicant's decision on enrollment.

Ehrenberg and Sherman use data collected on freshman admitted in 1981 in both Cornell's private endowed divisions (Arts and Sciences, Architecture, Art and Planning, and Engineering) and the state-supported statutory divisions. In addition to many other findings, they report: "Other things equal, a $500 increase in the scholarship offer at Cornell will raise the yield on accepted applicants by roughly 6½ to 8 percent in the endowed sector and 7 to 10 percent in the statutory sector" (p. 16). Contrary to Hoenack's findings and those of most other researchers using grouped data, Ehrenberg and Sherman found that students from low-income families have smaller (absolute value) elasticities of enrollment with respect to net cost than do students from higher-income families. They account for this difference by noting unique features of Cornell's financial aid packages which make Cornell substantially cheaper for low-income families.

Borus and Carpenter (1984) also use a probit model to analyze the probability that high school seniors go directly to college. Using data from the 1978 and 1979 National Longitudinal Survey of Youth Labor Markets Experience they consider the enrollment effect of demographic and location variables related to family background, economic status, attitude, and high school characteristics. The following factors were found to positively influence college enrollment: delayed plans for marriage by females, population growth in the south, and increasing education among the youths' fathers. While minority and poor youth were less likely to go directly to college from high school, it appears that factors such as father's education and lower scores on the ability measure were causal. High school characteristics appear to have a very limited influence on the probability of a student going directly to college after high school.

In the above probit model illustration and cited applications, students are faced with one decision involving only two options. This requires the assumption that colleges take all applicants or that the applicants are already admitted. Relaxation of these assumptions complicates the analysis but the intuitive explanation of the maximum likelihood procedure remains the same: namely, to find the line that best describes the unknown and unmeasurable benefit or utility of different choices, given that the deviations from this line follow a continuous distribution and given the observed discrete choices of the decisionmakers.

Radner and Miller relax the assumption that students face only two options in their postsecondary schooling decision. In their 1975 book they report on their cumulative work on the decision by individual high school graduates to go on or not go on to college and their choices among available institutions and institutional types (junior colleges, public four-year colleges, teacher colleges, private four-year colleges). They relate the relative frequencies of choices to the characteristics of the student and his or her alternatives. In particular, using the 1966 SCOPE data they consider the effect of ability, parent income, the selectivity of the college alternative, and out-of-pocket cost.

Instead of using a probit specification, Radner and Miller used a multinomial logit (or conditional logit) specification. The basic idea behind this specification is the following: The high school graduate (whose attributes are summarized by x) faces n alternatives each of which is characterized by a vector y_i. Utility is a random function of the attributes of the alternative and the attributes of the individual. Assuming V denotes average utility and ϵ is the deviation around it, we can write utility as

$$U(x, y_i) = V(x, y_i) + \epsilon_i$$

where $V(x, y_i) = Z_i\beta$ and Z_i is a vector of observations on the explanatory variables for the high school graduate and β is a vector of parameters.

The high school graduate will choose alternative i if the utility of that alternative exceeds the utility of each of the other alternatives. The probability of drawing an individual from the population of high school graduates who chooses alternative i is the probability that the utility of i exceeds the utility of all of the other alternatives.

$$P_i = Prob[\ U(x, y_i) > U(x, y_j)\ ] \text{ for all alternatives } j \neq i$$

$$= Prob[\ \epsilon_j - \epsilon_i < V(x, y_i) - V(x, y_j)\ ].$$

Convenient distribution assumptions on the ϵ's lead to the so-called conditional logit or multinomial logit functional form given by

$$P_i = e^{Z_i\beta} / (e^{Z_1\beta} + \ldots + e^{Z_J\beta})$$

where there are J alternatives. The odds in favor of choosing alternative i rather than j will be a function of the two explanatory variable vectors Z_i and Z_j. In particular, a base e logarithm transformation of the relative odds of choosing i over j shows the i to j odds to be a function of the Z's and the parameters in the β vector, i.e.,

$$Ln(P_i/P_j) = (Z_i - Z_j)\beta.$$

Radner and Miller's maximum likelihood estimations suggested that four factors affected the postsecondary choices of high school graduates: family income, cost of alternative options, academic ability, and selectivity of the alternative institutions for which the student is eligible.[9] Because the maximum likelihood technique gives choice probablities which are not linearly related to the explanatory variables, simple summary measures of these relationships are not possible. Nevertheless, Carlson et al. (1974) transformed some of Radner and Miller's early results to linear response coefficients calculated about the mean values of the independent variables. Their results suggest that a one-hundred-dollar increase in the cost of attendance in one institutional sector would decrease enrollment in that sector by from 3.26 to 0.71 percentage points, depending on family income and the particular institutional sector. As first detected by Hoenack (1967), Radner and Miller found that the cost elasticity for the University of California was greater in absolute magnitude for low-income groups than for high-income groups. Radner and Miller also report that "cost elasticity for all higher education options falls as income rises" (p. 66). In addition, they report that "At all levels of income, and at all ability levels, larger percentage changes in demand accompany higher cost institutions; demand is more elastic as cost rises" (p. 66).

Additional support for the idea that higher (absolute value) elasticities of demand are associated with low-income groups is found in Bishop (1977). Using a binomial logit specification and Project Talent data, Bishop assessed the individual characteristics affecting the decision to attend an institution of higher education. His sample of 27,046 male high school juniors in 1960 is divided into twenty subgroups which are defined by student ability and family income. Tuition, high admission standards, travel costs, and room and board cost are reported to have significant negative effects on enrollment. The highest elasticities of demand are found to occur in the low-income strata and lower-middle ability quartile. Calculated at mean values, Bishop reports "the tuition elasticity of the high-income stratum is -0.084; for the poverty stratum it is -0.393. Tuition elasticity was powerfully and nonlinearly related to ability: The high-ability quartile's tuition was -0.05; the lower-middle ability quartile's elasticity was $-0.47''$ (p. 295).

Following the lead of Bishop and Van Dyk (1977), Corman (1983) explored the demand for higher education of older adults in a discrete choice framework.[10] She also addresses the question as to whether or not college and postsecondary vocational training (voc-tech) are close substitutes. Using data from the 1975 Survey on Adult Education, a special questionnaire attached to the May 1975 Current Population Survey, she considered the schooling/work choices of individuals belonging to one of four groups: men, ages 18 to 22, women 18 to 22, men 25 to 44 and women 25 to 44. The options open to these individuals were (two or four-year) college, voc-tech, or not enrolling in any school. Corman argues that these three options cannot be ranked from highest to lowest on any universally accepted scale and thus she only considers unordered models. She uses a logit model where the probability that an individual chooses an alternative is equal to the probability that the net benefit from this alternative exceeds the net benefit from all other alternatives, regardless of the ranking of the other alternatives. The general demand equations estimated in this logistic model were

$$Ln(P_1/P_0) = f(S,E,C)$$

$$Ln(P_2/P_0) = g(S,E,C)$$

where P_1, P_2, and P_0 are the respective probabilities of enrolling in college, voc-tech or not enrolling at all. S is a vector describing costs and similar characteristics of the colleges and voc-tech schools in the Standard Metropolitan Statistical Area (SMSA) where the individual resides. E is a vector of employment characteristics describing the SMSA and C is a vector of the student's personal characteristics.

To avoid discussing effects in terms of utility and for the ease of the reader, Corman recalculates her raw logit results (by taking partial derivatives of the dependent variable evaluated at mean values of the independent variables) to obtain coeffecients which correspond to standard regression coeffecients for a change in the probability of attending given a change in an independent variable (see Table 3). For example, in Table 3, for mean ages eighteen to twenty-two, a one-hundred-dollar increase in college tuition lowers the probability of attending college by 1.55 percentage points while a thousand-dollar increase in family income raises the probability of attending college by 1.15 percentage points. However, Corman warns readers to be careful in interpreting her tuition results because she could not control for scholarship and loan programs in different states. She also notes that her tuition at voc-tech institutions represents a weighted average of tuition levels at all such schools in the SMSA where the student lives. She states that approximately eighty percent of these schools are privately operated. Tuition at the other school option (two-year or four-year college) was a weighted average of tuition charges at public four-year colleges and universities in the SMSA of the potential student resident.

TABLE 3
Changes in Enrollment Rates Associated with Changes in Tuition and Income

	Men		*Women*	
18-22 Years of Age	*College*	*School*	*College*	*School*
$100 increase in "own" price				
Absolute change in enrollment rate[a]	−1.55	−.07	−.82	−.12
Percent change in enrollment rate[b]	−4.29	−2.93	−4.04	−4.48
$100 increase in "cross" price[c]				
Absolute change in enrollment rate[a]	+.13	+.15	+.09	+.40
Percent change in enrollment rate[b]	+.35	+6.23	+.01	+14.92
$1000 increase in family income				
Absolute change in enrollment rate[a]	+1.15	−.10	+.78	−.15
Percent change in enrollment rate[b]	+3.18	−4.18	+3.87	−5.60
25-44 Years of Age				
$100 increase in "own" price				
Absolute change in enrollment rate[a]	−.69	+.07	−.52	−.01
Percent change in enrollment rate[b]	−9.77	+3.89	−8.47	−1.10
$100 increase in "cross" price[c]				
Absolute change in enrollment rate[a]	−.38	+.12	−.20	+.07
Percent change in enrollment rate[b]	−5.38	+6.67	−3.26	+7.69
$1000 increase in family income				
Absolute change in enrollment rate[a]	−.05	−.05	+.19	−.05
Percent change in enrollment rate[b]	−.71	−.71	+3.09	−5.49

[a] Expressed as percentage point change in the enrollment rate.
[b] Expressed as change in enrollment rate divided by the average enrollment rate.
[c] Refers to change in college (occupational school) enrollment associated with a change in occupational school (college) tuition.

Source: Adapted from Corman, (1983). "Postsecondary Education Enrollment Responses by Recent High School Graduates and Older Adults," *The Journal of Human Resources.*
© Copyright 1983 by the Board of Regents of the University of Wisconsin System.

After reviewing all the details and caveats involved in the data set and the method of estimation and results, Corman concluded that college and postsecondary vocational schools are close substitutes.[11] In addition, both younger and older adults respond to economic variables in the schooling choice. Thus, according to Corman, the human-capital model, with the modification that education is a good whose value depreciates, is supported. Corman argues that the robustness of her statistical model and of the modified human-capital model is supported by the fact that her estimates of the percentage-point change in college attendance resulting from a one-hundred-dollar increase in tuition, after converting to 1974 dollars, is within the range (−0.05 to −1.46) of effects calculated by Jackson and Weathersby (1975) in their comparative study. Furthermore, while Corman's estimates of tuition and income effects for recent graduates are a little low compared to those of Bishop (1977), Corman's estimates of the responsiveness of older adults to tuition changes are similar to those reported by Bishop and Van Dyk (1977) in their study of the enrollment behavior of older adults.

Although many refinements on the specification and estimation of random utility models have taken place since the original Radner and Miller work, (1975) these two researchers highlighted one of the problems which continues to plague this field: namely, where to draw the system boundaries on the number and type of decisions made by students and by schools. For instance, in commenting on Kohn, et al. (1972), Radner and Miller call attention to their own one-stage decision process versus the two-stage process assumed by Kohn, et al. In the Radner and Miller model students make one decision about all alternatives, including the no-school option. Kohn, et al. assume that in a first stage a student decides whether to go on for postsecondary education and then, in a second stage, decides which school to attend, if in the first stage he or she decided to go on. Although the difference in the way decisionmaking is assumed to occur did not greatly affect the direction of tuition results obtained by Bishop, Kohn, et al., and Radner and Miller, debate over this issue is not a trivial issue in fitting discrete choice models.

The effect of institution closings should have an effect on the demand for the remaining institutions. How the exclusion of this alternative is handled in a probit or logit model, however, will affect the estimation process.

In the two-stage model, removing an institution from a student's feasible set results in an increase in the probability of choosing one of the remaining institutions with no change in the probability of choosing no postsecondary education. In a one-stage model, the probability of all the remaining options increase, including the no-postsecondary-education option. Radner and Miller suggest that this effect on the remaining probabilities is important when considering the community college option versus work. They state, however, that "on a priori grounds we favor their two-stage model over our own single-stage model" (p. 70). Attempts to model the many stages and types of decisions made by individual decisionmakers characterize the recent work with random utility analysis.

Table 4 shows the types and sequence of decisions that researchers have examined with random utility models. As noted by Manski and Wise (1983), in theory the entire postsecondary-choice process could be analyzed with a single large statistical model. In practice, however, researchers have been successful in specifying and estimating only separate pieces of the puzzle. To the extent that the different types of decisions are treated as exogenous (determined outside the decision system) or independent, when in fact they are endogenous or dependent, biases in the estimation of related effects can be expected.

To appreciate the types of biases that might result from not estimating an entire decision system, consider the pedagogical example I used earlier. In analyzing the college/noncollege decision, I assumed that the students had already applied to and been accepted by colleges. But some students never apply to a college and are thus never considered for admission. If the intent is to estimate the probability that a student will elect to attend college, then not including those who didn't apply implies

TABLE 4
Sequence of Decisions Affecting Postsecondary School Choices

Decision and Decisionmaker	Choice	Alternatives
Decision 1 (student)	Application to college	Yes, no College quality
Decision 2 (institution)	Admission	Yes No
Decision 3 (institution)	Financial Aid	Yes, no How much
Decision 4 (student)	School or work	Universities Junior Colleges Work, etc.
Decision 5 (student)	Persistence in college	Persist to degree Drop out

Source: Manski and Wise (1983), *College Choice in America,* Table 2.1, p. 27.
Reprinted by permission, Harvard University Press.

that our estimates may be a biased representation of this probability. (As demonstrated by Garen, 1984, this selection-bias problem is not restricted to discrete choices.) More complete models, as first shown in Soss (1974) and more recently in Venti and Wise (1983), include estimates of the outcomes that a) a student who didn't apply would have applied, and b) the student would or would not have been admitted. Notice, however, that once these counterfactual outcomes have been included, one can raise a similar issue about the financial aid decision, as emphasized by Fuller, et al. (1982).[12] Expanding the decision process further into the past, as pointed out by Bishop (1977) and Abowd (1981), would imply that decisions about high school selection and high school course of study should also be made part of the system.

Conceptually there is no limit to the decisions that should be made part of the endogenous choice set. To capture all of the covariances among such things as application, admission and attendance choices, financial aid expectation, and earnings expectations, an entire system should be estimated simultaneously. As stated by Manski and Wise (1983), however, such a large-scale system would be difficult if not impossible to track, and to date no one has successfully estimated such a system. As exemplified by the modeling in their book, large systems must be broken into separate parts for estimation. (See Ghali, et al., 1977, for an interesting example of comprehensive modeling.)

Biakemore and Low (1983) constructed a model which takes account of two of the decision points in modeling the demand for higher education by individuals: an institution's decision to or not to grant financial aid, and the individual's decision to enroll or not enroll. They develop two equations to model this process. In the first, the enrollment decision is a function of family income, number of family siblings, dependent support, parental education, aptitude, unemployment rate, tuition and fees, number of institutions per capita and the likelihood of a scholarship. In the second, the scholarship decision is determined by the institution as a function of financial need and minority status, scholastic achievement, and institutional supply constraints. For estimation, they use the National Longitudinal Study of High School Seniors in 1972.

As stated by the authors, in estimating the probability of scholarship receipt, a potential sample-selection bias must be considered because only recipients are observed in the sample. If the error terms in the enrollment and scholarship equations are independent, no trouble is caused. But if an unmeasured factor influences both selection rules, the estimated scholarship equation is biased. The estimates derived from fitting the traditional probit function to the censored sample for the scholarship process are biased because the errors cannot be distributed normally (the errors are truncated because they do not include the individuals who are omitted) and they can be expected to correlate with explanatory variables in the equation. Using Heckman's (1976) procedure to adjust for sample-selection bias, they estimate the sample-selection process (the reduced form probability of enrollment), construct a hazard ratio (density to distribution functions based on the reduced form estimates) and use the hazard ratio as the adjustment factor (another independent variable) in the scholarship equation.

After all is said and done, Blakemore and Low conclude that affirmative action programs have had a substantial impact, particularly at the lowest GPA levels where white and nonwhite probabilities of receiving a scholarship differ most; nonwhites being more likely to receive a scholarship.[13] More interesting for my purpose here is their conclusion that prior researchers may have underestimated the income elasticity by ignoring the fact that an increase in income lowers the probability of receiving financial aid, thus offsetting the normal income effect. (See also Ehrenberg and Marcus for analysis of minimum-wage legislation on enrollment decisions.) This conclusion is a confirmation of results obtained by Catsiapis and Robinson (1982).

Catsiapis and Robinson (1982) and Catsiapis (1980) use the National Longitudinal data to model financial aid expected by individuals, including those who decided not to continue with postsecondary education. Catsiapis and Robinson argue that, in order to be observed in the sample of aid recipients, the student has to be both enrolled in college and to have had an expected value of aid exceeding the costs of applying. After correcting for both these sources of selection bias, they conclude:

> The effect of parental income is not apparent unless censoring is taken into account; similarly, the evidence of affirmative action programs is considerably strengthened. Ignoring the selection problem in this case will, therefore, yield an erroneous picture of financial aid available to students in the form of grants and scholarships.
>
> Most studies on the demand for higher education have not taken into account adequately the availability of financial aid. Kohn, Manski and Mundel (1974), for example, made an attempt to forecast the level of financial aid available to students at each of their college options, but since their method failed to yield reasonable results, no account of financial aid was taken in the specification of their model. (p. 366)

Fuller, et al. (1982) further refined the work of Kohn, et al. (1972). Their decision process starts with the student completing high school. The graduate decides among a discrete set of schools and a nonschool alternative. A multinimial logit model expresses the probability that a student will select a given alternative. As originally suggested in Chapman (1977), tuition, scholarships, and living expense are now the direct cost variables considered by the student in this decision. The student is also assumed to consider the cost of forgone earnings while in a post-secondary institution. Parental income and student ability also enter into the decision processes. Using data from the National Longitudinal Study of the High School Class of 1972, scholarship expectations were predicted in a two-equation model which explained college enrollment and the aid received by students who chose to enroll. Earnings expectations were predicted in a single-equation model which explained earnings of students who chose to enter the labor market (see also McMahon and Wagner, 1981). The scholarship model corrected for the selection bias associated with estimation based on only the observable realized scholarships. Arguing from the work of Willis and Rosen (1979) that the empirical evidence on the existence of selection bias in earnings after high school is mixed, the forgone-earnings model was estimated by ordinary-least-squares with an acknowledgement of possible selection bias.

Fuller, et al.'s estimated probability that student t selects any given alternative i from his or her choice set is

$$P_1 = \frac{exp\left(\sum_{k=1}^{25} \beta^k Z_{ti}^k\right)}{\sum_{j=1}^{J} exp\left(\sum_{k=1}^{25} \beta^k Z_{tj}^k\right)}$$

where i is one of the J alternatives ($j = 1, 2, \ldots, J$). For each of these alternatives, $Z_{ij}^1, Z_{ij}^2, \ldots, Z_{ij}^{25}$ is the value of the 25 variables in the system and $\beta^1, \beta^2, \ldots, \beta^{25}$ are the 25 parameters estimated. As demonstrated earlier, from this probability formulation the odds of choosing any alternative i over j can be shown to be a functions of the Z's and β's; i.e., $Ln(P_i/P_j) = (Z_i - Z_j)\beta$. Using this probability formulation, Fuller, et al. found that tuition, dormitory costs, and scholarship parameters associated with four-year colleges are close to one another and close to the tuition estimate for two-year colleges and vocational schools. The anomaly is the two-year college scholarship coefficient, which is larger in absolute value than any of the others. Commuting cost for off-campus students, measured by distance and included only for four-year schools, was negative and significant but small in magnitude. Expected forgone earnings detracted from the desirability of schooling alternatives. Although it was roughly of the same magnitude as the tuition effect, it tended to be slightly smaller for most students. They were also able to confirm Kohn, et al.'s conjecture that the effect of increases in school performance standards on the attractiveness of a school is first positive and then negative, implying that the optimum standard lies somewhere above the student's own ability. They also found that, all else equal, the probability that a student goes to college or a voc-tech institution rises with the percentage of his high school classmates doing likewise. Supporting McPherson's (1978) conclusion, they found that, all else equal, students tend to prefer privately controlled, four-year colleges to other postsecondary alternatives.

To help put into perspective their findings and those of their associates, Manski and Wise (1983) give a series of equivalencies for a student whose family income is $10,000 per year in 1972 dollars. All else equal, they conclude that a $100 decrease in tuition at a four-year college is approximately equivalent to: a $100-per-month increase in scholarship aid at a four-year college; a $100-per-month decrease in dormitory costs at a four-year college; a $250-per-month decrease in expected labor-force earnings; an increase in the average SAT of the college from 200 points below the student's SAT to an average equal to the student's SAT; a decrease in the average SAT of the school from 350 points above the student's SAT to 100 points above the student's SAT; a 30-point increase in the percent of a student's high school classmates who go to college. Also, a $100 decrease in tuition at a four-year college for a student whose family income is $10,000 is approximately equavalent to a $300 per month decrease in tuition at a four-year college for an individual whose family income is $30,000. This actual value in this last comparison, as acknowledged by Manski and Wise, is in part an artifact of their statistical specifications.

Tuition and Financial Aid Policies

The preceding sections reviewed much of the published literature on the college-going behavior of high school graduates. Emphasis was given to empirical studies which provide a descriptive explanation, regression explanations using group data, and discrete choice explanations of the demand for initial enrollment. This literature reflects a movement from explanations which are based only on tuition, income, demographic and other socioeconomic considerations to random-utility models which consider the manner in which costs (tuition effects adjusted for alternative forms of financial aid) are born by the individual. The construction of intricate discrete choice models of enrollment demand at individual institutions (e.g., Ehrenberg and Sherman, 1982, and Miller, 1981) and for sets of institutions (e.g., Manski and Wise, 1983) reveals a modeling component that has not received sufficient attention: namely, the supply conditions facing the student. How do institutions set their tuiton and why do institutions provide financial aid to students?[14] The answer to this question is important to understanding universities and to specifying the proper method of estimating the aid to be expected by potential enrollees.

Rather than specifying a simple utility function, which posits some grand social goal an institution is attempting to achieve by granting financial aid, Abowd (1981 and 1984) provides a market explanation of financial aid decisions. Abowd puts forward the idea that multifaceted schools use all their inputs to produce graduates along with certification, public service, basic and applied research, entertainment, and other outputs which are not unique products of the higher education industry. Unlike other competitive multiproduct suppliers, however, schools need to preserve their tax-exempt status and so do not sell equity stock. As a result schools do not have to follow the whims of the equity market in the allocation of resources. In generating income (from tuition, research grants and contracts, lump-sum subsidies, per student subsidies, income from endowments, and proceeds from direct sales) schools are better able than profit-maximizing firms to allocate resources in accordance with administrators' personal preferences. But competition among institutions may force schools to select cost-minimizing combinations of inputs. It is the restrictions on entry that enable schools to engage in price discrimination through tuition-setting and the granting of aid.

As the first example of the way institutions of higher education may use one activity as an input to another through price discrimination, consider how high-quality private universities ration admission places. These schools may offer admission to some students at a price below what could be realized if places were auctioned off to all qualified applicants. The extent to which observed tuition deviates from what would prevail in an auction may be viewed as a measure of the extent to which students are purchased as inputs to other production processes. This purchasing of students creates an incentive for potential applicants to invest in the acquisition of attributes desired by the schools. It also has implications for the appropriate price to use in estimating the demand for quality higher education. The appropriate price is now the observed tuition plus investment costs incurred by students to qualify for admission, controlling for the other variables known to affect demand. It also implies that curriculum choices made in high school may be endogenous to the system.

Next consider public schools offering admission to state resident students at a price below the price which could be obtained from comparable nonresident students. The selection process here represents a subsidy to the student, assuming residency definitions are based on student location rather than family location. (If residency definitions depend on parent location then the net subsidy depends on the family's tax payment.) Now the relationship between tuition and school quality reveals a community decision concerning how much of the competitive price of education the state will not finance publicly. For higher quality levels, every potential student may not be able to purchase enrollment in a public institution. Student options will be limited by the quality levels offered in the state. To the extent that students migrate to select desirable schools, the correct price to use in valuing the education purchase should include the cost of migration (as is already typical in cross-section studies).

The existence of high levels of quality in a state system can be expected to influence the choices made at all levels and between types of institutions since the public option is subsidized. The greater the diversity of subsidized public schooling options, the less likely it is that any student will find it desirable to forgo the subsidy and enroll in a private institution, unless that institution is willing to buy back some of the tuition, or accept some nonschooling option. Thus, it seems that the existence of subsidized public schools will influence the decision to attend private schools, and the distinction between these two options may influence the decision not to forgo postsecondary schooling altogether.

Abowd's theoretical market construction of the institution's (or state's) reasons for providing financial aid (or subsidies) is an improvement over the simple assumption that institutions such as Stanford or Cornell allocate financial aid on the basis of student quality, gender, or race considerations, because they derive utility from it. Unfortunately, in his empirical work Abowd was not able to model and estimate the many different products and services offered by a multiproduct university and the way these products and services affect financial aid decisions. In addition, he really never addressed how primarily undergraduate teaching institutions (which have little or no ability to use other activities to subsidize enrollments) compete with diversified universities (which have many other activities they can use to subsidize enrollments). Within Abowd's framework it should be possible to address and identify a change in the demand for one university service resulting from a change in another service. For example, a change in the demand for undergraduate enrollment at a quality institution may result from a reduction in demand for its research if overhead from research is used to subsidize student enrollment or if student quality is an input to the research of the institution. In such a model the constraint on available funds for grants and aid are not exogenous but are part of the system that determines institutional well being.

Summary

As my review of the literature makes clear, since the 1960s many researchers have estimated the demand for enrollment. Their work has been concerned with the demand for places within all private institutions, an individual private institution, all public institutions, an individual public institutions, as well as in all institutions of higher education. Demand curves for four-year institutions have been considered along with the demand for community colleges. Most of these studies have been interested in estimating the effect of costs and income on respective demand. Thus these studies can be used to shed light on the debate over the appropriate financing of higher education. As stated by Hearn and Longanecker (1985) the traditional argument for direct tuition subsidies to public higher education institutions is based on the belief that this is the least expensive way to achieve equitable access. Advocates of private education argue, however, that subsidized tuiton at public schools is fine for those who would not otherwise attend postsecondary institutions but across the board tuition subsidies and the expansion of public institutions puts private institutions at a competitive disadvantage in their traditional function of providing specialized education and training (see Anderson, 1975, and McPherson, 1978). Based on evidence such as that reported here, a growing number of economists have also entered this debate claiming that low postsecondary tuition as a public policy is both inefficient and inequitable (see Hansen, 1982, Hansen and Weisbrod, 1969, Hoenack, 1971, Windham, 1976, Manski and Wise, 1983, and Weiler, 1984). I will summarize what can be learned from studies of the demand for enrollment places.

Community and Other Two-year Institutions

While the tuition-cost elasticity of demand for community colleges and postsecondary vocational schools has been shown in many studies to be highly inelastic, the income effect appears highly elastic and able to swamp the cost effect. In addition, the tuition elasticity appears to greatly increase in absolute value as tuition approaches zero. At low tuition, low income, and low ability levels, a percentage increase in net tuition costs as the result of the removal of subsidized tuition can be expected to result in a greater percentage decrease in community college and vocational school enrollments. Higher tuition at these institutions would most likely result in greatly lower revenue and fewer low-income students in attendance. Given that high-income students have not opted for the community college alternative, it may be inferred that school closings would follow. There is, however, no direct empirical evidence to support this inference.

Four-Year Institutions

The price elasticity of four-year public institutions is possibly in the range of -0.6 to -1.2. Price increases matched by equal increases in financial aid or reduction in other costs such as dormitory fees will probably produce little change in the demand for four-year enrollments. A percentage increase in net costs at four-year institutions can be expected to result in an approximate equal percentage decrease in enrollments with little if any effect on revenue.

All else equal, potential students prefer private to public four-year institutions and are willing to pay a premium to attend private schools. The size of that premium is related to family income and financial aid availability. There is some evidence that the cross-elasticity between private and public institutions is positive but its magnitude may be highly sensitive to the institutions considered. While higher tuition costs may not affect the decision to enroll in college, as costs raise students may choose less expensive college options. The net tuition elasticity for private schools is probably greater (in absolute value) than that of like-quality but less expensive public schools.

Although low-ability students have a low probability of applying to four-year colleges, there is a high probability that if they apply they will be admitted. For example, Manski and Wise (1983) found that "People at the twenty-fifth percentile level in class rank and with a verbal and math SAT score totaling a mere 700 have only a 0.14 probability of applying to a four-year college, but would nonetheless have a 0.74 probability of admission to an average quality school were they to apply" (pp. 6-7).

Graduate Education

While Weiler (1984) claims that the demand for graduate education and professional training have a price elasticity of zero, there is evidence to the contrary. For example, in the case of medical schools, Sloan (1971) found a significant price response that suggests that "each dollar reduction in price may be expected on the average to generate from 4 to 14 applicants" (p. 481). In the case of MBA enrollments, Alexander and Frey (1984) report small but in some cases significant tuition effects.

Similarly, McClain, et al. (1984) found that the probability that an applicant accepts a position in Boston University's MBA program may be affected greatly by the amount of financial aid awarded. More recently Etherington and Smart (1986), in a large-sample study, found that next to completion of the undergraduate degree, receipt of financial aid had the greatest positive effect on graduate school enrollment. The demand for graduate and professional education appears sensitive to costs.

Older Students (Continuing Education)

The growing proportion of older individuals who enroll in nondegree, occupational programs is a new development of the 1970s. These students appear to respond to economic variables. Changes in tuition and income affect them much in the same way they affect younger students. Whether or not four-year colleges and postsecondary vocational schools are closer substitutes for older adults than for younger students is not clear.

Implications for Institutional Pricing Strategies

The above conclusions suggest that, at least in the case of some classes of public four-year institutions, the demand for places must be inelastic with respect to tuition. For instance Weiler states that such is the case at the University of Minnesota. The question to be raised, therefore, is: Why are these institutions and their overseeing state boards leery about raising their tuitions? (For noneconomic discussion of this question, see Hearn and Longanecker, 1985.) If enrollment demand is inelastic with respect to tuition, and the eligible population is relatively fixed, raising tuition implies fewer students enrolled but higher total revenue as long as subsidies to the institutions are not tied directly to total enrollments.

The Impact of Changing Levels of Financial Resources on the Structure of Colleges and Universities

JOSEPH FROOMKIN

There is no right level of resources required by American colleges and universities because these institutions do not have a clearly defined mission: They accommodate under one roof a teaching function and a scientific function, and no clear-cut standard has been set for the desirable level of activity for either function. No uniform curriculum is mandated in the United States for baccalaureate or advanced degrees. Higher education institutions set their requirements for graduation and decide on the level of resources to be expended for instruction. Nor is there any consensus about the level, content, and quality of research that colleges and universities are expected to perform. For an individual institution, the research and development effort is evaluated by fellow academics and, for the sector as a whole, it is judged by academia's ability to meet national goals for the advancement of scientific knowledge.

In this unstructured environment, it is not possible to set absolute standards for financial resources needed by American colleges and universities. Instead, one can only compare levels of resources which were available to higher education in the recent past and document where university administrators economized when the level of these resources diminished.

Trends in Resources

An Overview of the Past Forty Years

From the end of World War II until 1970, the higher education sector experienced very rapid growth. The number of degree-credit students quadrupled between 1946 and 1970—from 2.0 million in 1946 to 3.6

million in 1960 and 7.9 million in 1970. Enrollments grew at some 6 percent a year compounded during this period. Since 1970, the growth rate has decelerated to 2.4 percent, on the average. Between 1980 and 1984, the number of students in this category was practically stable, and in 1984 their number declined to 11.0 million.*

Non-degree-credit student enrollment grew at an even faster pace than degree-credit enrollment during the forty years since World War II. Although there were so few nondegree students in the late 1940s that it was believed inessential to count them, by the end of the 1950s they made up five percent of the total enrollment. By 1960, nondegree students numbered two hundred thousand and accounted for eight percent of the enrollment in higher education. Their share of enrollment is currently ten percent of the total. In 1984, 1.2 million nondegree students were enrolled in colleges and universities.

The growth in enrollments during the past forty years was made possible by a spectacular growth in the current resources made available to higher education. These increased some seventy-fold, in current dollars, between 1946 and 1984. In 1946, the total current revenues of institutions of higher education were reported to be $1.2 billion. In 1984, they were $86.1 billion. In constant prices, the increase was also impressive. We estimate that the 1946 revenues are the equivalent of $9.4 billion in 1984 prices. Thus the growth of revenues in real terms was more than nine-fold.

The resources expended per student on education have kept up very well despite the fast rate of growth. A number of studies have documented that the amount spent per full-time equivalent (FTE) student (a statistic derived by counting three part-time students as the equivalent of one full-time student) did not change significantly during the period of rapid growth or the current period of stable enrollments for 1966 to 1974, see Froomkin, 1978.

---

*In this chapter all financial and enrollment figures are for the academic year ending in June of the year cited. Statistics prior to 1966 are from the U.S. Bureau of the Census, *Historical Statistics.* For later years data are based on U.S. Department of Health, Education and Welfare, *Higher Education General Information Survey,* 1966-79, and U.S. Department of Education, *Higher Education General Information Survey,* 1980-85. Enrollment figures are from the opening fall enrollment of that year. Income statistics are from the U.S. Department of Commerce, *Survey of Current Business* for each appropriate year. The higher education price indexes, developed by D. Kent Halstead (Halstead, 1985a) were used to convert current to constant dollars. The series is updated and published currently by Research Associates of Washington, D.C. Additional sources are listed with the tables and described in the text.

Tuition and fees receipts grew at a more modest pace, from $925 million in 1946 (some $8 billion in current prices) to $19.7 billion in 1984, a mere 2.5-fold increase in the face of six-fold increase in total enrollment. Average tuition and fees grew more slowly than enrollments as a higher proportion of students attended low-tuition schools. Starting with the end of World War II, the high-tuition private sector enrolled a lower proportion of students every year until 1970. While half of the students in American colleges and universities were enrolled in private institutions in 1946, roughly one in four attend private institutions today.

After the end of World War II, states stepped up their appropriations to public colleges and universities thus enabling state schools to provide the majority of new places for a growing enrollment. State appropriations for the operation of colleges and universities increased from $225 million (around $2.0 billion in today's purchasing power) in 1946 to $23 billion in 1984.

Research and development and related contract work performed predominantly by universities grew even faster than other items of current revenue. In 1946 higher education institutions were paid $87 million, representing eight percent of their current revenues, to do research. In 1984, $12.0 billion of current revenues were derived from this source. After adjustment for the intervening price change, research receipts grew sixteen times in constant prices during that time.

Comparisons of the income statements of colleges and universities for 1946 and 1984 cannot be made with great precision because until 1966 financial statistics were not collected carefully and the earlier data may be incomplete or inaccurate.

Recent Trends in Revenue Sources of Higher Education

The revenues of postsecondary institutions are conventionally reported under the following headings: tuition and fees, appropriations of different levels of government (the most important of these are state appropriations to higher education institutions), research and development grants and contracts from different levels of government (the federal government provides the lion's share of these), private gifts and contracts, and endowment income. In addition, the revenues from sales of services related to education (mostly dormitory income), sales and services of auxiliary enterprises, the revenue from university-run hospitals, and from miscellaneous activities are also listed as revenue sources.

Revenue trends of institutions of higher education come into sharper focus if revenues from peripheral activities, such as dormitories, hospitals, and miscellaneous activities are netted out from the total. What remains are the moneys used for the principal functions of colleges and universities: instruction and research. For convenience, we call this figure adjusted current revenues (ACRs). The ACRs are further disaggregated into two parts: the money received for contract research, and the rest.

Tuition and fee receipts:

The average level of tuition charged to students depends upon (1) the share of students in public or private enrollment, since tuition levels are much lower in the public sector, and (2) the proportion of students attending part-time, since these students pay less tuition per capita.

In the twenty years since 1966, the year when sufficiently detailed data became available to calculate meaningful ratios, the amount of tuition charged per FTE student has been highly correlated to the level of per-capita disposable income (the regression equation for the whole period has an R^2 of over .9). Throughout most of the period, the average tuition was equal to twenty percent of the per-capita disposable income, with private institutions charging around forty-six percent and public institutions eleven percent of the income (see Table 1).

TABLE 1

Tuition and Fees per FTE Student in Current and Constant Dollars
and Percent of per-Capita Disposable Income

	1966	1970	1976	1979	1984
Current Dollars FTE					
All	573	749	1,043	1,233	2,175
Public	280	379	533	690	1,197
Private	1,148	1,537	2,392	3,005	5,381
Constant 1967 Dollars per FTE					
All	603	578	589	568	668
Public	302	313	301	318	368
Private	1,208	1,270	1,350	1,385	1,653
Percent of per Capita Disposable Income					
All	22.0	21.0	19.5	17.6	20.8
Public	10.7	11.4	10.8	9.9	11.5
Private	44.1	46.1	46.6	43.0	51.6

Source: See footnote, p. 190, and *The National Income and Product Accounts of the United States.*

The four-fold increase in tuition per FTE student in the eighteen years between 1966 and 1984 brought the institution only ten percent more resources per student. In 1979 the institutions did not anticipate the high rate of inflation and set the tuitions and fees too low. In 1984 private schools may have set their tuition higher than was warranted by past trends, possibly because they anticipated a higher rate of inflation.

The contribution of tuition and fees to adjusted institutional revenues net of receipts of grants and contracts for research and development is extremely stable over the years. The share of tuition and fees has remained practically constant as a percent of nonresearch ACRs in each type of institution. In public institutions it accounted for seventeen to twenty percent, and in private schools it neared or exceeded sixty percent of that figure (see Table 2).

TABLE 2
Tuition and Fees as Proportion (in percent) of Non-Research Revenues

	1966	1970	1976	1979	1984
All	35	33	29	30	33
Public	19	19	18	17	20
Private	61	61	59	61	60

Source: See footnote, p. 190.

The net contribution of tuition to institutional resources is reduced by awards of scholarships from unrestricted funds (other scholarship moneys from either state or government moneys channelled through institutions or specially endowed funds for this purpose cannot be used for any other purpose). In public schools, scholarships paid with unrestricted funds eroded the tuition and fees receipts by nearly four percent in 1966 and six percent in 1984. In 1976 and 1979, scholarships constituted a higher proportion of tuition than in 1984. This implies that in 1984 state schools were short of funds and cut down on scholarships. In private schools, scholarship funds from unrestricted sources increased consistently from under 8 to 10.5 percent during the same period. The percentage of tuition and fees remitted increased especially rapidly during the last five years (see Table 3).

The future level of tuition and fee receipts depends upon the rate of growth of the economy, the share of personal income taken by taxes, and, of course, enrollment levels. If and when the U.S. economy reduces unemployment levels to around four percent and the productivity of the labor force resumes its historical upward trend, some of the decline in

tuition and fees caused by projected future declines in enrollment may
be made up.

TABLE 3
Tuition Remission from Unrestricted Funds by Type of Higher Education
Institution for Selected Years, 1966 to 1984

	Millions of Dollars			Percent of Tuition Revenue		
	All	Public	Private	All	Public	Private
1966	184	39	145	6.7	4.4	7.8
1970	326	105	220	7.3	6.0	8.2
1976	687	276	410	8.2	7.9	8.8
1979	887	328	559	8.2	7.4	8.7
1984	1,738	518	1,220	8.8	6.4	10.5

Source: See footnote, p. 190.

Government appropriations:

One and half times as much current revenue comes from government
appropriations as from tuition and fees. Nine out of ten dollars provided
by governments come from state sources and benefit state schools almost
exclusively. Between 1966 and 1984, state appropriations to higher education increased nearly nine-fold. After taking account of the intervening inflation, the purchasing power of the state appropriation (deflated
by the Higher Education Price Index) was still two-and-a-half times
higher in 1984 than it was in 1946.

State appropriations since 1966 averaged roughly $1,000 in constant
1967 dollars ($3,500 in 1984 prices) per FTE student in public institu-
tions. This level of support has increasingly taxed the resources of the
states. Slightly under seven percent of the total revenue of states, or ten
percent of the tax revenues, was allocated to higher education during
the 1946-1984 period (see Table 4).

This rather impressive record failed to meet the expectations of
administrators of institutions of higher education who hoped that the
share of revenues, which rose from 2.6 to 4.9 percent between 1946 and
1966 and finally levelled off at 6.7 percent in 1976, would continue rising
to meet the growing needs and aspirations of state schools. An increasing
number of state legislatures have become more niggardly with respect to
their allocations to colleges and universities. Hard pressed for resources
to fund other programs, states with declining revenues did not hesitate
to cut appropriations to higher education during the last recession.

TABLE 4
Proportion of State Revenues Allocated to Higher Education Institutions,
Total and per FTE Student, Selected Years 1946-1984

	Percent of total rev.	Appropriation in current $	Appropriation in 1967 $	Per FTE
1946	n.a.	225	600	n.a.
1966	4.9	2,707	2,854	793
1970	6.5	5,669	4,782	933
1976	6.7	11,741	6,626	1,018
1979	6.7	15,837	7,301	1,073
1984	6.7	23,635	7,172	1,071

Source: U.S. Bureau of the Census, *State Government Finances;* see also footnote, p. 190.

National averages fail to depict the plight of institutions in roughly half the states. Between 1979 and 1985, twenty-eight states and the District of Columbia reduced their subsidy per FTE student in higher education. In five jurisdictions, Alabama, the District of Columbia, Florida, South Carolina, and Virginia, an increase in tuition more than offset the decline in the purchasing power of the state appropriations. The table below reproduces statistics for twenty-three states where appropriations per FTE decline as well. But in roughly half of the rest of the states tuition increases closed the gap only partially. In some states, tuition remained constant (see Table 5).

Generally the decline in support did not come about as a result of a significant cut in the proportion of tax resources allocated to higher education. Most states with declining support to higher education were either in the Northeast, in the industrial Midwest, or the agricultural Midwest. The three exceptions were Alaska, California, and Nevada, where local politics either put a ceiling on tax revenues or cut support to higher education. The reasons state appropriations per FTE student declined were that (1) states where economic activity was low reduced their appropriations, (2) states that benefited from the oil boom raised their appropriations very little or not at all, and (3) catch-up increases in low-expenditure Southern states failed to make up for losses elsewhere.

The variation of state appropriations for higher education in the past few years has highlighted once again these institutions' vulnerability to economic conditions. The proportion of state resources allocated to educational institutions has remained pretty constant. Thus, such states as Texas, which experienced dramatic increases in well-being, did not increase the proportion of revenue allocated to education during the period when oil prices were high, although their total funds for education increased. During the current funding cycle, as the price of oil declined causing a drop in state revenues, Texas imposed the same proportional funding cuts on institutions of higher education as it did on other functions of the state government.

TABLE 5

Trends in State Allocations per FTE Student to Higher Education
(in 1985 dollars) in States with Declining Support, 1979/80-1984/5

	Decline of Appropriation	Decline after Tuition Change	Percent Change in Tax Revenues
Alaska	502	113	−5.2
Arkansas	135	112	+0.1
California	298	−	−0.07
Florida	130	−	−0.4
Idaho	450	554	−0.3
Iowa	486	487	+0.1
Massachusetts	836	836	+0.4
Michigan	546	289	−1.2
Minnesota	623	368	−1.4
Missouri	650	465	−1.4
Nebraska	541	626	−0.09
Nevada	854	802	−0.8
New Hampshire	338	114	−0.5
North Dakota	585	570	−1.4
Ohio	311	125	−0.7
Oregon	164	31	−1.5
Pennsylvania	586	403	−0.1
South Carolina	266	−	+0.9
South Dakota	988	1,002	−2.1
Virginia	33	−	−0.5
Washington	426	487	−3.5
Wisconsin	737	924	−0.8
Washington, D.C.	211	126	−0.9
Wyoming	506	810	−2.4
United States	112	186	−0.1

Source: Halstead (1985b).

Government appropriations other than those by states play a very minor role in the current revenues of institutions of higher education. The major share of federal appropriations goes to Howard, Gallaudet College, and U.S. Service Schools. From 1979 on, these appropriations amounted to half a billion dollars a year in 1967 prices, a small fraction of the federal funds channelled to universities. About fifteen percent of these moneys, seventy-five million dollars a year, went to private schools. Federal moneys accounted for eight percent of the net revenues of public colleges and universities. Their share in private budgets was insignificant, a little over one percent.

Local expenditures, which include the District of Columbia's outlays for its higher education institutions, grew during the immediate postwar period when enrollment was booming, but they actually declined in real terms between 1976 and 1979. The decline was caused by the increased responsibility for higher eduation assumed by the states in New York, Illinois, Michigan, and California. The financial difficulties of big cities in these states caused states to take over city-controlled institutions.

By 1979, local expenditures, which were mostly for local junior colleges, had stabilized in real terms. In real terms they were slightly lower in 1984 than in 1979 (see Table 6).

TABLE 6
Federal and Local Government Appropriations (in Millions of Dollars)
for Selected Years, 1946-1984

| | Current Dollars | | | | | |
| | Federal | | | Local | | |
	All	Public	Private	All	Public	Private
1946	197	n.a.	n.a.	31	n.a.	n.a.
1966	560	460	100	296	295	1
1970	511	417	94	727	706	22
1976	906	782	185	1,419	1,419	3
1979	1,173	1,000	173	1,336	1,334	2
1984	1,426	1,216	210	1,826	1,824	2
	Constant 1967 Dollars					
1946	524	n.a.	n.a.	82	n.a.	n.a.
1966	589	484	105	311	310	1
1970	457	374	84	651	632	19
1976	511	441	71	801	799	2
1979	540	461	80	615	615	*
1984	438	374	64	561	561	*

*=less than one million dollars.
Source: See footnote, p. 190.

Gifts and endowments:

There is no way to estimate precisely the amount of resources from private gifts which add to the current income of colleges and universities. In the first place, the National Center for Education statistics changed the definition in the Higher Education General Information Survey (HEGIS) survey of revenues included under the rubric of gifts. In some years, gift moneys only were reported, in others, gifts and private contracts for research and development were lumped under this heading. In addition, a number of state-supported schools have established special foundations which are the principal recipients of private gifts, thus hiding them effectively from the scrutiny of state legislators.

There is no good way to obtain independent estimates for all of higher education. Statistics provided by a private source, the Council For Financial Aid to Private Education and the Association of Independent Schools collect information from only half of all institutions. In 1969/70, a year when the National Center published statistics on a comparable basis, the council reported $825 million dollars in gifts to support current operations. That same year, the National Center for Education Statistics reported a total of $671 million in gifts in their statistics of current revenue. The survey listed $147 million in gifts to public schools for current operations, while HEGIS statistics put this figure at $58 million. The survey's figure of $524 million in gifts to private schools was relatively close to the $559 million reported by the private sector.

In 1984, the council reported that $1,014 million of gifts for current operations was received by public institutions. This figure is close to the one reported by HEGIS which claims to include private contract revenues. In the case of private institutions, the council's $1,694 million figure is much lower than the one in HEGIS. One suspects that the reports of the council are not consistent from year to year.

The figures for private gifts shown in Table 7 were derived by subtracting from private gifts and contracts listed in HEGIS the amounts reported by the National Science Foundation for private sources for research and development for the years 1966, 1976, 1979 and 1984. HEGIS lumped private gifts and contracts under one heading in those years. In 1970, the actual amount reported in HEGIS can be used, this being the year when only gifts were supposed to be reported. It is possible that our figures may include some moneys for training or research, and they certainly do not include moneys collected by public institutions through separate foundations.

In all probability, gifts to public institutions should be doubled to take into account moneys which are channelled through alumni foundations outside of state control. Even so, these gifts do not account for more than three percent of adjusted revenue in 1970 and four percent today. It should be noted, however, that the public schools' share of total gifts to schools increased from ten to eleven percent during the 1970s to twenty-eight percent in 1984. State schools were successful in convincing donors that their needs were no longer being met by public funds alone and that they were deserving of private support. Is this the beginning of a trend?

Gifts to private schools doubled in real terms in the past eighteen years, a rate which exceeded the 1.5-times growth in real gross national product. This growth is consistent with what was reported in the past and should continue in the future. Roughly one dollar in six which is spent on instruction in the private sector comes from gifts. This ratio has remained fairly constant over time (see Table 7).

TABLE 7
Private Gifts to Institutions of Higher Education (in millions of dollars)
for Selected Years, 1966-1984

	Current Dollars			Constant 1967 Dollars		
	All	Public	Private	All	Private	Public
1966	463	65	327	486	68	343
1970	617	58	559	510	48	462
1976	1,512	116	1,396	853	66	787
1979	1,924	480	1,414	887	184	652
1984	3,328	937	2,391	1,022	287	734

Endowment income:

That part of endowment income which is used to pay for current expenses has grown more slowly than gift income. Nevertheless, it nearly doubled in real terms between 1966 and 1984. Although it grew most rapidly in both current and constant dollars in the public sector, its part of the budget is still less than one percent, even after research is netted out. In private institutions, endowment income in most years contributed slightly more than nine percent of current revenues, and thus played a more important part in the finances of these institutions (see Table 8).

In the past few years, the contribution of endowment to current revenues has grown apace. This is due to the way these contributions are programmed by institutions of higher education. Starting in 1966, institutions increasingly adopted a formula for withdrawals from endowment which took into account the erosion of the endowments' purchasing power because of the increase in prices and allowed transfers on the basis of a set percentage of the average change in the value of the endowment in the past five years.

TABLE 8
Endowment Income of Higher Education Institutions (in millions of dollars)
for Selected Years 1966-1984

| | Current Dollars | | | Constant 1967 Dollars | | |
	All	Public	Private	All	Public	Private
1966	276	24	253	290	25	266
1970	447	57	590	401	51	529
1976	687	96	591	387	54	333
1979	986	154	832	455	71	383
1984	1,874	315	1,559	575	97	478

Source: See footnote, p. 190.

What with inflation moderating, the stock market booming, and interest rates declining between 1982 and 1987, the value of most endowments has increased substantially, doubling on the average. Of course, they declined somewhat during the October 1987 market crash. Nevertheless, having scaled down their provisions for future inflation, most private school financial officers now anticipate that their endowments will provide one and a half times as much money to current revenue as they did in the past few years.

Other revenue:

Very little can be said about other revenue. This chapter will not deal with the revenues from auxiliary enterprises or hospitals which roughly equal expenses. The reporting of other revenue items is probably not consistent from year to year. Revenues from educational departments, auxiliary services, and other miscellaneous sources grew at roughly the same rate as all other revenues—8.7 times in current dollars and 2.5 times in constant dollars—between 1967 and 1984.

Such revenues increased somewhat faster in private institutions than in public colleges and universities. The share of other revenue in private institutions doubled—from 7.5 percent to 14.6 percent of adjusted current revenues. It fluctuated around the six percent level in public institutions. More recently, from 1979 to 1984, these revenues increased a little faster than the prices paid by institutions.

Grants and contracts and research and development:

Grants and contracts play a lesser role in the current revenues of institutions of higher education today than they did in the 1950s and 1960s. Their share of revenue decreased from twenty-two to sixteen percent in all institutions. This decline in importance is due primarily to the failure of grants and contracts to grow at the same pace as other parts of the adjusted current revenues of higher education institutions.

The slow-down in research and development outlays by the federal government, the main provider of funds in this area, was first noted with alarm at the end of the 1960s. What was deplored then was the stabilization of the level of the grants, rather than their decline. Since then, the purchasing power of research and development moneys available to higher education institutions did decline slightly in some years, but generally these declines were made up during the following budget cycle.

Current concerns of the higher education research community fall under two headings: (1) In the administration budget, defense research and development is scheduled to increase much faster than nondefense activities. The Reagan administration policies to fund generously military development, test, and evaluation and to curtail development in nondefense areas is causing some apprehension; (2) The possible across-the-board cuts which may be made to balance the budget could have serious consequences for the research effort at colleges and universities. Despite the lip service to basic research, there is a general feeling on campuses that the situation of academic research and development in science and engineering is likely to get worse rather than better as the administration's projections are not likely to be translated into appropriations.

Two series are often cited in describing the role of research and development in university budgets, one from the Financial HEGIS, the other from the National Science Foundation, Survey of Science Resources Series, *Academic Science, R&D Funds.* HEGIS reports moneys both for research and development in science and nonscience fields and for other government services, such as traineeships and nonresearch activities. The survey of science resources reports separately on research and development expenditures by institutions of higher education. A comparison of the two series for the past ten years reveals that, on the average, sixty percent of the grants and contracts are for scientific research and development (see Table 9).

The federal government dominates both the contract and grant funds reported by colleges and universities and the research and devel-

TABLE 9

Grants and Contracts in Current and Constant (1967) Prices (in millions of dollars)
and Share of Science Research and Development for Selected Years, 1966-1984

	Current	Constant	Share of Science R & D
1966	2,419	2,565	58
1970	3,263	2,735	58
1976	5,225	3,009	61
1979	7,198	3,401	64
1984	12,000	3,858	59

Source: See footnote, p. 190.

opment expenditures of colleges and universities reported by the National
Science Foundation. Nearly eighty percent of contracts and grants come
from federal sources, and the federal government contributes nearly
seventy percent of research and development moneys (see Table 10).

TABLE 10

Amounts (in millions of current dollars) of Grants and Contracts
and Research and Development and Reported Percentage of Federal Share

	Grants and Contracts		Research and Development	
	Millions of $	% Federal	Millions of $	% Federal
1970	2,643	81	1,647	71
1976	4,525	86	2,511	67
1979	5,715	79	3,595	67
1984	9,475	79	4,096	67

Source: Research and development figures are from National Science Foundation (1981).
Figures for 1984 are from an advance release of the same series. See also footnote, p. 190.

By contrast, state and local government shares declined. The proportion of research and development financed by the institutions' own
funds remained constant. And industry's contribution increased faster
than funds from other sources. Nevertheless, the role of industry in
research and development at universities is still minor: Its share grew
from three to five percent of the science research and development
budget between 1973 and 1984.

In the fifteen years since 1970, the share of different disciplines in
sciences and engineering in the research and development budgets has

remained fairly constant. The life sciences—the principal interest of the National Institutes of Health and a field where there is a great deal of excitement—claimed more than half of the resources in each of the last fifteen years. Engineering, somewhat neglected in the mid-1970s, has staged a comeback since that time: fourteen percent of the research and development budget was allocated to engineering disciplines both in 1970 and now.

A somewhat larger share of research and development budgets went to environmental sciences in 1984 than in 1970. The fastest growing item was computer sciences, though it still takes up only a small share of the budget. The proportion of the budget allocated to physical sciences declined between 1970 and 1976. It has gained since then, but by 1984 it had not yet regained the share of funding it commanded in 1970. The big losers were psychology, social sciences, and other sciences not separately listed, whose share declined substantially after 1970 (see Table 11).

TABLE 11
Percent of Total Research and Development Outlays
by Discipline for Selected Years 1970-1984

	1970	*1976*	*1979*	*1984*
Engineering	13.4	11.6	14.3	14.2
Physical sciences	13.2	10.1	11.2	11.7
Environmental sciences	5.4	7.7	8.4	7.6
Mathematics	—	1.4	1.5	1.5
Computer sciences	3.0	1.5	1.8	2.6
Life sciences	51.3	56.5	52.8	54.2
Psychology	2.5	2.1	1.9	1.7
Social & other sciences N.E.C.	11.0	9.5	8.0	6.4

Source: Research and development figures are from National Science Foundation (1981). Figures for 1984 are from an advance release of the same series.

The same source reports that despite the drastic restructuring of federal priorities in the last five years, the share of university research devoted to basic research, as contrasted to research and development, hardly changed at all: two-thirds of the higher education institutions' activities were devoted to basic research both in 1979 and 1984.

The scientific community's contention that research and development budgets are inadequate is based on the slow growth of these budgets, rather than their decline. In constant dollars, the scientific research and development activity funded by moneys other than those provided by the university itself increased some fifty percent in the years 1966 to

1984. During the period 1979 to 1984, the level of research appears to have been maintained, in constant prices, in all disciplines except the social sciences and sciences not elsewhere classified.

Why There Is Talk of a Financial Crisis

A superficial summary of the financial trends in the current revenues of higher education belies the pervasive talk of a financial crisis. Most items of current revenue have held up well, and their share in total revenue has not changed substantially. Nor are there any grounds for alarm when one looks at the financial conditions of higher education in another way, comparing the current revenues available per FTE student in 1966 and 1984. The resources available per FTE student have remained relatively level ever since 1970 in the public sector and have actually increased in the private sector (see Table 12).

TABLE 12
Resources Net of Research per FTE Student
by Type of Institution, for Selected Years, 1966-1980

	1966	1970	1976	1979	1980
All Institutions					
Current dollars	1,548	1,982	3,223	4,339	6,401
Constant 1967 $	1,625	1,775	1,919	2,000	1,967
Public Institutions					
Current dollars	1,391	1,832	2,965	4,017	5,747
Constant 1967 $	1,464	1,642	1,673	1,852	1,766
Private Institutions					
Current dollars	1,876	2,385	4,075	5,286	8,251
Constant 1967 $	1,975	2,370	2,300	2,437	2,535

Source: See footnote, p. 190.

The reason for the unease among administrators and faculty lies not in the resources they command, but in the prices which they pay for resources whose prices the university can influence: wages and salaries to professional staff.

Trends in Prices Paid for Inputs

During the years after World War II, educational institutions' costs increased faster than such common indicators of price change as the consumer price index (CPI) or the deflator used to calculate constant dollar values of the gross national product. This is no longer the case. Since 1971, the price of goods and services purchased by institutions and the CPI have tracked each other very closely. This was achieved by keeping down the salaries of the professional staff. These lagged behind the CPI by nearly twenty percent by the end of 1984. Professional salaries also fell behind total nonagricultural earnings during the past ten years (see Table 13). Since 1985 professionals in higher education have received wage increases which exceeded the rise in consumer prices.

TABLE 13
Professional Wages in Higher Education,
Selected Years 1970-1984 (index 1967 = 100)

	1970	1976	1980	1984
Professional Wages	121.4	161.6	202.1	266.6
Nonagricultural Wages	117.7	172.2	230.8	288.7
Consumer price index	116.3	170.5	246.8	311.1

Source: Halstead (1985a) and U.S. Department of Labor (1986).

Shrinking real incomes of professional staffs made it possible for both the resources per student and the level of research to be safe-guarded, on the average, during this difficult decade. From 1979 to 1984, as enrollments grew very slowly, the amount of money available to colleges and universities remained fairly constant in real terms. Those institutions and state-wide systems that had to learn to operate with less money each year found this a particularly difficult period. Even institutions whose current revenues increased did not feel affluent, since hardly any of them experienced an influx of funds at all comparable to that of the 1960s.

Slower Enrollment Growth

The financial adjustments required by a slow-down in the growth of enrollments in the late 1960s and early 1970s were documented in two studies by Earl F. Cheit (1971 and 1973). The first study documented the financial difficulties of a number of public and private institutions which were running deficits and did not cover current expenses. The surprising finding of the second study was that all the higher education institutions surveyed, including those that had been in financial difficulties two years previously, had managed to bring their expenditures and revenues into a state of precarious balance. This balance was achieved through an unprecedented cut in the rate of growth of expenditures per student, down, in real terms, from 4.0 percent a year, to 0.5 percent.

Clark Kerr, the former Chancellor of the University of California and then-Chairman of the Carnegie Commission on Higher Education, noted in his introduction to Cheit's (1973) study that this low rate of growth could not be sustained indefinitely without loss of quality. Cheit documented that these savings were through (1) the elimination of possibly marginal programs, (2) selective cutbacks in the number of faculty positions, and, (3) most important, general parsimony, especially in setting levels of faculty remuneration.

These conditions appear to have prevailed over the next twelve years. Between 1979 and 1984, the most recent five-year period for which financial data are available, instructional costs per student did not increase at all in real terms, and as the first part of this study documented, resources per student devoted to instruction remained constant. This 'miracle' was achieved by keeping faculty wages down.

Faculty wages had failed to keep up with average earnings in the United States since the early 1970s. Until then, the challenge facing administrators and department chairman was to recruit sufficient suitable staff to accommodate increasing numbers of students. In the mid-1970s, enrollments began to grow at a slower pace, and the demand for faculty slackened. Just as tuition receipts failed to reach expected levels, utility bills made unexpected demands upon institutions' budgets. The increase in the price of energy added one to two percent to the current expense budgets of colleges and universities.

Concurrently, tighter rules for reimbursement of overhead for government contracts reduced the resources available for faculty salaries or the maintenance of support activities. At the University of Chicago, one of the few institutions forthright enough to report the share of faculty salaries paid by government grants and contracts, the proportion of faculty salaries paid by this source of income declined from twenty-five percent of faculty compensation in 1972 to fourteen percent in 1980 (Gray, 1986a).

Impact of Slowdown in Economic Growth

The recent period of high unemployment and slow economic growth in the nation impacted educational institutions even more seriously. In 1977, a study I directed projected revenues for the period 1980 to 1985 for higher education institutions (Froomkin and McCully). In the public sector, the projected tuition level per FTE student for 1985 was expected to amount to $1,328 (in 1984 prices), and state aid per FTE student was projected at $4,594 (also in 1984 prices) for a full-employment economy where productivity grew at two and a half percent a year. The actual amounts for that year were $1,197 and $3,530 respectively. The difference between the total of projected tuition and state aid and the actual receipts amount to twenty-five percent of public institutions' budgets. These two revenue sources depend upon the level of economic activity and, while their relationship to economic variables did not change significantly, the shortfall was due to the poor performance of the economy.

The growth of tuition levels (in real terms) in private institutions was also kept down by high unemployment and the failure of productivity to increase. The average tuition level per FTE student was $5,750 in 1984, 6.4 percent less than projected. The shortfall reduced instructional revenues of private colleges and universities by 4 percent of their current revenue. An equal amount was lost because of the shortfall in gifts and endowment income.

Patterns of Cutbacks

It is possible to describe a pattern for cutbacks in institutions with shrinking resources. In those cases where resources were reduced less than twenty-five percent per FTE student: (1) Either the number of faculty members was frozen or the size of the faculty was allowed to shrink through attrition; (2) faculty salaries were allowed to lag behind the increase in the price level or the increase in real salaries of all professional workers; (3) tighter cost controls were introduced for all parts of the college and university budgets; (4) auxiliary enterprises, such as dormitories, bookstores, and university presses were made to break even or to contribute to the general revenue of universities; (5) maintenance was reduced to the extent that professors were forced to empty their own wastepaper baskets; and (6) some renovation of facilities was delayed and capital maintenance was deferred.

These measures were taken by all institutions. As a general rule the research universities, both public and private, did not reduce the number of course offerings, although in certain instances, especially in the graduate area, they deemphasized or eliminated graduate programs in their weak fields. For instance, Princeton's biology department reduced the scope of its graduate offerings to the four areas where it was traditionally strong. Georgetown University discontinued its graduate physics program. Simultaneous with the cutbacks, research universities established new programs. Princeton started an impressive computer science program, and Georgetown moved more resources into its graduate chemistry program.

Even public universities which are dependent on the fortunes of the state financial system are able to convince state legislators that some needs cannot be deferred. For instance, the University of California at Berkeley was the only institution to be given a waiver during the freeze on all construction projects decreed by Governor Edmund G. Brown, Jr., in 1982. It was allowed to build a new microelectronic research facility (McDonald, 1982). The following year, the chancellor of the university successfully lobbied the legislature to release construction funds for a new biology building that was needed to reorganize the biology department on that campus (Trow, 1983). Recognizing that one of its departments was in trouble, Berkeley took extraordinary and successful means to obtain resources to correct the situation.

The less selective institutions changed their character by discontinuing unpopular courses and offering others that were more likely to appeal to students. Many started undergraduate business programs, while others grafted a graduate business program onto their undergraduate offerings. It is not clear to what extent these innovations maintained enrollments in individual schools.

We have few documented instances of declines in revenue of more than twenty-five percent. The only publicized occurrence is that of the City University of New York. In this instance, one-sixth of the full-time faculty was dismissed. The scope of course offerings for the system as a whole did not shrink, but some students were forced to register in more than one undergraduate college to get the courses they wanted. In at least one of the four-year colleges, there was a long wait for registration in the science courses required for applicants to medical schools.

During the financial crisis of the 1970's and early 1980's in New York City, difficult decisions were made to keep the schools responsive to the needs of students: According to key documents about adjustments (kindly provided by Dean J. Magner of the Central Administration of the City University), Tenured faculty members in underenrolled programs were dismissed, while more junior staff members were retained in programs which the individual schools believed to be important and viable. Similarly in the Illinois higher education system, when total resources remained unchanged in constant dollars during the eight years 1974 to 1982, the resources allocated to computer sciences were allowed to triple and the health professions' budget was allowed to grow by 41 percent. These and other selective increases in professional courses were achieved with only slight declines in the budget of biological (5.9 percent) and physical sciences (1.2 percent) while mathematics and engineering budgets increased modestly in real terms. Programs in the humanities bore the brunt of the losses.

Impact of Cutbacks on Location of Science Research

The reluctance of institutions to drop departments or change the scope of graduate instruction translates into relative stability of the location of research. The universities with the highest dollar grants for research in 1970 were almost identical to those in 1982. Nevertheless, the share of research, region by region, has changed significantly during the past fifteen years. (National Science Foundation, 1972-81).

Three states, Arizona, Maryland, and Texas, significantly strengthened the research capabilities of their public systems. In Arizona, both the University of Arizona and the remainder of the system spent considerably more on research and development during the mid-1980s than in any earlier period. In Maryland, between 1977 and 1984, the University of Maryland at College Park moved twenty notches up in the ranking of all colleges and universities, based on their expenditures on research and development. It now ranks nineteenth. In Texas, both the University of Texas in Austin and Texas A&M University increased their research and development outlays faster than the national average, and a new network of medical schools, such as the University of Texas Health Sciences Center at Dallas, became important research centers in the course of the past ten years. The proportion of federal funds in research and development outlays declined in both Maryland and Texas and remained relatively constant in Arizona. The University of Maryland was particularly successful in attracting industry funds for its research program. Industry now contributes nearly ten percent of the College Park research and development budget, double its share ten years ago.

All three states financed their institutions generously enough to allow internal funds to finance part of the growth in research and development. It is not clear how long this trend will continue. In 1985 and 1986, economic conditions in Texas deteriorated and the University was scheduled to have its budget cut just as much as the other functions in the state. Its revenues were further affected by a decline in royalties from offshore wells which benefited the university. Since the final appropriation for the institution was not set at the time of writing this report, it is too early to pass any judgement on the effect of these cuts on the Austin campus. As to the Arizona campus, no published information on long-range plans is available.

On the other hand, institutions in the so-called rust belt of Illinois, Indiana, Michigan, Ohio, and Pennsylvania lost a share in the total research and development outlays. Their doctoral-granting institution's share, which declined slowly from 19 to 18 to 17 percent in 1970, 1975, and 1980, took a sharp drop to 14 percent in 1984. A significant part of this decline was due to a shift in federal funding away from the social sciences. The Universities of Chicago, Michigan and Pennsylvania State University were important performers of social science research and suffered from these cuts. In Michigan, the depression in the automobile industry resulted in no increase in research and development contributions from industry during the last five years, and, of course, translated itself into a decline of activity in real terms.

Conclusion

All higher education institutions experienced difficulties in balancing their income and expenditures during the five years ending in 1984. These difficulties were caused mainly by the slowdown in the economy. During this period of penury, budgets were balanced mostly at the expense of faculty compensation. Other functions of the university, such as construction, renovation of facilities, and maintenance also suffered. Most institutions managed to protect their instructional programs and, as far as we could determine, shifted resources from declining programs to new, emerging fields, mostly in the hard sciences.

On the whole, scientists and engineers fared quite well during this period of slow growth and shortages of money. The number of full-time scientists (including social scientists) and engineers did not decline significantly in any institution and increased slowly in others. Much of the credit for this is due to the federal government which maintained research and development funding at a fairly high level. During the next decade, if the resources earmarked for instruction fail to accommodate the size of the current postsecondary establishment, the vitality of research universities will have to be maintained by generous infusions of research moneys. Other means will have to be found to preserve the science and engineering capabilities of teaching institutions.

Will There Be Another Crisis?

The next expected threat to university finances is the decline in overall enrollments which started in 1984 and is likely to continue for close to a decade. There is no consensus on the possible magnitude of the decline in enrollments. A number of state boards of higher education have projected either level or slowly rising numbers of students, justifying these projections by assumptions of either higher participation rates of young persons 18 to 24, or growing rates of attendance of mature, mostly part-time, students.

These projections are highly optimistic. Current demographic projections do not anticipate the number of 18-24 year olds to increase until 1996, and a rather optimistic projection of enrollment places the number of FTE students in the year 2000 ten percent below the level of 1984. Decreases in enrollment due to demographic causes may be accentuated by a decline in interest in college education because the financial return for this investment is declining.

The decline in enrollment will affect higher education institutions unevenly, it is agreed. The most vulnerable ones are: (1) institutions in states where the number of 18-to-21 year-olds has declined most, i.e. states in the Northeast and the upper Midwest; (2) nonselective institutions which do not have much prestige; and (3) smaller, isolated, liberal arts colleges. By contrast, private institutions which are highly selective, such as Harvard, Yale, Chicago, etc., do not expect to have any trouble filling their freshmen classes, and neither do most of the flagship schools of state colleges, e.g. Berkeley in the University of California system, the University of Michigan at Ann Arbor, or the Austin campus of the University of Texas. By contrast, less-distinguished state universities and colleges and some liberal arts colleges have already experienced enrollment declines.

The prospect that enrollments may decline drastically are especially real for liberal arts schools. Among the current crop of freshmen, an increasing proportion shun such liberal arts majors as history or English and favor business or other practical subjects. The proportion of freshmen who planned to major in liberal arts subjects declined from 12 percent in 1975 to 8 percent in 1984. The proportion of freshmen planning to be physical science majors has remained relatively constant—18 percent in 1975 and 19 percent in 1984.

Institutional planners hesitate to forecast enrollment declines for individual institutions for fear of receiving the treatment usually given the messenger who brings bad news. As Frederick Balderston has stated repeatedly, most institutions prefer to devise schemes to beggar their neighbors rather than to plan for an orderly contraction.

The expected contraction of enrollments, two to four percent a year, and the consequent decline in tuition revenue and possibly state support, which is often calculated on a per-student basis, are not likely to affect the college and university budgets any more than the slow-down in economic growth in the early 1980s. However, the beggar-thy-neighbor policies of some schools may exacerbate some institutions' enrollment problems.

In Minnesota, where a twenty-three-percent decline in enrollment is anticipated, the Board of Higher Education convinced the state legislature to set appropriations for colleges and universities based on their enrollments two years before the budget cycle in question. This measure was designed to allow for an orderly contraction of staffs and facilities on campuses with declining enrollments.

If university resources depend mainly on the number of students, a prolonged depression will be experienced by higher education, more serious than anything in the past fifty years. Retrenchment to meet temporary difficulties has a very different impact than permanent retrenchment to accomodate conditions of a declining industry.

No models of higher education finances is easily available for the next decade when enrollments are likely to decline. In preparing such simulations, a number of alternative scenarios would have to be considered. Will the price of resources in higher education rise faster than the cost of living? From 1930 to 1967, the cost of these resources increased two-and-a-half percent per year in real terms (O'Neill, 1973). Between the early 1970s and the mid 1980s, the increase in the price of these resources has been close to zero.

If resource costs resume their upward trend, it is possible to anticipate a postsecondary sector where (1) the wages of staff increase as fast as earnings in the total economy, and employment declines in proportion to enrollment, or (2) the wages of staff remain stagnant and the employment stabilizes at current levels.

The fewer students and the scantier resources will be distributed among roughly the same number of institutions. If past experience is any guide, it is highly unlikely that public sector institutions will close. Even in New York City, which experienced the most serious financial crisis of any system, with its budget cut by some thirty percent during the financial crisis of 1976 and 1977, local politics made it impossible to implement the City University administration's proposal to close one of the four-year schools and downgrade others to two-year status. In California, where community college enrollment declined by one-third after tuition was imposed, not one of the colleges closed its doors.

One would expect some closings among private-sector schools, especially those that are dependent on tuition. During the past decade, one four-year institution closed its doors or merged with another institution each year. Most of these institutions were small, with enrollments under five hundred students. None offered engineering programs. It appears that there is unbelievable tenacity among private institutions, and as long as they can attract a minimum number of students, their doors will remain open.

The staying power of weak or unpopular institutions may have an undesirable effect on the rest of the postsecondary sector. Fewer students are likely to enroll in the stronger institutions, and these institutions may find it more difficult to shift resources to meet students' changing demands for new majors. In the recent past, when resources were tight but enrollments were still rising, some institutions could no longer accommodate the demand for certain programs. Thus, Berkeley placed a ceiling on the number of students in engineering, and Iowa tried a novel approach to discouraging applications: the university extended the engineering bachelor's curriculum to five years.

Among administrators of research universities there is an abiding conviction that students follow resources for research and development. As long as the lion's share of funds for research and development comes from the federal government, the prospects of leading universities depend more on federal policy than on whether they are privately controlled or state institutions. Institutions with the most prestige and the leading research universities are generally believed to have a competitive edge in attracting both undergraduate and graduate students. But it is not certain that this advantage will hold during a prolonged period of decline in enrollments. No one wishes to discuss the circumstances which may weaken these institutions: a prolonged depression, federal fiscal austerity translated into cuts for research and development funds, and the decreased attractiveness of academic programs due to aging and disgruntled faculty.

The viability of public research universities will continue to depend on the level of state appropriations, determined by the levels of economic activity. Private research institutions also would benefit from prosperity. But in the final analysis it is the volume of federal funds which will determine whether all research universities prosper. The failure of either the executive or Congress to offer a convincing plan to balance the budget does not augur well for the long-range science policy of the government and, consequently, the health of these institutions.

It may not be enough for the prestigious schools, which have had less trouble attracting students, to maintain current enrollment levels. In her report to the faculty, Hanna H. Gray, the President of the University of Chicago, mentioned the university's plans to increase its undergraduate enrollment and also attempt to attract more students to its graduate programs (Gray, 1986b). The University of Chicago has the highest proportion of tenured instructional staff in arts and sciences of the six leading private universities: 82 percent, compared to 81 percent at Stanford, 69 percent at Princeton, 64 percent at Harvard, 59 percent at Columbia, and 57 percent at Yale. To afford an infusion of new blood, the university is forced to expand.

The high proportion of tenured faculty, and the consequent high costs, are as real a threat as any of the others to research university finances. The intellectual imperatives by which these universities live will force them to hire new staff to make sure that their research capability is preserved. These new hires may very well destroy the newly achieved balance between revenues and expenses.

A financial crisis in higher education is likely to come about as enrollments decline and schools start competing with each other. The united front of college presidents may disintegrate, and, horrors of horrors, both state and federal lawmakers may dare to look at the costs and benefits of instruction beyond high school.

CHAPTER 9

College and University Adjustments to a
Changing Financial Environment

PAUL T. BRINKMAN

Colleges and universities are complex entities in a complex world. At any given time, the financial circumstances of these institutions depend on a host of environmental factors and a variety of institutional responses and adjustment strategies. No single factor is decisive, nor is any one response inevitable.

The first part of this chapter consists of an overview of the environmental factors that affect the financial status of institutions of higher education (IHE). The second part focuses on the need for adjustments to the financial environment, various adjustment behaviors, and the implications of those behaviors for science and engineering education.

The Financial Environment for Higher Education

The environmental factors that determine the financial circumstances of IHE exert their influence through the revenues that IHE receive, the prices of the goods and services they purchase, the technology they use, and the societal demands imposed on them. In what follows, each of these types of evironmental factors will be discussed briefly in conceptual terms and some indication given as to how these factors have been changing.

Revenues

Revenues have an immediate and important effect on the financial status of IHE. The importance of a particular revenue source varies greatly by sector and type of IHE. It can even vary considerably among IHE of the same type, and, of course, it can also change over time.

The revenues for IHE come from the following sources: students, government, private donors, corporations, and financial markets. Students provide revenues in the form of payments for tuition, room and board, and books and supplies. State and local governments provide revenue directly through appropriations and indirectly through financial aid to students. The federal government provides revenue directly through support of research activities and through appropriations to a handful of IHE. Indirect federal support is provided through financial aid to students. Individuals and foundations give gifts to IHE for operations, capital, and scholarships. Corporate donors do likewise. Corporations also may contract with IHE for research and development. Financial markets provide revenue through returns on investment of the IHE funds. Most private IHE depend heavily on tuition and other student-related revenue, while public IHE typically receive a large portion of their funds from state appropriations.

Students are a key source of revenue for virtually all IHE. At private IHE, tuition can account for two-thirds or more of educational and general (E&G) revenue. On average, in 1984 tuition accounted for 65 percent of E&G revenue at private teaching IHE and 39 percent at private IHE with substantial research or public service activities. Even at public IHE the numbers were not small: 20 percent and 17 percent for teaching and multiproduct IHE, respectively (Christal, 1986). The amount of revenue from students depends in part on enrollment which for most institutions, is largely a function of the size and structure of the student pool and the participation rate of potential students. The latter depends on sociocultural mores, the ability of students to pay for tuition and other expenses, and the rate of return on a college degree. Real gains in personal income, substantial amounts of student financial aid, and attractive rates of return to a college education have helped maintain fairly robust enrollment, as enhanced participation rates in recent years have countered declines in the pool of traditional college-age students.

The picture that emerges for state government as a revenue source for higher education is dramatically different depending on whether one takes a national versus a state perspective or the perspective of a particular state in one year rather than another. Collectively, state revenues have increased faster than general price inflation and state expenditures. In the aggregate, in other words, states seem to be better off now than a decade ago with respect to cash flow. At the same time, the share of state expenditures going to higher education has been fairly stable. However, many individual states have been in and out of serious financial trouble at one time or another in the past decade, which has lead to abrupt and often substantial changes in appropriations for public higher education. The pattern will likely continue.

Federal revenues have increased faster than inflation, but have not kept up with federal expenditures. Attempts to reduce budget deficits are a threat to the two largest categories of federal support for higher education: student aid and research grants and contracts. From the mid 1970s through the mid 1980s, federal student aid increased dramatically in overall dollar terms. Since the late 1970s, however, student loans have grown in importance relative to nonrepayable grants as a share of federal student aid. The full consequences of this development are as yet unknown. Federal funding for university-based research has increased in real terms over the past decade, with considerable impact on a number of IHE.

Private IHE depend more heavily than do public IHE on private and corporate donations, but IHE in the public sector are increasing their efforts to generate more revenues from these sources. Both private and corporate giving to higher education have been strong. Total contributions from individuals rose from $1 billion in 1975 to $2.6 billion in 1984 (Council for Financial Aid to Education, 1985), an increase of thirty-three percent in constant dollars. Total contributions from corporations rose from $357 million in 1975 to $1.27 billion in 1984, an eighty-one percent increase in real terms. Although these contributions are running at record levels, they constitute a modest share (typically less than ten percent even for private IHE) of total IHE revenues.

Like other institutions, IHE have access to a wider variety of financial instruments than ever before. The yields on investments vary greatly from one time period to the next. The revenue is small for most IHE, but, like many private or corporate gifts, it is prized because it is not linked to any particular workload or output and can be used for virtually any purpose.

Prices

The price of purchased goods and services is one of several environmental factors that affect the financial status of IHE by increasing or decreasing expenditures. Typically, the largest single expenditure for operations is faculty salaries. Other major expenditures include the salaries of other personnel, retirement benefits, utilities, supplies, library materials, and equipment. On occasion, IHE undertake major capital construction projects. Perhaps the most dramatic changes in the financial environment in the past ten years have been in the movement of prices in the economy as a whole. One consequence was that faculty salaries fell far behind general price inflation during the late 1970s and early 1980s. The current period of relatively low inflation is giving IHE a chance to restore faculty purchasing power. Their efforts in this regard, however, are contributing to a situation in which higher education costs are going up faster than inflation, which reflects poorly on higher education's public image. Efforts to put retirement plans, such as Social Security, on a sounder actuarial basis have also pushed up labor costs.

Technological change

Technological changes that can influence the financial status of IHE occur in areas such as instruction, research, data processing, and energy conservation. The increasing pace of technological developments presents a special problem for IHE. Whereas such developments often lead to productivity gains for other industries, and thus, all else equal, lower unit costs, in many instances they lead to higher costs for IHE.

The impact of both price changes and technological developments is modulated by institutional choice and may be immediate or delayed. For instance, an increase in faculty salaries nationally does not necessarily entail proportional increases in salaries at particular IHE. IHE have some latitude in how they will respond, depending on how competitive they wish to be in a given instance. Similarly, the effects of changes in instructional technologies can be slow in coming, because IHE can elect to delay implementing new technologies—indefinitely if they so choose. New research technologies are more difficult to delay if IHE wish to remain competitive. In contrast to the delayed effect of some changes in prices or technology, a decision by a major revenue source to change the amount of funding it provides usually has an immediate impact on the receiving IHE.

Social Change

As society changes, the demands it makes on its institutions change. The effect on higher education can be modest or substantial or somewhere in between. As Bowen (1980) has conceptualized the issue, social change affects higher education along three paths: IHE may be forced to respond by governmental action; they may be pressured into responding by pressure groups; or they may respond voluntarily to social demands.

IHE are large, formal organizations whose work can take them into highly regulated areas. For example, they are subject to all the usual governmental regulations having to do with safety in the workplace, affirmative action, and minimum wages. In addition, many IHE are subject to regulations concerning animal rights, participation in sports, disposal of hazardous waste materials, and even the operation of nuclear reactors. Compliance with these regulations is never free and sometimes quite expensive. Performance monitoring is another area of possible governmental action. It was once limited to certifying entry into some of the professions, but it now extends in a few instances to mandatory testing and curriculum content at the undergraduate level.

In addition to governmental action, there are numerous other societal demands that have financial implications for higher education. Student interests can change quickly and dramatically, often leaving IHE with misplaced resources. Industry too puts pressure on IHE, and in certain technological, equipment-intensive fields, accommodating the needs of industry can be costly.

Higher education can become a focal point for broad social movements, with significant consequences for institutional costs. The egalitarianism of the 1960s brought an influx of undeprepared students into college. Expenditures for remedial education (to say nothing of opportunity costs) soared and remain controversial to this day. The effects can run in the other direction as well. The same social currents, for instance, also led to a vast increase in federal student aid which gave a boost to institutional revenues through increased enrollments (and, some would argue, the opportunity to raise tuition more than otherwise). The women's movement brought both new regulations and new students. Today it is widely expected that universities will lead the way to regional economic development, an expectation that will inevitably force institutional behavior to change and institutional costs to increase.

Institutional Adjustments and Their Implications

In this second section, we look first at some evidence that IHE have found it necessary to make adjustments to changing financial circumstances. The focus then turns to mechanisms and typical behaviors engaged in by IHE as they adjust to deteriorating financial circumstances, and the section concludes with a discussion of what may happen to science and engineering programs when such adjustments are made.

Evidence for Financial Adjustments

Questions about the financial condition of IHE are complicated by the fact that such conditions are highly localized. Some IHE can be in serious financial trouble while others may be doing quite well. The history of an institution, its funding base, its local environment, the management and planning tools it has in place, and the competition it faces are among the factors that can influence institutional financial strength.

In view of the importance of these local effects, rather than averages, counts that summarize the performance of various IHE by sector and type can provide a better indication of whether adjustments are likely to have been needed.

TABLE 1
Institutions with Decreased Instructional Expenditures*
per FTE Student, 1975 to 1984

Type of Institution	Number in Sample	Number with Decrease =			Percent with Decrease =		
		Any	>10%	>20%	Any	>10%	>20%
Public							
Research	50	15	6	3	30	12	6
Other doctoral	53	24	14	5	45	26	9
Teaching	50	36	24	11	72	48	22
Private							
Research	23	6	3	2	26	13	9
Other doctoral	33	13	5	1	39	15	3
Teaching	50	27	14	10	54	28	20

*In constant dollars, using the Higher Education Price Index.
Data source: Higher Education General Information Survey.

TABLE 2
Institutions with Decreased Education and General Expenditures*
per FTE Student, 1975 to 1984

Type of Institution	Number in Sample	Number with Decrease =			Percent with Decrease =		
		Any	>10%	>20%	Any	>10%	>20%
Public							
Research	50	21	7	1	42	14	2
Other doctoral	53	20	8	3	38	15	6
Teaching	50	28	15	6	56	30	12
Private							
Research	23	5	3	0	22	13	0
Other doctoral	33	6	2	0	18	6	0
Teaching	50	20	12	4	40	24	8

*In constant dollars, using the Higher Education Price Index.
Data source: Higher Education General Information Survey.

To develop such data, samples of the following three types of IHE were drawn from both the public and private sectors: universities that offer a broad range of doctoral programs and emphasize separately budgeted research; universities that offer a broad range of doctoral programs but are only moderately engaged in separately budgeted research; and IHE devoted primarily to teaching. With respect to the first two types, the samples used in the analysis include most of the population. By contrast, the randomly drawn samples of public and private teaching institutions represent only a small portion of the roughly 360 public and 730 private four-year IHE in the population.

As indicated in Tables 1 and 2, a considerable number of IHE in both sectors experienced constant-dollar declines in expenditures per FTE student for the period from 1975 to 1984. Declines were more prevalent for some segments than others, with teaching IHE in both sectors faring less well than the more comprehensive IHE. A substantial portion of public IHE did not keep up with inflation. However, only modest proportions of IHE of any type experienced declines of more than twenty percent in instructional expenditures—a condition indicating the need for serious adjustments. The corresponding proportions for E&G expenditures are smaller. Another way of addressing the need for adjustment is through data on the number of IHE experiencing revenue shortfalls. In a recent survey of a representative sample of IHE, forty-five percent of all institutions reported a revenue shortfall during the period from 1981 to 1984 (Andersen, 1985).

While the late 1970s and early 1980s are remembered as a time when some IHE underwent financial difficulties, many IHE actually increased the resources at their disposal during that period (see Tables 3 and 4). Except for public teaching IHE, from one-third to nearly two-thirds of the IHE in the various samples managed to increase their E&G expenditures by ten percent or more in real terms. One-fourth to one-third of the private IHE experienced E&G expediture increases in excess of twenty percent.

Over the period from 1975 to 1984, the distribution of revenues from various sources also changed. In terms of averages by type of IHE, tuition revenues became an increasingly important component of (adjusted) E&G revenues for all six institutional types (see Table 5). For public IHE, this is most clearly seen in the relationship between revenues from state appropriations and revenues from tuition. Tuition still far from equals state and local appropriations as a source of revenue, but the trend since 1975 is clearly in that direction. (Given the increasing availability of state student aid, however, the actual share of governmental assistance may be a different story.) About two-thirds of the public IHE sampled experienced growth in the share of revenues from tuition (see Table 6).

TABLE 3
Institutions with Increased Instructional Expenditures*
per FTE Student, 1975 to 1984

Type of Institution	Number in Sample	Number with Increase =			Percent with Increase =		
		Any	>10%	>20%	Any	>10%	>20%
Public							
Research	50	35	19	11	70	38	22
Other doctoral	53	29	15	9	55	28	17
Teaching	50	14	8	4	28	16	8
Private							
Research	23	17	13	9	74	57	39
Other doctoral	33	20	17	9	61	52	27
Teaching	50	23	13	8	46	26	16

*In constant dollars, using the Higher Education Price Index.
Data source: Higher Education General Information Survey.

TABLE 4
Institutions with Increased Educational and General Expenditures*
per FTE Student, 1975 to 1984

Type of Institution	Number in Sample	Number with Increase =			Percent with Increase =		
		Any	>10%	>20%	Any	>10%	>20%
Public							
Research	50	29	18	8	58	36%	16%
Other doctoral	53	33	20	13	62	38	25
Teaching	50	22	10	7	44	20	14
Private							
Research	23	18	10	6	78	43	26
Other doctoral	33	27	21	11	82	64	33
Teaching	50	30	21	13	60	42	26

*In constant dollars, using the Higher Education Price Index.
Data source: Higher Education General Information Survey.

TABLE 5
Proportion of Revenues from Various Sources, 1975 and 1984

A. Public Institutions

Type of Institution	Tuition/State and Local Appropriations		State and Local Appropriations/ Adj. E&G* Revenue	
	1975	1984	1975	1984
Research	.259	.316	.628	.594
Other doctoral	.351	.362	.655	.639
Teaching	.327	.379	.716	.685

B. Private Institutions

Type of Institution	Endowment Income/ Tuition Revenue		Tuition/ Adj. E&G* Revenue	
	1975	1984	1975	1984
Research	.431	.300	.414	.438
Other doctoral	.180	.178	.605	.645
Teaching	.094	.110	.705	.736

*E&G revenue less government grants and contracts.
Source: Higher Education General Information Survey.

TABLE 6
Institutions with Changes in the Proportion of Adjusted* E&G
Revenue Coming from Tuition, 1975 to 1984

Type of Institution	Number in Sample	Percentage w/ Any Increase	Percentage w/Increase >5 Percentage Points	Percentage w/Decrease >5 Percentage Points
Public				
Research	50	80	26	8
Other doctoral	53	68	14	9
Teaching	50	64	32	18
Private				
Research	23	35	26	9
Other Doctoral	33	45	24	9
Teaching	50	62	32	18

*E&G revenue less government grants and contracts.
Data source: Higher Education General Information Survey.

Tuition traditionally has been the single largest source of revenue at private IHE. From 1975 to 1984 the proportion of E&G revenue from tuition increased slightly, on average, for the three types of private IHE (see Table 5); however, fewer than half of the research and other doctoral IHE experienced growth in the proportion of E&G revenues from tuition (see Table 6). About one-fourth to one-third of the IHE experienced an increase that exceeded five percentage points. A much smaller percentage of IHE saw a decline of more than five percentage points. The corresponding figures for public teaching IHE are similar.

In summary, at many IHE there have been modest shifts during the past decade in the way funds are raised and expended. Shifts in the relationship between capital and operating expenditures may have occurred as well, and they may well be more significant than what has been happening to, or within, the operating budget. Unfortunately, the available data are not definitive. The extent to which assets in the broad sense of the term—equipment, buildings, faculty, and programs—have been sacrificed on behalf of balancing the operating budget is worth further research.

Adjustment Mechanisms

The reponse of IHE to their financial environment is a broad and complex topic. The focus in what follows is restricted to their response to a deteriorating financial environment. There is a modest literature on this theme and the possibility of an accompanying decline in institutional capacity and output would likely be of interest to the federal government.

The range of institutional responses to fiscal problems is moderately extensive. Conceptually, the responses can be categorized as being designed to either *resist* the problem or *adapt* to it (Mingle and Norris, 1981).

There are several related types of responses that fit the notion of resisting a deteriorating environment and its consequences, but in one form or another they all are directed toward raising additional revenue. A classic example is strengthening student recruitment. If the institution's financial problems can be traced to enrollment, as is often the case, then better student recruitment is one solution and this approach has been taken by many IHE. In a recent American Council on Education (ACE) survey (Andersen, 1985), it was reported that two-thirds of all IHE (excluding research universities) experiencing revenue shortfalls during the last few years reacted by increasing student recruitment efforts. Similarly many institutions will attempt to improve student retention as a means of generating additional revenue. In that same survey, two-thirds of the IHE reported using this tactic.

Increases in tuition are also used frequently to ward off financial difficulty, but there are major differences among IHE in their respective abilities to increase net tuition revenue substantially. For example, among private IHE there are great differences in the price elasticity of tuition. Some private IHE have a pool of student applicants from which they select a subset for acceptance. Increasing tuition may not affect the total number of registrants at all. Other private IHE essentially take all students who wish to attend. Their enrollments may be very sensitive to tuition hikes. Public IHE too differ with respect to their tuition options. Differences in tuition elasticities are again present, as are differences in cross-price elasticities, but also important are differences in the locus of authority to set tuition. For example, Michigan universities responded to their fiscal crises in part by raising tuition, while Washington's public universities, when faced with a similar problem, could only hope that the legislature would increase tuition. In general, there is a trend toward greater reliance on tuition especially at public IHE (see Tables 5 and 6).

A related strategy is to increase the diversification of revenue sources. IHE that depend heavily on one revenue source have fewer options in dealing with a revenue shortfall. Some public IHE are in this position with respect to state appropriations. Many private IHE are similarly, or even more heavily, dependent on revenue from tuition. Thus, a move to strengthen fund-raising form private sources, for example, is a means not only of raising more revenue in the short run, but of building a more secure (because more diversified) revenue base for the future. Sixty-nine percent of the IHE in the ACE survey (Andersen, 1985) adopted this resistance strategy to revenue decline.

IHE have a propensity for short-term or one-time cost-cutting measures when revenue shortfalls first occur. These measures, which can be viewed as a combination of resistance and adaptation, are often based on the premise that the financial problems will soon be resolved—at least by the next budget cycle. Some typical actions of this kind include reducing travel budgets, delaying equipment purchases, delaying or reducing library acquisitions, freezing vacant positions, laying off staff for short periods of time, and deferring special projects. These actions are reported time and again in the accounts of what transpires in IHE when they first encounter financial problems. For example, when Michigan State University had to cut about $10 million from a $204 million budget in 1980, they furloughed all but essential personnel for two days and deferred new projects (Hyatt, et al., 1984). At Penn State, considerable emphasis was placed on nonpersonnel cuts during the first round of budget reductions (Mortimer, 1981). Three years of financial problems at the University of Idaho show that IHE may also adopt short-term cost cutting measures—such as eliminating travel budgets—even after the initial round of budget reductions, provided that the second- or third-round budget problems are thought to be short-term (McKinney, 1982).

Adapting to fiscal stress, or to a deteriorating environment more generally, is not the same as capitulation or resignation. Adaptation in this context means reconciling institutional goals to the new circumstances (Mingle and Norris, 1981). Several concepts can serve to organize the various responses. IHE can *reduce* the rate of growth of some budget categories, or they can engage in *retrenchment* activities involving *across-the-board* cuts or *selective* cuts or some combination thereof. Alternatively, they can *reallocate* resources (these alternatives are discussed at length in Mortimer and Tierney, 1979). By definition, reallocation is a selective process.

Reduction and retrenchment strategies include using more part-time faculty, reducing the number of staff, letting the student-faculty ratio increase, consolidating administrative structures, eliminating programs, and limiting course offerings. Reallocation involves strengthening some programs and weakening others and may involve the closure of one or more programs. Retrenchment and reallocation in particular can result in modest changes in institutional mission. In 1977, after making across-the-board cuts in response to previous revenue shortfalls, the University of Michigan created a priority fund by further reducing each unit's 1976 budget. The fund was used to develop new areas and to increase the resources of high-priority programs (Hyatt, et al., 1984).

At many IHE adapting to a new financial environment has entailed, as a preliminary step, enhancing the institution's management and planning capabilities (the extensive efforts in the Wisconsin system of public IHE, for instance, are described in Smith, 1980). Practices such as program review, formal planning structures, cash-management techniques, and contingency funds have become much more widespread than they were a decade or two ago. Of the four practices mentioned, the first three can now be found on three-fourths of the nation's campuses, while contingency funds are used at half of the IHE (Andersen, 1985). Short-term, incremental cutbacks and deferred expenditures do not require these mechanisms, but long-term, relatively permanent adjustments do.

The reports of IHE that have faced financial problems indicate that they frequently attempt to protect the instructional budget during the initial round of cost-cutting measures. In the case of Ohio State University, for instance, not only was instruction protected during the first round of required cutbacks, but certain financial mangement rules were changed to free up additional funds for instruction (Ihrig, 1983). However, instruction was not exempted in the second round of budget reductions.

Once committed to serious reduction, retrenchment, or reallocation, most IHE can make very substantial adjustments. Further research would be needed to determine which of the adjustments have a truly lasting effect, that is, which of them survive when institutional finances return to more favorable levels. For example, are retrenched programs or other major commitments likely to be restored? Do planning and program review processes atrophy when the impetus of financial difficulty is removed?

What are the factors that influence how an institution of higher education is likely to react to a deteriorating financial environment? Hyatt et al. (1984) devloped the following list of important internal and external factors:

- duration of the fiscal crises;
- degree of management flexibility available to the institution;
- diversification of institutional revenue sources;
- historical level of recurring program support;
- ability of administration to communicate with all of the institution's constituent groups.

One of the first things IHE do when confronted with a fiscal problem is to estimate how long the problem is likely to last. As indicated earlier, the tendency is to continue doing business as usual, albeit at a smaller scale, if the problem is judged to be short-term. This often entails across-the-board cuts. If the problem is judged to be long-term, or if in fact it proves to be long-term, the chances increase that IHE will feel it necessary to begin to do things differently. Selectively reducing some areas while strengthening others is a response to a perceived longer-term problem.

Timing affects the likelihood that across-the-board cuts will be, or even can be, used. For example, public IHE are especially vulnerable to mid-year reductions. Because they are at the mercy of state financing decisions, their financial status can change abruptly. Such changes are likely to lead to the imposition of available one-time measures. Often the choices are quite narrow because of binding contractual arrangements, especially those with faculty and students. It has been estimated that less than half of a college or university budget is subject to reduction once a fiscal year has begun (Hyatt, et al., 1984). When a longer warning time has been given, a situation more likely to occur in the private sector, IHE are more likely to respond with strategic measures that focus on recurring costs and the full range of expenditures.

The difficulties of dealing with budget problems can be mitigated considerably by advance preparation. One mode of preparation is to have contingency funds on hand that can be used to cover a budget deficit. IHE can also build more flexibility into their contractual arrangements with faculty and staff. In addition, if they have established ongoing planning and priority-setting activities, they may be in a position to take selective, targeted steps in the event of a revenue shortfall. IHE without plans must first develop them, while relying heavily on across-the-board measures in the interim.

One of the major advantages that private IHE have in facing a financial crisis is their relatively large degree of flexibility in handling their financial resources. Public IHE have varying degrees of flexibility depending on the state and even the system within a state, but almost none have the flexibility available to their private counterparts. Some of the critical attributes of flexibility are the following: being able to carry forward funds from one fiscal year to the next; being able to transfer funds among budgetary units and expenditure categories; and being able to reduce costs through techniques such as capturing the salaries of vacant faculty and staff positions. On occasion, states will react to continued financial pressure on their public IHE by giving them greater financial management flexibility (Carter and Blanton, 1983).

IHE that have had to work their way through fiscal problems may be better prepared to handle them in the future, but they may also find their future options somewhat restricted. Indeed, a protracted series of difficult fiscal situations could leave an institution without any easy fixes. It seems reasonable to suggest that many public and private IHE have used up much of their 'organizational slack' in coping with previous revenue shortfalls, and will have to make substantive organizational changes if revenues drop off again. To put it another way, IHE that have relied on across-the-board cuts in the past may have considerable difficulty in continuing to rely on that strategy in the face of new difficulties, unless, of course, they have several good years in between. IHE that historically have been well funded and have not had to face previous financial problems can use across-the-board cuts much more easily.

Management style and the groundwork that has been laid ahead of time may or may not permit decisive steps to be taken. While the most appropriate response to fiscal stress may be apparent to an administrator, there may be little or no chance of implementing the right decision if the institution is fragmented into adversarial camps. The point is not that there is one right way to run these complex, hard-to-manage organizations, but that certain options may not be available if the institution is poorly run to begin with. Across-the-board cuts may be the only viable option politically under certain circumstances.

Implications for Science and Engineering

Has there been or is there likely to be a shakeout among IHE in various categories, with the less competitive going out of business? The odds of any college or university going out of business entirely are very small, especially if the relevant set of IHE consists of those institutions that currently are making a noticeable contribution to training in science and engineering. The political problems surrounding the closing of a public IHE are so great that few public officials are willing to advocate closure. Private IHE, too, do not go out of business easily. One reason is that various constituencies are likely to come to the rescue when a truly serious crisis develops. Furthermore, since only minimal accreditation requirements offer a basic standard, IHE can retrench to very great extent befor they dip below minimum performance standards.

This is not to say that IHE have not closed in the past or will not continue to do so in the future. During the 1980s, for instance, there were five to ten closures each year. But in the same period, there were four or five times as may new IHE created or newly accredited. Between 1981 and 1984, the total number of accredited colleges and universities of all kinds increased by two percent (Broyles and Fernandez, 1984). Those that did close would have to be described as marginal contributors to science and engineering.

What factors determine whether across-the-board cuts in IHE tend to reduce the size or the quality of an activity or both, especially with regard to science and engineering activities? Across-the-board cuts often mean that open positions are not allowed to be filled. This adjustment by attrition poses a considerable long-run threat to the mission and objectives of an institution (Bowen and Glenny, 1981). In either the short or long run, science and engineering departments are at relatively high risk of being adversely affected because they are more likely, it would seem, to have open positions due to the loss of faculty to higher-paying jobs in industry. Across-the-board cuts (by function) hit supply budgets and support staff especially hard because they are less well protected contractually. This entails a disproportionately negative effect on science and engineering departments because they are the largest consumers of these goods among academic departments. Across-the-board cuts hit fast-changing disciplines harder than other disciplines; this again puts the sciences and engineering at a disadvantage. Such cuts almost always mean that little or no funds are available for new programs, innovations, new equipment, or new facilities, all of which are likely to be needed most often in the science and engineering disciplines. Presumably, any effects on program quality would be negative.

In what circumstances have or will cutbacks tend to eliminate entirely some individual activities or subactivities within an institution, especially science and engineering activities? There appear to be four circumstances that pave the way for the elimination of activities. One is the sharpness of the financial setback. The sharper or more dramatic the financial crisis, the more likely it is that an institution will move decisively and selectively. A gradual erosion in financial status typically is accompanied by a ratcheting down of all activities. A sharp reversal can change the prevailing psychology and allow for elimination of activities. A second circumstance that can lead to the same effect is a major decrease in demand for an activity. In good financial times, low demand is much more tolerable than when financial cutbacks are required.

A third situation that leads to program elimination is the confluence of the loss of soft money for a particular program along with general financial problems. In good financial times, a program that has been around awhile may be retained with institutional funds when its primary or original funding runs out. When resources are tight, such a program has much less chance against other programs that are already funded through institutional sources. Finally, the presence of a rigorous program review activity on the campus will facilitate program elimination (Buchanan, et al., 1978). Such activity pinpoints strengths and weakness in terms of student demand, faculty productivity, and centrality to institutional mission (a concise description of these elements of program review being used in a period of financial distress can be found in Shirley, 1982). These appraisals can lead to program elimination even in relatively good financial circumstances, but not as frequently.

Because science and engineering programs are affected more readily by the life-cycle phenomenon, some of them may be more vulnerable to elimination than other kinds of programs. This is especially true for subspecialties in the more applied fields. For example, a basic physics program typically would be less in jeopardy than a concentration in electric power generation within an electrical engineering program.

In situations where severe cutbacks are required, science and engineering programs offer an attactive target because of their expense. Cutting one of them can have a major impact on the budget. (It was just this sort of reasoning that apparently led to the elimination of all engineering programs at the University of Denver several years ago.)

Another way in which science and engineering programs can become targets for elimination is through a strategic planning process in which an institution commits itself to be especially strong in some but not all areas. On average, it is more expensive to be very good in science and engineering than in many other fields. Thus other fields will look more attractive in a period of financial cutback. On the other hand, high-tech programs are very attractive now, in part because they are likely to attract outside funding.

Available national data on IHE do not permit a straightforward analysis of the amount of resources directed toward instruction in science and engineering at different points in time during the past decade. Two resource-related issues would be useful to examine: (1) whether the proportion of institutional resources going to science and engineering education has changed, especially at IHE that have experienced financial problems; and (2) whether instruction in science and engineering has become any more or less efficient. The first question would be the easier of the two to address. The key ingredient would be a sample of IHE (including some that experienced financial difficulties) willing to share department level expenditure data for recent and past years. Given data availability, the complexity of the project would be a function of how inclusive one wished to be in recording expenditures; direct costs would be the simplest, but something could be learned by including indirect and capital costs as well. Addressing the second issue, relative efficiency, would require not only a sample of IHE and expenditure data, but data that would adequately convey the output flowing from those expenditures. Given the availability of the full data set, appropriate data analysis techniques, such as Data Envelopment Analysis, would permit an assessment of relative efficiency over time, and thereby allow for a deeper understanding of the effects of unfavorable financial conditions.

Has there been or is there likely to be any tendency for concentration of some fields or specialties of science and engineering research or training in only a few IHE? This is a difficult question to answer with any degree of precision, but there are two forces pushing greater concentration. One is the emphasis on strategic planning now quite widespread among IHE and state higher education agencies. Combined with reduced resources, it tends to lead IHE toward a more narrow, sharply defined focus. As the President of Michigan State University said after several years of serious financial problems, "we no longer can be all things to all people" (Hyatt, et al., 1984, p. 63). The literature on state coordination of higher education contains the same theme: To have an effecent and effective state higher education system, it is necessary to delineate clearly the mission of each of the state's public IHE. Such delineation often has a limiting or restricting effect, especially on regional colleges and universities.

A second force, which interacts with the first, is that more and more science is becoming 'big science,' requiring considerable resources to be done right. Over the long run, unless there is an abundance of resources, this condition may reduce participation by IHE in some particularly expensive fields.

There are counteracting forces. IHE traditionally have shown a strong inclination to expand into new areas and to offer a wide if not comprehensive set of programs. The lure of economic development may lead to additional funds that IHE can use to remain competitive in the big-science fields.

As an indication of the current situation, a current listing of graduate and professional programs shows that of 256 programs there are only fifteen that are offered by fifteen or fewer IHE (Conley and Frary, 1984). Eight programs are offered by 6 or fewer IHE. The definition of *program* makes considerable difference, of course. In this case, it is a major concentration in which one can obtain a degree; for example, architectural engineering.

In any case, in view of the absence of extensive national planning for higher education in the United States, most of the decisions regarding program offerings will be done locally, or, at best, in conjunction with state plans. The distribution and concentration of science and engineering programs, then, may not be optimum from a national perspective, although market forces and the intervention of agencies such as the National Science Foundation will probably maintain some degree of rationality in the system.

Notes and References

Introduction

References

Bowen, Howard R. 1977. *Investment in Learning: The Individual and Social Value of Higher Education*. San Francisco: Jossey-Bass.

Clotfelter, Charles T. 1976. "Public Spending for Higher Education: An Empirical Test of Two Hypotheses." *Public Finance* 31: 177-95.

Coombs, Philip H. 1985. *The World Crisis in Education: The View from the Eighties*. New York and Oxford: Oxford University Press.

Economics of Education Review Special Issue: Student Financial Aid and Public Policy 1988. Estelle James and Stephen A. Hoenack, eds., 7(1).

Grubb, Norton W. 1988. "Vocationalizing Higher Education: The Causes of Enrollment and Completion in Public Two-Year Colleges, 1970-1980." *Economics of Education Review*. 7: 301-319.

Hoenack, Stephen A. 1988. "Incentives, Outcome-Based Instruction, and School Efficiency." In *Microlevel School Finance: Issues and Implications for Policy*. David H. Monk and Julie Underwood, eds., Cambridge: Ballinger.

———— and Daniel J. Pierro. 1990. *An Econometric Model of a Public University's Income and Enrollments*. To appear in *The Journal of Economic Behavior and Organization*.

Jones, Beau Fly and William G. Spady. 1985. "Enhanced Mastery Learning and Quality of Instruction." In *Improving Student Achievement Through Mastery Learning Programs*, D. U. Levine, ed., San Francisco: Jossey-Bass.

Leslie, Larry L. and Paul T. Brinkman. 1988. *The Economic Value of Higher Education*. New York: American Council on Higher Education/Macmillan.

McKenzie, Richard B. and Staaf, Robert J. 1974. *An Economic Theory of Learning: Student Sovereignty and Academic Freedom*. Blacksburg, Virginia: University Publications.

Psacharopoulos, George. 1980. *Higher Education in Developing Countries: A Cost-Benefit Analysis*. World Bank Staff Working Paper no. 440, Washington, D. C.

_____ and Maureen Woodhall. 1985. *Education for Development: An Analysis of Investment Choices*. New York and Oxford: Oxford University Press.

Rubin, S. E. and William G. Spady. 1984. "Achieving Excellence Through Outcome-Based Instructional Delivery." *Educational Leadership*, 8 (May): 27-44.

Solmon, Lewis C. 1975. "The Definition of College Quality and Its Impact on Earnings." *Exploring Economic Research* 2: 537-87.

Spady, William G. 1982. "Outcome-Based Instructional Management: A Sociological Perspective." *The Australian Journal of Education*, 26: 123-43.

Chapter One

References

Astin, Alexander W. 1973. "Measurement and Determinants of the Outputs of Higher Education." In L. Solmon and P. Taubman (eds.), *Does College Matter?* New York: Academic Press.

Astin, Alexander W. 1968. "Undergraduate Achievement and Institutional Excellence." *Science*, 161 (3842) (August 16): 661-8.

Becker, William E., Jr. 1983. "Economics Education Research: Part II, New Directions in Theoretical Model Building." *Journal of Economic Education* 14 (2) (Spring): 4-11.

_____. 1975. "The University Professor as a Utility Maximizer and Producer of Learning, Research, and Income." *Journal of Human Resources* 10 (Winter): 107-15.

Breneman, David W. 1976. "The Ph.D. Production Process." In J. Froomkin, D. Jamison, and R. Radner, eds., *Education as an Industry*. Cambridge: Ballinger.

Bresler, Jack B. 1968. "Teaching Effectiveness and Government Awards." *Science* 160 (3824) (April 12): 164-68.

Carlson, Daryl. 1975. "Examining Efficient Joint Production Processes." In R. A. Wallhaus, ed., *Measuring and Increasing Academic Productivity*. San Francisco: Jossey-Bass.

Carnegie Commission on Higher Education. 1971. *New Students and New Places.* New York: McGraw-Hill.

Cohn, Elchanan. 1979. *The Economics of Education.* Cambridge: Ballinger.

Coleman, James S., et al. 1966. *Equality of Educational Opportunity.* Washington: U.S. Government Printing Office.

Cootner, Paul H. 1974. "Economic Organization and Inefficiency in the Modern University." In K. G. Lumsden, ed., *Efficiency in Universities: The La Paz Papers.* Amsterdam: Elsevier.

Dunworth, John, and Anthony Bottomley. 1974. "Potential Economics of Scale at the University of Bradford." *Socio-Economic Planning Sciences* 8:1 (February): 47-55.

Garvin, David A. 1980. *The Economics of University Behavior.* New York: Academic Press.

Gulko, Warren W. and Khateeb M. Hussein. 1971. "A Resource Requirements Prediction Model (RRPM-1)." *Technical Report No. 17.* WICHE (Western Interstate Commission on Higher Education): Boulder.

Hanushek, Eric A. 1979. "Conceptual and Empirical Issues in the Estimation of Education Production Functions." *Journal of Human Resources* 14(3) (Summer): 351-88.

Hayes, John R. 1971. "Research, Teaching and Faculty Fate." *Science* 172 (3980) (April 16): 227-30.

Heim, John and Lewis Perl. 1974. 06The Educational Production Function. Ithaca, N.Y.: Institute of Public Employment, Cornell University.

Hopkins, David S. P. 1971. "On the Use of Large-Scale Simulation Models for University Planning." *Review of Educational Research* 41(5) (December): 467-78.

———— and William F. Massy. 1981. *Planning Models for Colleges and Universities.* Stanford: Stanford University Press.

Lau, Lawrence J. 1979. "Educational Production Functions." In Douglas M. Windham, ed., *Economic Dimensions of Education.* National Academy of Education.

Levin, Henry M. 1976. "Concepts of Economic Efficiency and Educational Production." in J. Froomkin, D. Jamison, and R. Radner, eds., *Education as an Industry.* Cambridge: Ballinger.

Lewis, Darrell R., Bruce R. Dalgaard, and Carol M. Boyer. 1985. "Cost-Effectiveness of Computer-Assisted Economics Instruction." *American Economic Review* 75(2) (May): 91-96.

Lumsden, Keith G. (ed.). 1974. *Efficiency in Universities: The La Paz Papers.* Amsterdam: Elsevier.

Manahan, Jerry. 1983. "An Educational Production Function for Principles of Economics." *Journal of Economic Education* 14 (2) (Spring): 11-16.

National Research Council Committee on an Assessment of Quality-Related Characteristics of Research-Doctorate Programs in the U.S. 1982. *An Assessment of Research-Doctorate Programs in the United States.* Washington, D.C.: National Academy Press.

Nerlove, Marc. 1972. "On Tuition and the Costs of Higher Education: Prolegomena to a Conceptual Framework." *Journal of Political Economy* 80(3) (May-June): S178-S218.

Oliver, Robert M., and David S. P. Hopkins. 1976. "Instructional Costs of University Outputs." In J. Froomkin, D. Jamison, and R. Radner, eds., *Education as an Industry.* Cambridge: Ballinger.

Polachek, Solomon W., Thomas J. Kniesner, and Henrick J. Harwood. 1978. "Educational Production Functions." *Journal of Educational Statistics* 3(3) (Autumn): 209-31.

Radner, Roy and Leonard S. Miller. 1975. *Demand and Supply in U.S. Higher Education.* New York: McGraw-Hill.

Sengupta, J. K. 1975. "Cost and Production Functions in the University Education System: An Econometric Analysis." In H. Correa, ed., *Analytical Models in Educational Planning and Administration.* New York: David McKay.

Solmon, Lewis C. 1973. "The Definition and Impact of College Quality." In L. Solmon and P. Taubman, eds., *Does College Matter?* New York: Academic Press.

Southwick, L., Jr. 1969. "Cost Trends in Land Grant Colleges and Universities." *Applied Economics* 1 (August): 167-82.

Voecks, Virginia W. 1962. "Publications and Teaching Effectiveness." *Journal of Higher Education* 33 (April): 212-25.

Wallhaus, Robert. 1975. "The Many Dimensions of Productivity." In R. A. Wallhaus, ed., *Measuring and Increasing Academic Productivity.* San Francisco: Jossey-Bass.

WICHE. 1970. "The Outputs of Higher Education: Their Identification, Measurement, and Evaluation." Boulder Col.: Western Interstate Commission for Higher Education.

Chapter Two

* The author is grateful for the extensive assistance of Dr. Ana Maria L. Rodrigues. He also benefited from discussions with numerous colleagues at several universities.

References

American Association for the Advancement of Science. 1987. *AAAS Report XI: Research and Development, FY 1987.* Washington D.C.

Baker, William B. 1985. "Statement on Higher Education's Facilities and Instrumentation Needs." Subcommittee on Science, Research and Technology, U.S. House of Representatives, October 22, (unpublished, Office of the President, University of California).

Balderston, F. E. 1985. "Academic Program Review and the Determination of University Priorities." Netherlands Institute for Advanced Study. Wassenaar, Netherlands. Published in revised form, *International Journal of Institutional Management in Higher Education* (Fall).

————. 1974. *Managing Today's University.* Jossey-Bass Publishers, San Francisco.

Balderston, F. E. , and M. McPherson. 1980. "The Forecaster's Art and the Young Investigator Problem: What We Have Learned and What We Need to Know." In Michael McPherson, *The Demand for New Faculty in Science and Engineering.* Commission on Human Resources, NAS, Washington, D.C.

Chemical Engineering News. 1984. "University Research Costing Changes Urged," 62 (17): 28-56.

Cheit, E. and Lobman T. 1979. *Foundations in Higher Education: Grant Making from Golden Years through Steady State.* Carnegie Council on Policy Studies in Higher Education, Berkeley.

Colvig, R. 1986. "Berkeley Rates Among Top Schools in NSF Fellowships." Berkeleyan, 14 (33) (May 7): 1

Congress of the United States, Office of Technology Assessment. 1985. *Demographic Trends and the Scientific and Engineering Work Force.* Government Printing Office, Washington D.C.

Culliton, B. 1986. "David Packard Tackles OMB on Indirect Costs." *Science* 232 (April 18): 315.

Day, Douglas N., Jr. 1976. "The Management of Organized Research Units at the University of California, Berkeley: Size, Politics, and Interdisciplinarity." CP-399, July, revised March 1977. Center for Research in Management, Berkeley.

Froomkin, Joseph, ed. 1983. *The Crisis in Higher Education.* Academy of Political Science, New York.

Kaiser, H. 1985. "Time to Close the R&D Funding Gap." AGB Reports 27 (4) (July/August):

Massachusetts Institute of Technology. 1985. *Report of the Treasurer, Year Ended June 30, 1985.*

National Academy of Sciences, Ad Hoc Committee on Government-University Relationships in Support of Science, Committee on Science, Engineering and Public Policy. 1983a. *Strengthening the Government-University Partnership in Science.* National Academy Press, Washington, D.C.

National Academy of Sciences. 1983b. *An Assessment of Research Doctorate Programs in the United States: Biological Sciences; Mathematical & Physical Sciences; Humanities; Engineering and Social and Behavioral Sciences.* National Academy Press, Washington D.C.

———. 1985. *Research Briefings.* National Academy Press, Washington D.C.

———. 1986. "Government-University-Industry Research Roundtable: Report of a Conference." National Academy of Sciences, National Academy of Engineering and Institute of Medicine, Washington, D.C.

National Commission on Research. 1980. *Funding Mechanisms Balancing Objectives and Resources in University Research.* Washington, D.C.

National Science Board. 1984. 1985. 1986a. *Science Indicators.* Government Printing Office, Washington, D.C.

———. 1986b. *Academic Research Facilities: Financing Strategies.* National Academy Press, Washington, D.C.

National Science Foundation. 1985. *Science and Engineering Personnel: A National Overview* (NSF 85-302). Washington D.C.

Nelson, R. R. and S. G. Winter. 1982. *An Evolutionary Theory of Economic Change.* The Belknap Press of Harvard University Press, Cambridge.

New York Times. 1986. "Oil Glut May Drown Texas Universities' Hope of Joining Elite." (May 20): 8.

Peterson, P. E. 1986. "Commissionitis in Higher Education." *The Brookings Review,* 4 (Winter/Spring): 21-6.

Stanford University. 1985. *Annual Financial Report.* Stanford News and Publications Services, Palo Alto.

State of California. 1986. *Governor's Budget.*

———. 1985-86. *Legislative Analyst's Analysis of the Budget Bill for 1985-86.*

United States General Accounting Office. 1986. *Federal Funding Mechanisms in Support of University Research.* Gaithersburg, Maryland.

University of California. 1980. *Partnership Between Universities and the Federal Government.* Office of the Executive Assistant to the President, Berkeley.

———. 1982. "Interim Guidelines on Industry-University Relations," Office of the President, University of California, Berkeley.

———. 1985-86. *Regents' Budget.* Regents of the University of California, Berkeley.

Von Neumann, J. 1955/1986. "Can We Survive Technology? John Von Neumann on Technological Prospects and Global Limits." *Population and Development Review* 12 (1) (March): 117-126.

Chapter Three

* Supplemental funding for this chapter was provided by the Avron B. and Robert F. Fogelman Academic Excellence Fund. The definitions of goals in this chapter are based on research that was first published in the *Journal of Higher Education*, Vol. 59, No. 6 (Nov/Dec 1988), 611-633. Copyright 1988 Ohio State University Press. All rights reserved.

References

Becker, W. E. and D. M. Waldman. 1987. *Econometric Modeling in Economic Education Research*. Boston; Kluwer-Neijhoff Publishing.

Berdahl, R. and S. K. Gove. 1982. "Governing Higher Education: Faculty Roles on State Boards." *Academe* 68 (May/June): 21-24.

Bowen, H. R. 1980. *Investment in Learning* San Francisco: Jossey-Bass.

——— . 1984. "Opportunities for Optimism." *Change* 12 (April): 18-13.

Cohn, E. 1979. *The Economics of Education*. Cambridge: Ballinger Publishing Company.

Coleman, J.S., et al. 1966. *Equality of Educational Opportunity*. Washington D.C.: Government Printing Office.

Conrad, C. 1974. "University Goals: An Operative Approach." *Journal of Higher Education* 45 (7)(October): 504-16.

Elgart, L. D. and L. Schanfield. 1984. "Private Colleges in the 1980s." *The Educational Forum* 48(Summer): 449-57.

Fallows, S. 1983. "Federal Support for Graduate Education in the Sciences and Engineering." Paper prepared for the Ad Hoc Committee on Government-University Relationships in Support of Science, National Academy of Sciences.

Fenske, R. H. 1980. "Setting Institutional Goals and Objectives." in P. Jedamus, M. Peterson and Associates (eds.), *Improving Academic Management*. San Francisco: Jossey-Bass.

Ferguson, C. E. *Microeconomic Theory*. 1969. Homewood: Richard D. Irwin. Chapters 1 and 2.

Freeman, R. 1971. *The Market for College Trained Manpower*. Cambridge: Harvard University Press.

Gardner, J. W. 1965. *Remarks at the Inauguration of James R. Perkins as President of Cornell University*. October.

Hoenack, S. A., and D. J. Berg. 1980. "The Role of Incentives in Academic Planning." *New Directions for Institutional Research* 28: 73-95.

Kohler, H. 1986. *Intermediate Microeconomics: Theory and Applications*. Glenview: Scott, Foresman and Company.

Mann, W. R., and D. R. Fusfeld. 1970. "Attitude Sophistication and Effective Teaching in Economics." *Journal of Higher Education* (Spring).

Mayeske, G. W., et al. 1972. *A Study of Our Nation's Schools*. Washington: U.S. Office of Education.

McPherson, M. S. 1983. "Value Conflicts in American Higher Education: A Survey." *Journal of Higher Education* 34 (May/June): 243-74.

Perkins, H. 1984. "Defining the True Functions of the University: A Question of Freedom versus Control." *Change* 16 (July/August): 20-29.

Pratt, L. K. and D. R. Reichard. 1983. "Assessing Institutional Goals." *New Directions for Institutional Research* 10 (March): 53-66.

Rugg, E. A., T. Warren, and E. L. Carpenter. 1981. "Faculty Orientations Toward Institutional Change." *Research in Higher Education* 15 (Fall): 161-73.

Tuckman, H. P. and C. F. Chang. 1988. "Conflict, Congruence, and Generic University Goals." *Journal of Higher Education* 59 (November/December): 611-33.

Wallin, F. W. 1983. "Universities for a Small Planet— A Time to Reconceptualize Our Role." *Change* 15 (March): 7-9.

Zumeta, W. 1985. *Extending the Educational Ladder: The Changing Quality and Value of Postdoctoral Study*. Lexington: D. C. Heath and Company.

Chapter Four

References

Alpert, Daniel. 1985. "Performance and Paralysis: The Organizational Context of the American Research University," *Journal of Higher Education* 56: 241-81.

Balderston, Frederick. 1974. *Managing Today's University*. San Francisco: Jossey-Bass.

———. 1983. "Strategic Management Approaches for the 1980s: Navigating in the Trough." In *The Crisis in Higher Education*, ed. Joseph Froomkin. New York: Proceedings of the Academy of Political Science.

Baldridge, J. 1971a. *Power and Conflict in the University*. New York: Wiley.

———. 1971b. *Academic Governance*. Berkeley: McCutchan.

Baumol, William J. 1967. *Business Behavior, Value and Growth*. New York: Harcourt, Brace.

Becker, William E. 1979. "Perspectives from Economics: The Economic Consequences of Changing Faculty Reward Structures." In *Academic Rewards in Higher Education*, eds. Darrell Lewis and William Becker. Cambridge: Ballinger.

Ben-David, Joseph. 1971. *American Higher Education, Directions Old and New*. New York: McGraw-Hill.

Breneman, David. 1970. *An Economic Theory of Ph.D. Production: The Case at Berkeley*. Berkeley: Ford Foundation Program for Research in University Administration, University of California.

Brown, David. 1967. *The Mobile Professors*. Washington, D.C.: American Council on Education.

Caplow, Theodore and Reece McGee. 1958. *The Academic Marketplace*. New York: Basic Books.

Chubb, John and Terry Moe. 1985. "Politics, Markets and the Organization of Schools," Brookings Institution, mimeo.

Cohen, Michael and James March. 1974. *Leadership and Ambiguity*. New York: McGraw-Hill.

Colander, David C. and Aijo Klamer. 1987. "The Making of an Economist." *The Journal of Economic Perspectives* 1: 95-111.

Cootner, Paul. 1974. "Economic Organization and Inefficiency in the Modern University." In *Efficiency in Universities: The La Paz Papers*, ed. Keith Lumsden. Amsterdam: Elsevier.

Doi, James I. 1974. "Assessing Faculty Effort." In *New Directions for Institutional Research*. San Francisco: Jossey-Bass.

Dornbusch, Sanford. 1979. "Perspectives from Sociology: Organizational Evaluation of Faculty Performances." In *Academic Rewards in Higher Education*, ed. Darrell Lewis and William Becker. Cambridge: Ballinger.

Doyle, Kenneth. 1979. "Use of Student Evaluations in Faculty Personnel Decisions." In *Academic Rewards in Higher Education*, ed. Darrell Lewis and William Becker. Cambridge: Ballinger.

Ehrenberg, Ronald and Daniel Sherman. 1984. "Optimal Financial Aid Policies for a Selective University." *Journal of Human Resources* 19: 202-30.

Garvin, David. 1980. *The Economics of University Behavior*. New York: Academic Press.

Gross, E. and P. Grambusch. 1968. *University Goals and Academic Power* Washington, D.C.: American Council on Education.

————. 1974. *Changes in University Organization: 1964-71.* New York: McGraw-Hill.

Hagstrom, Warren. 1971. "Inputs, Outputs and the Prestige of American University Science Departments." *Sociology of Education* 44 (Fall): 375-97.

Hoenack, Stephen. 1977. "Direct and Incentive Planning within a University." *Socio-Economic Planning Sciences* 11: 191-204.

———— and David Berg. 1980. "The Roles of Incentives in Academic Planning." *New Directions for Institutional Research* 28: 73-95.

———— and Alfred Norman. 1974. "Incentives and Resource Allocation in Universities." *Journal of Higher Education* 45 (January): 21-37.

———— and Daniel Pierro. 1990. "An Econometric Model of a Public University's Income and Enrollments." *Journal of Economic Behavior and Organization.* Forthcoming.

————, William Weiler. Rebecca Goodman, and Daniel Pierro. 1986. "The Marginal Costs of Instruction." *Research in Higher Education* 24: 335-418.

Hopkins, David and William Massy. 1981. *Planning Models for Colleges and Universities.* Stanford: Stanford University Press.

James, Estelle. 1978. "Product Mix and Cost Disaggregation: A Reinterpretation of the Economics of Higher Education." *Journal of Human Resources* 13: 157-86.

————. 1983. "How Nonprofits Grow: A Model." *Journal of Policy Analysis and Management* 2(Spring): 350-65. Reprinted in *The Nonprofit Sector: Economic Theory and Public Policy.* ed. Susan Rose-Ackerman. New York: Oxford University Press, 1986.

————. 1986. "Cross Subsidization in Higher Education: Does it Pervert Private Choice and Public Policy?" In *Private Education: Studies in Choice and Public Policy*, ed. Daniel Levy. New York, Oxford: Oxford University Press.

———— and Gail Benjamin. 1988. *Public versus Private Education: The Japanese Experiment.* London: Macmillan.

———— and Egon Neuberger. 1981. "The University Department as a Nonprofit Labor Cooperative." *Public Choice* 36: 585-612.

———— and Susan Rose-Ackerman. 1986. "The Nonprofit Enterprise in Market Economies." In *Fundamentals of Pure and Applied Economics*, ed. J. Lesourne and H. Sonnenschein. London: Harwood.

Jencks, Christopher and David Reisman. 1968. *The Academic Revolution.* New York: Doubleday.

Katz, D. A. 1973. "Faculty Salaries, Promotions and Productivity at a Large University." *American Economic Review* (June): 469-77.

Leslie, Larry and Garey Ramey. 1986. "State Appropriations and Enrollments." *Journal of Higher Education* 57: 1-19.

Levy, Daniel. 1986. *Higher Education and the State in Latin America: Private Challenges to Public Dominance.* Chicago: University of Chicago Press.

Lewis, Darrell and William E. Becker. 1979. *Academic Rewards in Higher Education.* Cambridge: Ballinger.

Manns, Curtis and James March. 1978. "Financial Adversity, Internal Competition and Curriculum Change at a University." *Administrative Science Quarterly* 23: 541-52.

March, James and Johan Olsen. 1976. *Ambiguity and Choice in Organizations.* Bergen: Universitetsforlaget.

Mayhew, Lewis B. 1970. *Graduate and Professional Education, 1980: A Survey of Institutional Plans.* New York: McGraw-Hill.

McKenzie, Richard B. 1979. *The Political Economy of the Educational Process.* Boston: Martinus Nijhoff.

O'Donoghue, M. 1971. *Economic Dimensions in Education.* Chicago: Aldine.

Peltzman, Sam. 1976. "The Effect of Government Subsidies-in-Kind on Private Expenditures: The Case of Higher Education." *Journal of Political Economy* 84: 1-27.

Pfeffer, Jeffrey and William Moore. 1980. "Proven University Budgeting: A Replication and Extension." *Administrative Science Quarterly* 25: 637-53.

Pfeffer, J. and G. Salancik. 1974. "Organizational Decision-Making as a Political Process: The Case of a University Budget." *Administrative Science Quarterly* 19 (December): 135-50.

Richman, Barry and Richard Farmer. 1974. *Leadership, Goals and Power in Higher Education.* San Francisco: Jossey-Bass.

Salancik, G. and J. Pfeffer. 1974. "The Bases and Use of Power in Organizational Decision-Making: The Case of a University." *Administrative Science Quarterly* 19 (December): 453-73.

Siegfried, John and Kenneth White. 1973. "Teaching and Publishing as Determinants of Academic Salaries." *Journal of Economic Education* 4 (Spring): 90-99.

Tuckman, Howard. 1979. "The Academic Reward Structure in American Higher Education." In *Academic Rewards in Higher Education*, ed. Darrell Lewis and William Becker. Cambridge: Ballinger.

————— , James Gapinski and Robert Hagamann. 1977. "Faculty Skills and The Salary Structure in Academia: A Market Perspective." *American Economic Review* 67 (September): 692-701.

Verry, Donald and Bleddyn Davies. 1976. *University Costs and Outputs.* Amsterdam: Elsevier.

Vladeck, Bruce. 1976. "Why Nonprofits Go Broke." *The Public Interest* 42 (Winter): 86-101.

Williamson, Oliver. 1964. *The Economics of Discretionary Behavior.* Englewood Cliffs: Prentice-Hall.

—————. 1975. *Markets and Hierarchies.* New York: Free Press.

Zemsky, Robert, Randall Porter, and Laura Oedel. 1978. "Decentralized Planning to Share Responsibility." *Educational Record* 59 (Summer): 229-53.

Chapter Five

References

Adams, C. R., R. L. Hankins, and R. G. Schroeder. 1978. "The Literature of Cost and Cost Analysis in Higher Education." Volume 1 in *A Study of Cost Analysis in Higher Education.* Washington, D.C.: American Council on Education.

Allen, R. H., and P. T. Brinkman. 1983. *Marginal Costing Techniques for Higher Education.* Boulder, Col.: National Center for Higher Education Management Systems.

Baumol, W. J., J. C. Panzar, and R. D. Willig. 1982. *Contestable Markets and the Theory of Industry Structure.* New York: Harcourt Brace Jovanovich.

Borgmann, C. W., and J. W. Bartram. 1969. *Mineral Engineering Education in the West.* Boulder, Col.: Western Interstate Commission for Higher Education.

Bottomley, A. 1972. *Costs and Potential Economies.* Studies in Institutional Management in Higher Education, University of Bradford. Paris: Organization for Economic Co-Operation and Development.

Bowen, H. R. 1980. *The Costs of Higher Education: How Much Do Colleges and Universities Spend Per Student and How Much Should They Spend?* San Francisco: Jossey-Bass.

————— and G. K. Douglass. 1971. *Efficiency in Liberal Education.* New York: McGraw-Hill.

Brinkman, P. T. 1981a. "Factors Affecting Instructional Costs at Major Research Universities." *The Journal of Higher Education* 52: 265-79.

———. 1981b. *Marginal Costs of Instruction in Public Higher Education.* Ph.D. dissertation, University of Arizona.

———. 1984. *A Comparison of Expenditure Patterns in Four-Year Public and Private Institutions.* Mimeo. Boulder, Col.: National Center for Higher Education Management Systems.

———. 1985. *Instructional Costs Per Student Credit Hour: Differences by Level of Instruction.* Mimeo. Boulder, Col.: National Center for Higher Education Management Systems.

——— and L. L. Leslie. 1986. "Economies of Scale in Higher Education: Sixty Years of Research." *Review of Higher Education* 10: 1-28.

Broomall, L. W., B. T. Mahan, G. W. McLaughlin, and S. S. Patton. 1978. "Economies of Scale in Higher Education." Blacksburg, V.: Virginia Polytechnic Institute and State University, Office of Institutional Research. (ERIC No. ED 162604.)

Brovender, S. 1974. "On the Economics of a University: Toward the Determination of Marginal Cost of Teaching Services." *Journal of Political Economy* 82: 657-64.

Buckles, S. 1978. "Identification of Causes of Increasing Costs in Higher Education." *Southern Economic Journal* 45: 258-65.

Butter, I. H. 1966. *Economics of Graduate Education: an Exploratory Study.* Ann Arbor: The University of Michigan, Department of Economics. (ERIC No. ED 010639.)

California Coordinating Council for Higher Education. 1969. *Meeting the Enrollment Demand for Public Higher Education in California through 1977—the Need for Additional College and University Campuses.* Sacramento: Coordinating Council for Higher Education.

Calkins, R. N. 1963. *The Unit Costs of Programmes in Higher Education.* Ph.D. dissertation, Columbia University.

Carlson, D. E. 1972. *The Production and Cost Behavior of Higher Education Institutions.* Ford Foundation Program for Research in University Administration. Berkeley: University of California. (ERIC No. ED 081375).

———. 1975. "Examining Efficient Joint Production Processes." In R. A. Wallhaus, ed., *Measuring and Increasing Academic Productivity.* New Directions for Institutional Research, no. 8. San Francisco: Jossey-Bass.

Carnegie Commission on Higher Education. 1972. *The More Effective Use of Resources.* New York: McGraw-Hill.

Christensen, L. R., D. W. Jorgenson, and L. J. Lau. 1973. "Transcendental Logarithmic Production Frontiers." *Review of Economics and Statistics* 55: 28-45.

Cohn, E. 1979. *The Economics of Education.* Cambridge: Ballinger.

Cohn, E., S.L.W. Rhine, and M. C. Santos. 1989. "Institutions of Higher Education as Multi-Product Firms: Economies of Scale and Scope." *The Review of Economics and Statistics* 71 (May): 284-90.

Corrallo, S. B. 1970. *An Analysis of Instructional Expenditures for Institutions of Higher Education in the Northeast United States.* Ph.D. dissertation, State University of New York at Buffalo.

Dean, J. 1976. *Statistical Cost Estimation.* Bloomington, Ind.: Indiana University Press.

Gibson, T. T. 1968. *Unit Costs of Higher Education: A Study of the University of Colorado.* Ph.D. dissertation, University of Colorado.

Gonyea, M. A. 1978. *Analyzing and Constructing Cost.* New Directions for Institutional Research, no. 17. San Francisco: Jossey-Bass.

Gray, R., and K. Weldon. 1978. *An Experiment with Convex Production Functions.* Boulder, Col. National Center for Higher Education Management Systems.

Health Resources and Services Administration. 1986. *Cost Estimating Model for Baccalaureate Nursing Education Programs.* Washington, D.C.: U.S. Department of Health and Human Services.

Henderson, J. M. and R. E. Quandt. 1971. *Microeconomic Theory: A Mathematical Approach.* New York: McGraw-Hill.

Hoenack, S. A., W. C. Weiler, R. D. Goodman, and D. J. Pierro. 1986. "The Marginal Costs of Instruction." *Research in Higher Education* 24: 335-417.

James, E. 1978. "Product Mix and Cost Disaggregation: A Reinterpretation of the Economics of Higher Education." *Journal of Human Resources* 13: 157-86.

Lave, J. R. and L. B. Lave. 1970. "Hospital Cost Functions." *American Economic Review* 60: 379-95.

Lyell, E. H. 1979. "The Cost Structure of Higher Education: Implications for Governmental Policy in Steady State." Paper presented at the Annual Meeting of the American Educational Research Association, San Francisco, April. (ERIC No. ED 172634.)

Maynard, J. 1971. *Some Microeconomics of Higher Education.* Lincoln: University of Nebraska Press.

Mayo, J. W. 1984. "Multiproduct Monopoly, Regulation, and Firm Costs." *Southern Economic Journal* 51 (July): 208-12.

McFadden, D. 1978. "Cost, Revenue, and Profit Functions." In *Production Economics: A Dual Approach to Theory Application*, vol. 1, edited by M. Fuss and D. McFadden. Amsterdam: North-Holland Publishing Co.

McLaughlin, G. W., J. R. Montgomery, A. W. Smith, and L. W. Broomall. 1980. "Size and Efficiency." *Research in Higher Education* 12: 53-66.

Metz, G. E. 1964. *Current Fund Expenditures.* Atlanta: Commission on Colleges, Southern Association of Colleges and Schools.

Middlebrook, W. T. 1955. *California and Western Conference Cost and Statistical Study for the Year 1954-1955.* Berkeley: University of California.

O'Neill, J. 1971. *Resource Use in Higher Education: Trends in Output and Inputs, 1930-1967.* Berkeley, Calif.: Carnegie Commission on Higher Education.

Pauly, M. V. 1978. "Medical Staff Characteristics and Hospital Costs." *Journal of Human Resources* 13: 77-111.

Razin, A., and J. Campbell. 1972. "Internal Allocation of University Resources." *Western Economic Journal* 10: 308-20.

Russell, J. D., and F. W. Reeves. 1935. "The Evaluation of Higher Institutions." *Finance*, vol. 7. Chicago: University of Chicago Press.

Scherer, F. M. 1980. *Industrial Market Structure and Economic Performance*, 2d ed. Chicago: Rand McNally.

Sengupta, J. K. 1975. "Cost and Productivity Functions in the University Education System: An Econometric Analysis. In H. Correa, ed., *Analytical Models in Educational Planning and Administration.* New York: David McKay.

Shepard, R. W. 1953. *Cost and Production Functions.* Princeton, N.J.: Princeton University Press.

Siegel, B. N. 1967. *Costing Students in Higher Education—A Case Study.* Eugene, Ore.: University of Oregon. (ERIC No. ED 014143.)

Smith, J. D. 1980. *Impact of Health Programs on Instructional Expenditures in Higher Education.* Boulder, Col.: National Center for Higher Education Management Systems.

Smith, N. S. 1978. *An Economic Analysis of the Costs of Instruction in the Michigan System of Higher Education.* Ph.D. dissertation, Michigan State University.

Stevens, E. B., and E. C. Elliot. 1925. "Unit Costs of Higher Education." *The Educational Finance Inquiry*, no. 13. New York: Macmillan.

Stommel, M. 1985. *Effects and Consequences of Organization Size: A Study of Land-Grant Institutions.* Ph.D. dissertation, Michigan State University.

Terman, F. E. 1969. "Economic Factors Relating to Engineering Programs." *Journal of Engineering Education* 59: 510-14.

Tierney, M. L. 1980. "An Estimate of Departmental Cost Functions." *Higher Education* 9: 453-68.

To, Duc-Le. 1987. *Estimating the Costs of a Bachelor's Degree: An Institutional Cost Analysis.* Washington, D.C.: Office of Educational Research and Improvement, U.S. Department of Education.

Verry, D., and B. Davies. 1976. *University Costs and Output.* Amsterdam: Elsevier.

Witmer, D. R. 1972. "Cost Studies in Higher Education." *Review of Educational Research* 42: 99-125.

Chapter Six

Notes

1. For a private institution, such costs depend on its competitive situation, while the costs facing a public university's legislature depend either on the constraints it imposes or, if these are loose enough, on its demand function. Such constraints could be the institution's awareness that the legislature will take actions the university wants to avoid if its cost per student to the legislature exceeds a certain amount. For example, a legislature might open or expand competing institutions or intervene to impose workload requirements within the institution.

2. Surveys of the literature on descriptive studies of instructional costs can be found in Adams, Hankins, and Schroeder (1977, vol. 1) and Powell and Lamson (1970). The concepts of this approach to costing were developed in the 1930s. However, interest in these studies grew in the 1960s when the National Center for Higher Education Management Systems (formerly Western Interstate Commission for Higher Education) developed its Resource Requirements Prediction Model which in turn was based on a model developed by Weathersby (1967). This work included the use of regression analyses for the calculation of allocation formulas and workload requirements. The aggregation categories and instability of regression coefficients of this type of model have come under criticism (Hopkins, 1971), and it is not in widespread use. Presently, however, many, if not most research universities make essentially the same calculations using accounting formulas and their historical enrollment data.

3. Incentive-based budgeting systems have been suggested as an alternative to centralized internal planning based on cost data and other measures of departmental performance. See Hoenack and Berg (1980) and the references cited therein.

4. Nerlove's (1972) paper remains one of the best available theoretical discussions of the jointness of research and instruction. Becker's (1979) work

advances understanding of productive behavior in higher education by analyzing the optimal behavior of academic personnel, given the production tradeoffs and incentives facing them.

5. It was pointed out by James (1978, p. 166) that "in 1972, only seven percent of all university faculty positions were located in organized research." She suggested that her data underestimated the costs of nonsponsored research because of unpaid summer research activity.

6. The lack of complexity of two-year and four-year institutions may result in relatively tight constraints facing their personnel. As a result, it is possible that estimated cost functions roughly approximate costs facing their faculties and support staffs. However, there remains the problem of identifying these functions vis-à-vis demand. Larger two- and four-year institutions may well face lower marginal valuations of their services. Models of demand and supply are needed in which each equation is identified on a priori grounds, and then, when estimated, there should be empirical tests of each equation's overidentifying restrictions.

7. A recent economic study (Garvin, 1980) provides an empirical analysis of the determinants—including sponsored research funding—of quality rankings or "prestige" in American universities. Although the equations in this study combine the behavior of departments, academic administrators, and funders, they provide some insights into the costs of enhancing quality.

Abowd (1977) provides another approach to the economic analysis of quality in higher education. He estimated a model of the American higher education market based on Sherwin Rosen's (1974) theoretical model of implicit markets. The implicit prices in both the demand and supply equations of this model are derived from an estimated market relationship between tuition and quality. The Rosen model provides many useful insights into markets for higher education. However there are problems in applying this model. These include the difficulty of measuring quality (Abowd simply used instructional expenditures per student), the difficulty of finding variables that are justified as a priori overidentifying zero restrictions, and some estimation problems (see Brown and Rosen, 1982).

References

Abowd, John M. 1984. *An Econometric Model of the U. S. Market for Higher Education.* New York: Garland Publishing Company.

Adams, Carl R., Russell L. Hankins, and Roger G. Schroeder. 1978. *A Study of Cost Analysis in Higher Education*, vols. 1-4, Washington, D.C.: American Council on Education.

Albright, Brenda. 1982. "Capital Renewal in the 1980's: A State Perspective." In Robert A. Wilson, ed., *Responses to Fiscal Stress in Higher Education.* Tucson: Center for Study of Higher Education, University of Arizona.

Baumol, William J., John C. Panzar, and Robert D. Willig. 1982. *Contestable*

Markets and the Theory of Industry Structure. New York: Harcourt Brace Jovanovich.

Becker, William E. 1979. "Perspectives from Economics: The Economic Consequences of Changing Faculty Reward Structures." In Darrell Lewis and William E. Becker, eds., *Academic Rewards in Higher Education*, chap. 2. Cambridge, Mass.: Ballinger.

Berg, David J., and Stephen A. Hoenack. 1987. "The Concept of Cost-Related Tuition and Its Implementation at the University of Minnesota." *Journal of Higher Education* 58(3)(May/June): 276-305.

Berliner, Joseph S. 1957. *Factory and Manager in the U.S.S.R.* Cambridge: Harvard University Press.

Blau, Peter M. 1963. *The Dynamics of Bureaucracy: A Study of Interpersonal Relations in Two Government Agencies*, chap. 3, 2d ed., Chicago: University of Chicago Press.

Blaug, Mark 1981. "The Economic Costs and Benefits of Overseas Students." In Peter Williams ed., *The Overseas Student Question*. London: Heinemann Educational Books.

Bowen, Howard R., 1980. *The Costs of Higher Education*. San Francisco: Jossey-Bass.

Brinkman, Paul T. 1981a. "Factors Affecting Instructional Costs at Major Research Universities." *Journal of Higher Education* 52(3) (May/June): 265-79.

————. 1981b. *Marginal Costs of Instruction in Public Higher Education*. Ph.D. Dissertation, University of Arizona.

———— and Larry L. Leslie. 1986. "Economies of Scale in Higher Education: Sixty Years of Research." Unpublished manuscript.

Brown, James N., and Harvey S. Rosen. 1982. "On the Estimation of Structural Hedonic Price Models." *Econometrica* 50: 756-68.

Butter, Irene H. 1966. *Economics of Graduate Education: An Exploratory Survey*. Washington, D. C.: U. S. Office of Education.

Charles River Associates. 1986. *Capital Intensity in University Scientific Research*, CRA Report No. 820-06. Sponsored by the National Science Foundation, Division of Policy Research and Analysis. Boston: Charles River Associates.

Cohn, Elchanan, Sherrie L.W. Rhine, and Maria C. Santos. 1989. "Institutions of Higher Education as Multi-Product Firms: Economies of Scale and Scope." *The Review of Economics and Statistics* 71 (May): 284-90.

Executive Office of the President, Office of Management and Budget. 1982. "Principles for Determining Costs Applicable to Grants, Contracts, and

Other Agreements with Education Institutions," Government Printing Office. Washington, D.C.: Circular no. A-21, August.

Garvin, David A. 1980. *The Economics of University Behavior.* New York: Academic Press.

Goodman, Rebecca D. 1985. "A Neglected Element of Institutional Costs Analysis: A Study of the Costs of Federally Sponsored Research." Minneapolis: Management Information Division, University of Minnesota.

Hoenack, Stephen A. 1983. *Economic Behavior Within Organizations.* Cambridge and New York: Cambridge University Press.

─────── and David J. Berg. 1980. "The Roles of Incentives in Academic Planning." In Richard B. Heydinger, ed, *Academic Planning for the 1980's, New Directions for Institutional Research,* vol. 28. San Francisco: Jossey-Bass.

─────── and Daniel J. Pierro. 1990. "An Econometric Model of a Public University's Income and Enrollments." To appear in the *Journal of Economic Behavior and Organization.*

Hoenack, Stephen A., William C. Weiler, Rebecca D. Goodman, and Daniel Pierro. 1986. "The Marginal Costs of Instruction." University of Minnesota. *Research in Higher Education.* 24 (No. 4): 335-418.

Hopkins, David S. P. 1971. "On the Use of Large-Scale Simulation Models for University Planning." *Review of Educational Research* (5) (December): 467-78.

Hyatt, James A. 1983. "A Cost Accounting Handbook for Colleges and Universities." Washington, D. C.: National Association of College and University Business Officers.

James, Estelle. 1978. "Product Mix and Cost Disaggregation: A Reinterpretation of the Economics of Higher Education." *Journal of Human Resources* 13: 157-186.

─────── and Egon Neuberger. 1981. "The University Department as a Non-Profit Labor Cooperative." *Public Choice* 36: 585-612.

Jenny, Hans H., with Geoffrey C. Hughes and Richard D. Devine. 1981. *Hang-Gliding or Looking for an Updraft: A Study of College and University Finance in the 1980's-The Capital Margin.* Wooster, Oh. and Boulder, Col.: The College of Wooster and John Minter Associates, Inc.

Lumsden, Keith G., 1974. *Efficiency in Universities: The La Paz Papers.* Amsterdam: Elsevier.

National Association of College and University Business Officers. 1980. "Costing for Policy Analysis." Washington, D. C.: National Center for Higher Education Management Systems.

National Science Foundation. 1984. *Federal Support to Universities, Colleges and Selected Non-Profit Institutions.* Washington, D.C.: National Science Foundation.

Nerlove, Marc. 1972. "On Tuition and the Costs of Higher Education: Prolegomena to a Conceptual Framework." *Journal of Political Economy* 80 (3 pt. 2) (May/June): S178-S218.

O'Neill, June. 1971. *Resource Use in Higher Education.* Berkeley, Ca.: Carnegie Commission on Higher Education.

Powell, John H., Jr., and Robert D. Lamson. 1970. *Elements Related to the Determination of Costs and Benefits of Graduate Education.* Washington, D. C.: The Council of Graduate Schools.

Robinson, Daniel D. 1986. *Capital Maintenance for Colleges and Universities.* Washington, D. C.: National Association for College and University Business Officers.

Rosen, Sherwin. 1974. "Hedonic Prices and Implicit Markets: Product Differentiation in Pure Competition." *Journal of Political Economy* 82: 34-55.

Russell, John Dale. 1954. *The Finance of Higher Education.* Chicago: University of Chicago Press.

Verry, Donald, and Bleddyn Davies. 1976. *University Costs and Outputs.* Amsterdam: Elsevier.

Weathersby, George B. 1967. "The Development and Application of a University Cost Simulation Model." Berkeley, Ca.: Office of Analytical Studies, University of California.

Witmer, David R. 1971. "Cost Studies in Higher Education." *Review of Educational Research* 42 (1): 99-127.

Woodrow, Raymond J. 1972. "Government-University Financial Arrangements for Research." *Science* 176(May 25): 885-9.

Chapter Seven

* In the development of this chapter Suzanne Becker, Eileen Collins, Masanori Hashimoto, Stephen Hoenack, and Catherine Melfi provided helpful comments and suggestions. Mary K. Welsh's patience and skill in word processing is also appreciated.

Notes

1. In the preparation of this review, an attempt was made to secure bibliographic information on enrollments, research, and service from the major online computer services. Searches were made on ERIC (Educational Resource Infor-

mation Center), H. W. Wilson's Education Index, AWPE (Abstracts of Working Papers in Economics), ELI (Economic Literature Index). ABI/INFORM (Abstracted Business Information), SOCIAL SCISEARCH (Social Science Index). In most cases the search was limited to key word searches of the type "Research, within two words of higher education" or "Enrollments, within two words of postsecondary." In the case of ELI the search was done by codes fields. Document retrieval was restricted to U.S. education. All of the computer searches were conducted by Pat Riesman, Indiana University reference librarian.

The online computer searches and document retrievals produced a glut of quantitative information on enrollment demand for higher eduation, a sizeable fraction of which is reviewed here. These searches, however, did not turn up a substantial body of literature on the quantitative aspects of the applied or basic research demand for higher education or the service demand for higher education. While this finding may be interesting, its implications are unclear. Our inability to find a well-defined body of literature on the research and service demands for institutions of higher education may reflect our inappropriate use of word limiters (although we tried many different combinations), the online computer services' poor classification systems, or their omission of significant bodies of literature (although ERIC currently shows itself to be relatively good in most other educational areas) or the actual lack of research in the area. This issue should be pursued further.

2. Leslie et al. (1981) provided demographic information on 554 liberal arts colleges for the 1965-77 period. They show data that suggest that many of the less-than-top-quality full-time, undergraduate, single-purpose institutions are becoming increasingly part-time, graduate, and occupationally oriented. When taken as a group, their data suggest that liberal arts colleges show more stable FTE (full-time equivalent) enrollment patterns than all institutions nationally.

3. Using trend analysis Rusk et al. (1982) state that short-run variations in economic activity had considerably more impact on enrollment during the mid 1970s than during the 1960s. They feel that enrollments have not slackened to the degree that some of the 'long-term analysts' had forecasted. Instead, what has developed is an increased sensitivity of enrollment to changes in labor-market conditions.

4. Moor (1979) provides an economic-demographic model and projections for enrollments in the state of Michigan. First, Moor determined the economic and demographic phenomena that jointly determine the size and distribution of the pool feeding higher education. Next he determined participation rates and then made enrollment projections. He concludes that Michigan enrollments will remain stable through the 1980s and then decline steadily until the mid-to-late 1990s; four-year institutions will fare better than two-year institutions.

5. For survey information on the perception of institutions as to who their competitors are, see Zammuto (1985). An interesting conclusion of Zammuto's is that competition was highest for major doctoral institutions and lowest for specialty institutions.

6. Weinschrott (1977) and Chisholm and Cohen (1982) are extremely critical of attempts to standardize and compare demand estimates from highly disparate time-series and cross-section studies, in which different variables as well as different equational forms are employed. To get an appreciation of the problem, consider how an elasticity is calculated. For demonstration purposes, consider the calculation of an enrollment/cost elasticities in the following diagram.

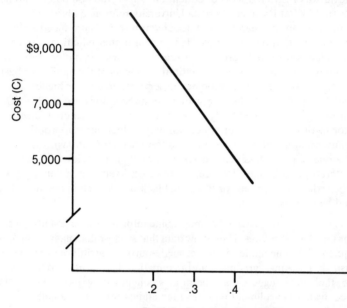

Participation Rate R = (E/P)

The participation rate (R) is defined by enrollment (E) divided by the eligible population (P) and college cost is C. The enrollment/cost elasticity is defined by $\alpha = (\delta R/R)/(\delta C/C)$, where δ indicates change. For example, a cost rise from $5,000 to $7,000 is associated with an elasticity value of

$$\alpha = \frac{\delta R/R}{\delta C/C} = \frac{(.3-.4)/.4}{(7000\text{-}5000)/5000} = -0.625$$

which indicates that a 1% rise in cost is associated with a 0.625% decrease in the participation rate. Alternatively, a cost rise from $7,000 to $9,000 is associated with an elasticity value of

$$\alpha = \frac{\delta R/R}{\delta C/C} = \frac{-.1/.3}{2000/7000} = -1.167$$

which indicates that a 1% rise in cost is associated with a 1.167% decrease in the participation rate. In general, a demand elasticity less (greater) than negative one implies that revenue will fall (rise) as price rises and quantity falls. For the above enrollment demand this is true if the eligiblity population remains fixed. A college receives revenue on the basis of enrollment (E) and not the participation rate (E/P).

While elasticity changes along the above linear (straight line) demand curve, the effect of a $100 increase in cost is always associated with a 0.5% reduction in the participation rate, i.e.,

$$a \ (\delta C/C)R \ = \ \delta R \ = \ -0.625(100/5000) \ (.4) \ = \ 0.005$$
$$a \ (\delta C/C)R \ = \ \delta R \ = \ -1.167(100/7000) \ (.3) \ = \ 0.005$$

Alternatively, if the demand curve is a rectangular hyperbola, as shown in the diagram below, then revenue and elasticity are constant along the curve (because $\delta C/C$ always equals $\delta R/R$), but the change in the participation rates resulting from a $100 increase in cost will depend on the starting point.

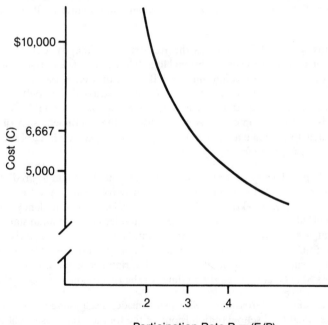

Participation Rate R = (E/P)

Other demand curve specifications give rise to different properties. On the basis of only the above two demand curves, however, it can be seen that any identical cost adjustment made to differently specified demand curves can be expected to produce different consequences.

Leslie and Brinkman (1987) acknowledge the concerns of Weinschrott, Chisholm and Cohen but proceed to recalculate the original Jackson and Weathersby

(1975) standardized enrollment effects. They then apply Glass et al.'s (1981) meta-analysis to standardized etimates obtained from twenty-five different studies. Unfortunately, consensus values obtained from meta-analysis have no known statistical properties and do not negate the problems raised by Weinschrott, Chisholm, and Cohen.

7. In OLS estimation, the proportion of the eligible population can be predicted to be greater than one or less than zero since OLS does not recognize these bounds. This problem can be overcome by using transformations of this proportion, see Cohn and Morgan (1978) for an example of the logistic transformation.

8. This zero mean and unit variance normalization of ϵ is not essential and is not used in real world applications but is convenient for pedagogical purposes. In the absence of this assumption, the β's are interpreted as parameters which have been divided by the standard deviation of ϵ. Since the scaling of the dependent variable is not observable, the scaling of the β's is never known. Thus, individual predicted utility levels are not meaningful but relative utility comparisons are.

9. Weinschrott (1977) criticizes the Radner and Miller specification for being more of an illustration of conditional logit "than a serious attempt to obtain the relevant parameters for policy analysis." Because they enter the ratio of cost to income as an explanatory variable, they have constrained the coefficient of costs and income to be equal in magnitude, though opposite in sign. We do not know if it is cost or income that is giving rise to the coefficient sign of this variable; a negative price elasticity may be due to the positive effect of income or the negative effect of cost.

10. Bishop and Van Dyk's regression equation enabled them to predict the effect of alternative tuition levels on total adult enrollment. They found that "lowering tuition from $400 to zero doubled the local college attendance rate of adults. Establishing a new two-year college in a standard metropolitan statistical area without one also doubled adult enrollment. None of the characteristics of local public four-year institutions was found to have a significant effect on adult enrollment. A supplementary logit analysis of variations of the average attendance across SMSAs confirmed the findings of the regression analysis" (p. 57).

11. Shakotko and Grossman (1980) also consider a schooling-choice model in which the vocational school option is one of the four alternatives available to recent high school graduates. (The other three are universities, junior colleges, and no postsecondary education.) Because they do not include variables for the price of each schooling alternative, unlike Corman they cannot estimate the price elasticities. Similar to Corman, however, they did find a negative relationship between income and vocational school attendance. More recently Strickland et al. (1984) reported a price elasticity of -1.8 for urban institutions (including old normal schools) and an insignificant price elasticity of -0.17 for the three major universities in the state of Virginia.

12. Most early studies of enrollment demand defined the cost variable to be net of financial aid. Thus tuition and financial aid where constrained to have the same coefficient, although opposite in sign. Carroll et al. (1977) was one of the first to attempted to model explicitly the effect of financial aid in the sequential decisions a student may make about post-high school alternatives.

13. Similar to Blakemore and Low's analysis of financial aid across institutions is Miller's (1981) study in which Stanford University's financial aid policy is considered in conjunction with enrollment decisions and admissions policies. Miller finds that "high school achievers are attracted to Stanford, loans offered instead of grants repel admitted applicants, and the higher a minority student's SAT score (for those with over approximately 500 points) the more they are attracted by Stanford's offers" (p. 130). Miller concludes, "the analysis shows that Stanford prefers to include minority members as a part of its community" (p. 131).

14. Heath and Tuckman (1987) review several of the more recent studies of the effect of financial aid on the college-going decision. Surprisingly, researchers are continuing to treat financial aid as if it were exogenous to the system. In assessing whether he or she will receive financial aid, a student must consider why an institution awards aid and whether he or she is a likely candidate for that aid based on the institution's interests.

References

Abowd, John M. 1981. *An Econometric Model of Higher Education.* Chicago: University of Chicago Press, pp. 1-56.

———. 1984. *An Econometric Model of the U.S. Market for Higher Education.* New York: Garland Publishing Co.

Agarwal, Vinod B., and Donald R. Winkler. 1985. "Foreign Demand for United States Higher Education: A Study of Developing Countries in the Eastern Hemisphere." *Economic Development and Cultural Change* 33(3): 623-44.

Ahlburg, Dennis, Eileen M. Crimmins, and Richard A. Easterlin. 1981. "The Outlook for Higher Education: A Cohort Size Model of Enrollment of the College Age Population, 1948-2000." *Review of Public Data Use* 9: 211-27.

Alexander, Elmore R., III, and Donald E. Frey. 1984. "An Econometric Estimate of the Demand for MBA Enrollment." *Economics of Education Review* 3(2): 97-103.

American Council on Education. 1982. Foreign Students and Institutional Policy: Toward an Agenda for Action: A Report of the Committee on Foreign Students and Institutional Policy, Washington, D.C.: American Council on Education.

Anderson, Charles Arnold, Mary Jean Bowman, and Vincent Tinto. 1972. *Where*

Colleges Are and Who Attends: Effects of Accessibility on College Attendance. New York: McGraw-Hill.

Anderson, Richard E. 1975. "Private/Public Higher Education and the Competition for High Ability Students." *The Journal of Human Resources* 10(4): 500-11.

Baird, Leonard L. 1984. "Relationships between Ability, College Attendance, and Family Income." *Research in Higher Education* 21(4): 373-95.

Becker, William E., and Donald M. Waldman. 1987. "The Probit Model." In William Becker and William Walstad, eds., *Econometric Modeling in Economic Education Research.* Boston: Kluwer-Nijhoff.

Bishop, John. 1977. "The Effect of Public Policies on the Demand for Higher Education," *Journal of Human Resources* 12(3)(Summer): 285-307.

Bishop, John, and Jane Van Dyk. 1977. "Can Adults Be Hooked on College? Some Determinants of Adult College Attendance." *Journal of Higher Education* 48(1)(January/February): 39-62.

Blakemore, Arthur E., and Stuart A. Low. 1983. "Scholarship Policy and Race-Sex Differences in the Demand for Higher Education." *Economic Inquiry* 21(4)(October): 504-19.

Borus, Michael E., and Susan A. Carpenter. 1984. "Factors Associated with College Attendance of High School Seniors." *Economics of Education Review* 3(3): 169-76.

Bowen, William B. 1977. "Economic Problems Confronting Higher Education: An Institutional Perspective." *American Economic Review* 67(1)(February): 96-100.

California Postsecondary Education Commission. 1980. *The Price of Admission: An Assessment of the Impact of Student Charges on Enrollments and Revenues in California Public Higher Education.* Sacramento: California Postsecondary Education Commission.

Campbell, Robert, and Barry N. Siegel. 1967. "Demand for Higher Education in the United States, 1919-1964." *American Economic Review* 57(June): 482-94.

Carlson, D., J. Farmer, and G. Weathersby. 1974. "A Framework for Analyzing Postsecondary Education Financing Policies." Washington, D.C.: Government Printing Office, May.

Carroll, R., B. Mori, D. Relles, and D. Weinschrott. 1977. *The Enrollment Effect of Students' Aid Policies.* Monograph R-2005-NIE/LE. Santa Monica, Cal.: Rand Corporation, June.

Carter, Allan M. 1976. *Ph.D.'s and the Academic Labor Market.* New York: McGraw-Hill.

Catsiapis, George. 1980. "Subsidization and Investment in Postsecondary Education with Application Using the U.S. National Longitudinal Study of the 1972 High School Class." Ph.D. dissertation, University of Chicago.

———, and Chris Robinson. 1982. "Sample Selection Bias with Multiple Selection Rules: An Application to Student Aid Grants." *Journal of Econometrics* 18: 351-68.

Chapman, R. 1977. "Buyer Behavior in Higher Education: An Analysis of College Choice Decision Making Behavior." Ph.D. dissertation, Carnegie-Mellon University.

Chisholm, M., and B. Cohen. 1982. *A Review and Introduction to Higher Education Price Response Studies.* Boulder, Col.: National Center for Higher Education Management Systems.

Chishti, Salim. 1984. "International Demand for American Higher Education." *Research in Higher Education* 20(3): 329-44.

Christiansen, Sandra, John Melder, and Burton A. Weisbrod. 1975. "Factors Affecting College Attendance." *Journal of Human Resources* 10(Spring): 174-88.

Clowes, Darrel, A., Dennis E. Hinkle, and John C. Smart. 1986. "Enrollment Patterns in Postsecondary Education, 1961-1982." *Journal of Higher Education* 57(2)(March/April): 121-33.

Cohn, Elchanan, and J. Michael Morgan. 1978. "The Demand for Higher Education: A Survey of Recent Studies." *Higher Education Review* 1(2)(Winter): 18-30.

Corazzini, Arthur J., D. Dugan, and H. Grabowski. 1972. "Determinants and Distributional Aspects of Enrollment in U.S. Higher Education." *Journal of Human Resources.* 7(1)(Winter): 39-59.

Corman, Hope. 1983. "Postsecondary Education Enrollment Responses by Recent High School Graduates and Older Adults." *The Journal of Human Resources* 18(2): 247-67.

Dresch, Stephen P. 1975. "Demography, Technology, and Higher Education: Toward a Formal Model of Educational Adaptation." *Journal of Political Economy* 83(3)(June): 535-69.

Ehrenberg, Ronald G., and Alan J. Marcus. 1982. "Minimum Wages and Teenagers' Enrollment-Employment Outcomes: A Multinominal Logit Model." *The Journal of Human Resources* 17(1): 39-58.

Ehrenberg, Ronald G., and Daniel R. Sherman. 1982. "Optimal Financial Aid Policies for a Selective University," Working Paper no. 1014. Cambridge, Mass.: National Bureau of Economic Research, November.

Etherington, C., and J. Smart. 1986. "Persistence to Graduate Education. *Research in Higher Education* 24: 287-303.

Feldman, P., and S. Hoenack. 1969. "Private Demand for Higher Education in the United States." *The Economics and Financing of Higher Education in the United States.* The Joint Economic Committee.

Frances, Carol. 1984. "1985: The Economic Outlook for Higher Education." *AAHE Bulletin* 37(4)(December): 3-6.

Freeman, Richard B. 1971. *The Market for College-Trained Manpower: A Study in the Economics of Career Choice.* Cambridge, Mass.: Harvard University Press.

————. 1976a. *The Over-Educated American.* New York: Academic Press.

————. 1976b. "Overinvestment in College Training?" *The Journal of Human Resources* 10(3): 287-311.

————. 1977. "The Decline in The Economic Rewards to College Education." *The Review of Economics and Statistics* 59: 18-29.

Fuller, Winship C., Charles F. Manski, and David A. Wise. 1982. "New Evidence on the Economic Determinants of Postsecondary Schooling Choices." *The Journal of Human Resources* 17(4): 477-95.

Fuller, Winship C., Charles F. Manski, and David A. Wise. 1983. "Impact of the BEOG Program on College Enrollments." In Elhanan Helpman, Assaf Razzin, and Efraim Sadka, eds., *Social Policy Evaluation: An Economic Perspective.* New York: Academic Press.

Galper, Harvey, and Robert M. Dunn, Jr. 1969. "A Short-Run Demand Function for Higher Education in the United States." *Journal of Political Economy* 77 (September/October): 765-77.

Garen, John. 1984. "The Returns to Schooling: A Selectivity Bias Approach with a Continuous Choice Variable." *Econometrica* 52(5)(September): 1199-1218.

Ghali, Moheb, Walter Miklius, and Richard Wada. 1977. "The Demand for Higher Education Facing an Individual Institution." *Higher Education* 6(4): 477-87.

Glass, Gene V., Barry McGraw, and Mary Lee Smith. 1981. *Meta-Analysis in Social Research.* Beverly Hills, Cal.: Sage Publications.

Glenny, Lyman A. 1980. "Demographic and Related Issues for Higher Education in the 1980s." *Journal of Higher Education* 51(July-August): 363-80.

Hansen, W. Lee. 1982. "Economic Growth and Equal Opportunity: Conflicting or Complementary Goals in Higher Education." Discussion Paper no. 706-82.

Madison, Wis.: Institute for Research on Poverty, University of Wisconsin, Madison.

Hansen, W. Lee, and Burton A. Weisbrod. 1969. *Benefits, Costs, and Finance of Public Higher Education.* Chicago: Markham.

Hearn, James C., and David Longanecker. 1985. "Enrollment Effects of Alternative Postsecondary Pricing Policies." *Journal of Higher Education* 56(5) (September/October): 485-508.

Heath, Julia A., and Howard P. Tuckman. 1987. "The Effects of Tuition Level and Financial Aid on the Demand for Undergraduate and Advanced Terminal Degrees." *Economics of Education Review* 6(3): 227-38.

Heckman, James J. 1976. "The Common Structure of Statistical Models of Truncation, Sample Selection and Limited Dependent Variables, and a Simple Estimator for Such Models." *Annals of Economic and Social Measurement* 5(4)(Fall): 475-92.

Hight, Joseph E. 1970. "The Supply and Demand of Higher Education in the U.S.: The Public and Private Institutions Compared." Paper presented to the Econometric Society (December).

————. 1975. "The Demand for Higher Education in the U.S., 1927-72: The Public and Private Institutions." *The Journal of Human Resources* 10(4): 512-20.

Hoenack, Stephen A. 1967. "Private Demand for Higher Education in California." Mimeo, Berkeley Office of Analytical Studies, University of California.

————. 1971. "The Efficient Allocation of Subsidies to College Students." *American Economic Review* 61(June): 302-11.

————, and William C. Weiler. 1975. "Cost-Related Tuition Policies and University Enrollments." *Journal of Human Resources* 10(3)(Summer): 332-60.

————, and William C. Weiler. 1979. "The Demand for Higher Education and Institutional Enrollment Forecasting." *Economic Inquiry* 17(1)(January): 89-113.

Hopkins, Thomas D. 1974. "Higher Education Enrollment." *Economic Inquiry* 12 (March): 53-65.

Hossler, Don. 1984. *Enrollment Management: An Integrated Approach.* New York: College Entrance Examination Board.

Howe, Wayne J. 1988. "Education and Demographics: How Do They Affect Unemployment Rates?" *Monthly Labor Review* 111(1)(January): 3-9.

Hu, T., and E. W. Stromsdorfer. 1973. *Demand and Supply of Higher Education in Massachusetts.* Study submitted to the Massachusetts Board of Higher Education. Boston, Mass.: Board of Higher Education.

Iwai, Stanley, and William D. Churchill. 1982. "College Attrition and the Financial Support Systems of Students." *Research in Higher Education* 17(2): 105-13.

Jackson, Gregory A., and Weathersby, George B. 1975. "Individual Demand for Higher Education: A Review and Analysis of Recent Empirical Studies." *Journal of Higher Education* 46(6)(Nov./Dec.): 623-52.

Kohn, M., C. F. Manski, and D. Mundel. 1972. "A Study in College Choice." Paper presented at the North American Regional Meeting of the Econometric Society, Toronto (December).

———. 1974. *An Empirical Investigation of Factors Which Influence College-Going Behavior.* Rand Report R-1470-NSF. Santa Monica: Rand Corp.

Lehr, Dona K., and Jan M. Newton. 1978. "Time Series and Cross-Sectional Investigations of the Demand for Higher Education." *Economic Inquiry* 16(3)(July): 411-22.

Leslie, Larry L., and Paul T. Brinkman. 1987. "Student Price Response in Higher Education: The Student Demand Studies." *Journal of Higher Education* 58(2)(March/April): 181-204.

———, Arthur Grant, and Kenneth Brown. 1981. "Patterns of Enrollment in Higher Education 1965 to 1977. Topical Paper no. 19, Center for the Study of Higher Education, College of Education, University of Arizona, January.

Manski, Charles F., and David A. Wise. 1983. *College Choice in America.* Cambridge: Harvard University Press.

McClain, D., B. Vance, and E. Wood. 1984. "Understanding and Predicting the Yield in the MBA Admissions Process." *Research in Higher Education* 20: 55-76.

McMahon, Walter W., and Alan P. Wagner. 1981. "Expected Returns to Investments in Higher Education." *The Journal of Human Resources* 16(2): 274-85.

McPherson, Michael S. 1978. "The Demand for Higher Education." In David W. Breneman and Chester E. Finn, Jr., eds., *Public Policy and Private Higher Education.* Washington: Brookings Institution.

Miller, Leonard S. 1981. "College Admissions and Financial Aid Policies as Revealed by Institutional Practices." *Economic Inquiry* 19(January): 117-31.

Moor, James R., Jr. 1979. *The Demand for Higher Education in Michigan: Projections to the Year 2000.* Lansing, Michigan: President's Council, State College and Universities.

Murphy, Kevin, and Finis Welch. 1988. "Wage Differentials in the 1980s: The Role of International Trade," Paper presented at The Mont Pelerin Society General Meeting, September 9.

Open Doors. 1980-81. "Report on International Educational Exchange." New York Institute of International Education.

Patton, Carl V. 1981. "Higher Education Revenue Sources." *Academe: Bulletin of the AAUP* 67(6)(December): 387-8.

Peng, S. S. 1977. "Trends in the Entry to Higher Education: 1961-1972." *Educational Researcher* 6(January): 15-19.

Radner, Roy, and Leonard S. Miller. 1975. *Demand and Supply in U.S. Higher Education.* New York: McGraw-Hill.

Rusk, James J., Larry L. Leslie, and Paul T. Brinkman. 1982. "The Increasing Impact of Economic Conditions upon Higher Education Enrollments." *Economics of Education Review* 2(1)(Winter): 25-48.

Scott, Charles E. 1979. "The Market for Ph.D. Economists: The Academic Sector." *American Economic Review* (Proceedings) 69(2): 137-42.

Sewell, William H. 1971. "Inequality of Opportunity for Higher Education." *American Sociological Review* 36(5)(October): 793-809.

———, and Vimal P. Shah. 1967. "Socioeconomic Status, Intelligence, and the Attainment of Higher Education." *Sociology of Education* 40(1)(Winter): 1-23.

———, and Vimal P. Shah. 1968. "Social Class, Parental Encouragement, and Educational Aspirations." *American Journal of Sociology* 73(March): 559-72.

Shakotko, Robert, and Michael Grossman. 1980. "Physical Disabilities and Post-Secondary Educational Outcomes." Working Paper no. 609, National Bureau of Economic Research, Cambridge (December).

Sloan, F. 1971. "The Demand for Higher Education: The Case of Medical School Applicants. *Journal of Human Resources* 6(4)(Fall): 466-89.

Soss, Neal M. 1974. "The Demand for College Education: The Application Decision." Ph.D. dissertation, Princeton University.

Spies, Richard R. 1973. *The Future of Private Colleges, the Effect of Rising Costs of College Choice.* Princeton: Industrial Relations Section, Princeton University.

Strickland, D., V. Bonomo, G. McLaughlin, J. Montgomery, and B. Mahan. 1984. "Effects of Social and Economic Factors on Four-Year Higher Education Enrollments in Virginia." *Research in Higher Education* 20: 35-53.

Tannen, Michael B. 1978. "The Investment Motive for Attending College." *Industrial and Labor Relations Review* 31(4)(July): 489-97.

Tierney, M. 1980. "The Impact of Financial Aid on Student Demand for Public/Private Higher Eduation." *Journal of Higher Education* 51: 527-45.

Tuckman, Howard P., and W. Scott Ford. 1972. *The Demand for Higher Education: A Florida Case Study.* Lexington, Mass: Lexington Books.

U.S. Bureau of the Census. 1965, 1967, 1969, 1971, 1973, 1975, 1978, 1980, 1982-1987. *Money Income of Families in the United States,* Series P-60, Washington, D.C.

Viehland, Dennis W., Norman S. Kaufman, and Barbara M. Krauth. 1982. "Indexing Tuition to Cost of Education: The Impact on Students and Institutions." *Research in Higher Education* 17(4): 333-43.

Venti, Steven F., and David A. Wise. 1983. "Individual Attributes and Self-Selection of Higher Education: College Attendance Versus College Completion." *Journal of Public Economics* 21(1): 1-32.

Weiler, William C. 1984. "Using Enrollment Demand Models in Institutional Pricing Decisions." In Larry H. Litten, ed., *Issues in Pricing Undergraduate Education.* San Francisco, Jossey-Bass.

Weinschrott, David J. 1977. *Demand for Higher Education in the United States: A Critical Review of the Empirical Literature.* Monograph R-2195-LE, Rand Corporation, Santa Monica, Cal., December.

Willis, Robert J., and Sherwin Rosen. 1979. "Education and Self-Selection." *Journal of Political Economy* 87(5, pt. 2)(October): S7-S36.

Windham, Douglas M. 1976. "Social Benefits and the Subsidization of Higher Education: A Critique." *Higher Education* 5(3): 237-52.

Winkler, Donald R. 1984. "The Fiscal Consequences of Foreign Students in Public Higher Education: A Case Study of California." *Economics of Education Review* 3(2): 141-54.

Wish, John R., and William D. Hamilton. 1980. "Replicating Freeman's Recursive Adjustment Model of Demand for Higher Education." *Research in Higher Education* 12(1): 83-95.

Zammuto, Raymond F. 1985. "Characteristics of Enrollment Competition in Higher Education." Paper presented at the Annual Meeting of the Association for the Study of Higher Education, Chicago (March).

Chapter Eight

References

American Association for the Advancement of Science, Intersociety Working Group. 1986. *AAAS Report XI: Research and Development, FY 1987.* Washington, D.C.

Cheit, Earl F. 1971. *The New Depression in Higher Education: A Study of Conditions at 41 Colleges and Universities.* New York, N.Y.: McGraw Hill.

————. 1973. *The New Depression in Higher Education—Two Years Later.* New York, N.Y.: McGraw Hill.

Froomkin, Joseph. 1972. *The Financial Prospects of the Postsecondary Sector, 1975 to 1990.* Washington, D.C.: Joseph Froomkin Inc.

————. 1978. *A Review of Financial Conditions of Higher Education 1971 to 1975.* Washington, D.C.: Joseph Froomkin Inc.

———— and Clinton McCully. 1977. *A Review of Financial Developments in Higher Education, 1970/71-1974/5, and a Prognosis for 1980 and 1985.* Processed. Washington, D.C.: EPRC for Higher Education and Society (February): 38.

Gray, Hanna H. 1986a. "The State of the University." *The University of Chicago Record,* Vol. XX, No. 1 (April 10): 2.

————. 1986b. "A Report of the Size and the Composition of the University of Chicago." *The University of Chicago Record,* Vol. XX, No. 1 (April 10): 17.

Halstead, Kent. 1985a. *Higher Education Prices and Price Indexes, 1985 Supplement.* Washington, D.C.: U.S. Department of Education, National Institute of Education (May).

————. 1985b. *How States Compare in Financing Higher Education, 1984-5.* Washington, D.C.: U.S. Department of Education, National Institute of Education (May).

McDonald, Kim. 1982. "California Pushing Research in Microelectronics." *Chronicle of Higher Education* (April 7): 11.

National Science Foundation. 1981. *Academic Science, R & D Funds,* Survey of Science Resources Series, Washington, D.C.: G.P.O.

O'Neill, June A. 1973. *Resource Use in Higher Education.* New York: McGraw-Hill.

Trow, Martin A. 1983. "Reorganizing Biological Sciences at Berkeley." *Change,* vol. 15, No. 8 (November/December): 50.

U.S. Bureau of the Census. 1976. *Historical Statistics of the United States, Colonial Times to 1970, Bicentennial Edition,* Part I, H339-350 H716-727 and H728-738. Washington, D.C.: G.P.O.

U.S. Bureau of the Census. *State Government Finances,* Series GF No.3. Washington, D.C.: G.P.O.

U.S. Department of Commerce. 1977. *The National Income and Product Accounts of the United States, 1929-76.* Washington, D.C.: G.P.O.

U.S. Department of Commerce. 1985. *Survey of Current Business.* Washington, D.C.: G.P.O. (April and July).

U.S. Department of Health, Education, and Welfare, Office of Education, National Center for Education Statistics. 1966-79. *Higher Education General Information Survey.* Annual. Washington, D.C.: G.P.O.

U.S. Department of Education, National Center for Education Statistics. 1980 and 1984. *Higher Education General Information Survey.* Washington, D.C.: computer printouts.

U.S. Department of Labor, Bureau of Labor Statistics. 1986. *Economic Report of the President.* Transmitted to Congress February 1986. Washington, D.C.: G.P.O. Tables B-42 and B-45.

Chapter Nine

References

Andersen, Charles J. 1985. *Conditions Affecting College and University Financial Strength.* Washington, D.C.: American Council on Education.

Bowen, Frank, and Lyman Glenny. 1981. "The California Study." In Larry L. Leslie and James Hyatt, eds., *Higher Education Financing Policies: States/ Institutions and Their Interaction.* Tucson, Ariz.: Center for the Study of Higher Education.

Bowen, Howard R. 1980. *The Costs of Higher Education.* San Francisco: Jossey-Bass.

Broyles, Susan G., and Rosa M. Fernandez. 1984. *Education Directory of Colleges and Universities 1983-84.* Washington, D.C.: National Center for Education Statistics.

Buchanan, W. and others. 1978. "Review of Academic Degree Programs: Striving to Keep Higher Education Viable in a Time of Limited Resources." Paper presented at the Annual Forum of the Association for Institutional Research, Houston, May.

Carter, Edward A., and Jack C. Blanton. 1983. "Institutional Management Flexibility: A Strategy for Dealing with Funding Reductions." In Robert A. Wilson, ed., *Survival in the 1980s: Quality, Mission, and Financing Options.* Tucson, Ariz.: Center for the Study of Higher Education.

Christal, Melodie E. 1986. *Higher Education Financing in the Fifty States: Inter-*

state Comparisons Fiscal Year 1984, 5th ed. Boulder, Col.: National Center for Higher Education Management Systems.

Conley, Diane, and Andrea C. Frary. 1984. *Graduate and Professional Programs: An Overview 1985,* 19th ed. Princeton, N.J.: Peterson's Guides.

Council for Financial Aid to Education. 1985. *Voluntary Support of Education 1984-85.* New York: Council for Financial Aid to Education.

Hyatt, James A., Carol Herrnstadt Shulman, and Aurora A. Santiago. 1984. Reallocation: Strategies for Effective Resource Management. Washington, D.C.: National Association of College and University Business Officers.

Ihrig, Weldon E. 1983. "Resource Reallocations at the Ohio State University." In Robert A. Wilson, ed., *Survival in the 1980s: Quality, Mission, and Financing Options.* Tucson, Ariz.: Center for the Study of Higher Education.

McKinney, David L. 1982. "The Idaho Experience." In Robert A. Wilson, ed., *Responses to Fiscal Stress in Higher Education.* Tucson, Ariz.: Center for the Study of Higher Education.

Mingle, James R., and Donald M. Norris. 1981. "Institutional Strategies for Responding to Decline." In James Mingle and Associates, *Challenges of Retrenchment.* San Francisco: Jossey-Bass.

Mortimer, Kenneth P. 1981. Pennsylvania's Retrenchment Battle. *AGB Reports,* 23 (March-April): 28-34.

Mortimer, Kenneth P., and Michael L. Tierney. 1979. *The Three "R's" of the Eighties: Reduction, Reallocation, and Retrenchment.* Washington, D.C.: American Association for Higher Education.

Shirley, Robert C. 1982. The SUNY-Albany experience. In Robert A. Wilson, ed., *Responses to Fiscal Stress in Higher Education.* Tucson, Ariz.: Center for the Study of Higher Education.

Smith, D. K. 1980. *Preparing for a Decade of Enrollment Decline: The Experience of the University of Wisconsin System.* Atlanta, Ga.: Southern Regional Education Board.

Contributors

FREDERICK E. BALDERSTON is Professor of Business Administration, University of California, Berkeley. His research interests include strategic planning, university administration and planning, financial regulation, and marketing systems. He is the author of *Managing Today's University* (Jossey-Bass), *Thrifts in Crisis* (Ballinger), and numerous articles in scholarly and professional journals. From 1966-70 he served as Vice President—Business and Finance and as Vice President—Planning and Analysis in the central administration of the University of California. He was Associate Dean of the School of Business at Berkeley in 1983 and from 1979-81.

WILLIAM E. BECKER is Professor of Economics at Indiana University, Bloomington. His Ph.D. is from the University of Pittsburgh, 1973. He is the editor of *The Journal of Economic Education*. His articles appear in *American Economic Review, American Journal of Agricultural Economics, Journal of Finance, Journal of Human Resources, Journal of Risk and Insurance, Monthly Labor Review, Review of Economics and Statistics* and other journals. He is also the coauthor of *Business and Economics Statistics* (Addison Wesley), *Academic Rewards in Higher Education* (Ballinger), and *Econometric Modeling in Economic Education Research* (Kluwer-Nijhoff). He is working currently on a book on higher education and economic growth.

PAUL BRINKMAN is a senior associate at the National Center for Higher Education Management Systems in Boulder, Colorado. He received his Ph.D. degree in higher education administration from the University of Arizona in 1981. His research interests are in the economics and financing of higher education. He is a frequent contributor to higher education literature, including a recent book, *The Economic Value of Higher Education* with Larry Leslie (Macmillan).

CYRIL F. CHANG is Professor of Economics at Memphis State University. He holds a doctorate in economics from the University of Virginia and specializes in the economics of higher education and health care economics. He is the author or coauthor of over 30 articles published in a variety of academic and professional journals including the *Journal of Higher Education, Research in Higher Education, Economics of Education Review,* the *Journal of Economic Education,* the *Journal of Health Politics, Policy and Law,* and the *Journal of Health Care Marketing.*

JOSEPH FROOMKIN is the head of a small group of consultants whose main interest is accelerating technological change in industry. Dr. Froomkin is the coauthor of *Technology and Jobs* (Praeger), and the author of *Aspirations, Enrollments, and Resources,* (Government Printing Office) *Needed: A New Federal Policy for Higher Education,* (Institute for Educational Leadership) and numerous articles on education, technological change and tax policy in underdeveloped countries. He is also the editor of and contributor to *The Crisis in Higher Education,* (The Academy of Political Science.) He was awarded a Ph.D. in Finance from the School of Business of the University of Chicago and has held academic, business and government positions, including that of Assistant Commissioner of Education for Program Planning and Evaluation from 1966 to 1969.

STEPHEN A. HOENACK is Professor in the Humphrey Institute of Public Affairs and Director of the Management Information Division at the University of Minnesota. He received his Ph.D. in Economics from the University of California at Berkeley. He is the author of *Economic Behavior Within Organizations* (Cambridge University Press) and has written extensively on the economics of higher education. Mr. Hoenack is an associate editor of *Economics of Education Review.* In 1988-89 he was on leave to the World Bank.

DAVID S.P. HOPKINS is Assistant Vice President for Management and Financial Planning at Stanford University. He earned an A.B. in Biology from Harvard in 1964, and an M.S. in Statistics from Stanford in 1967, and a Ph.D. in Operations Research from Stanford in 1969. He is coauthor of *Planning Models for Colleges and Universities* (Stanford University Press), and an author or coauthor of numerous articles in *Management Science, Operations Research, The New England Journal of Medicine,* and other journals. He serves on the Council of the Operations Research Society of America, is an associate editor of *Operations Research* and is a director of The Alan Guttmacher Institute.

ESTELLE JAMES is Professor of Economics, State University of New York, Stony Brook. She is the author of *Public Policy and Private Education in Japan* (Macmillan), *The Nonprofit Sector in International Perspective* (Oxford) and numerous articles on the economics of education and nonprofit organizations.

HOWARD P. TUCKMAN is the Distinguished Professor of Economics at Memphis State University where he teaches in the Executive M.B.A. program. He is the author of eight books and over one hundred and ten journal articles. An expert in the fields of economic education, human resources, medical economics, public finance, and strategic planning, he has held national offices in economic associations and currently serves on the editorial boards of several journals.

Author Index

Subject Index